CW01507264

Call Me Brother

The Story of a New Zealand
Doctor in Bangladesh

First published in 2022 by the New Zealand – Kailakuri Link Group, Auckland, New Zealand

ISBN: 978-0-473-63125-3

Front cover image: Doctor Edric Baker.
Back flap: Village health worker Lakhoni Hagidok weighing a baby.
Photos from the Kailakuri Healthcare Project.
Front flap: Edric supporting a patient who is learning to walk again.
Photo by Judy Walter.

Edited by Deborah Shepard
Proofread by Stephanie Day
Cover, maps and typesetting by Emma Bevernage
Printed by Crayons Bangladesh Limited, Dhaka, Bangladesh
on PEFC-certified paper

PEFC
PEFC/39-32-20002

Promoting
Sustainable Forest
Management

www.pefc.org

For Peter Wilson,
a faithful friend to Edric

For the Kailakuri family of
paramedics, patients and supporters

And for all those seeking inspiration
to live out their ideals

NEW ZEALAND

Auckland ●

● Whakatāne

● Taupō

● Paraparaumu
● Wellington

● Christchurch

● Dunedin

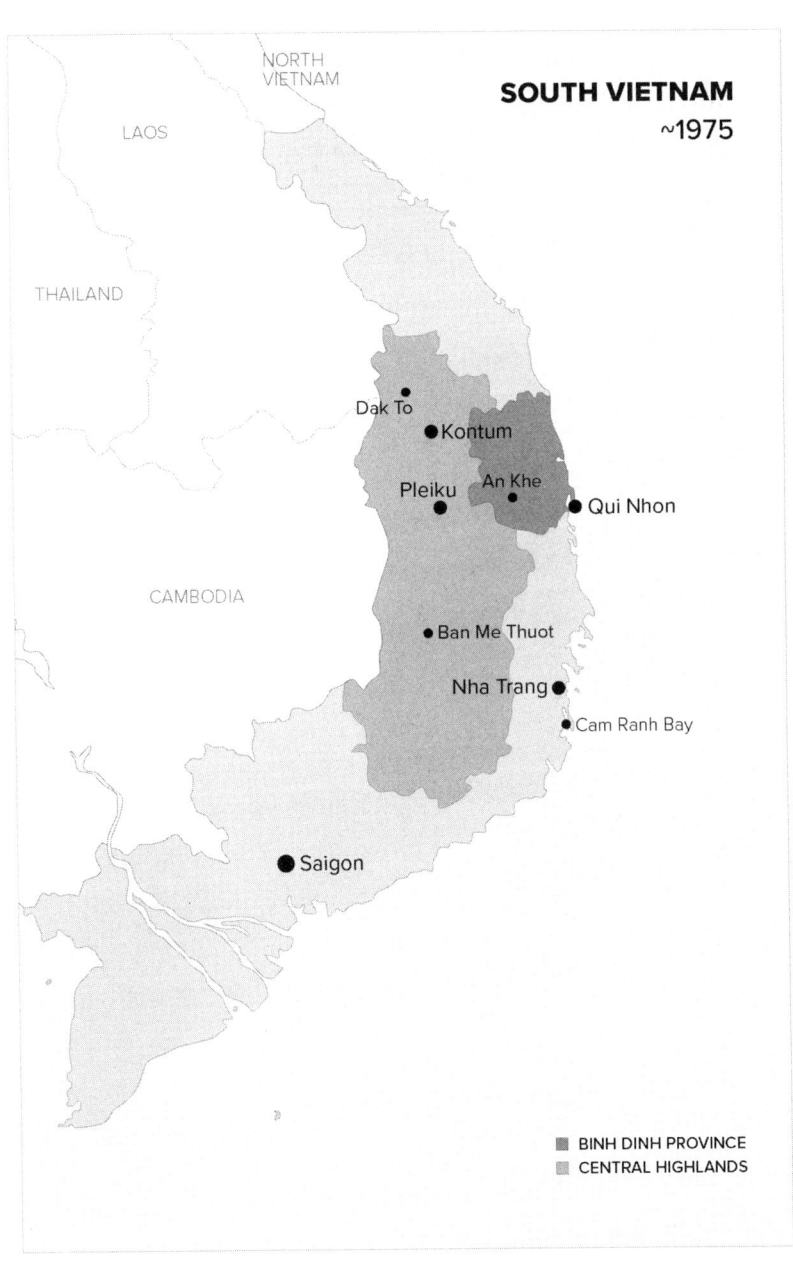

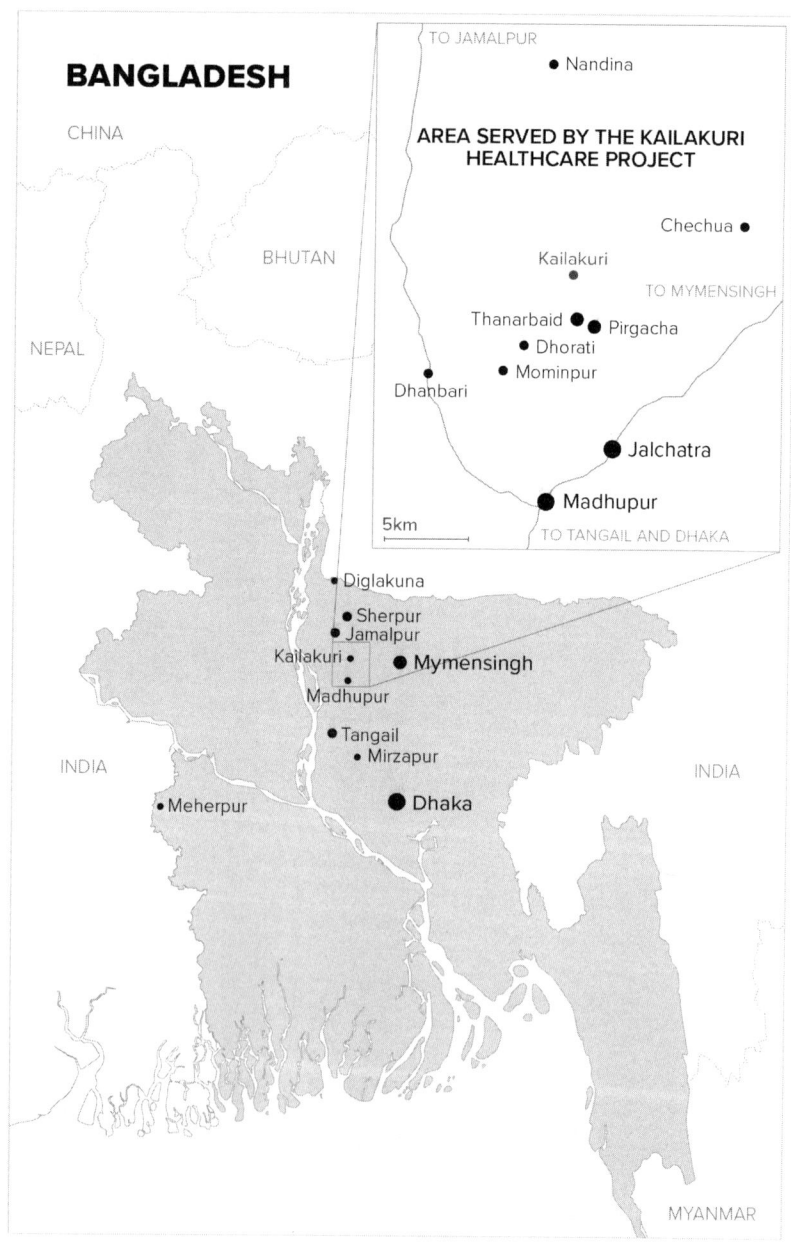

BANGLADESH

CHINA

BHUTAN

NEPAL

INDIA

INDIA

MYANMAR

Diglakuna
Sherpur
Jamalpur
Kailakuri
Mymensingh
Madhupur
Tangail
Mirzapur
Meherpur
Dhaka

TO JAMALPUR

Nandina

AREA SERVED BY THE KAILAKURI
HEALTHCARE PROJECT

Chechua

Kailakuri

TO MYMENSINGH

Thanarbaid
Pirgacha
Dhorati
Mominpur

Dhanbari

Jalchatra

5km

Madhupur

TO TANGAIL AND DHAKA

Contents

'Greater love has no one than this:
to lay down one's life for one's friends.'
~ Jesus

'Live with, eat with and work with the people.'
~ Slogan in a Viet Cong prison camp

Prologue

The one and only day I spent with Edric Baker was on a bus on 20 July 2012. In order to interview him, I had flown from Christchurch to Wellington, then boarded a ten-hour intercity bus. I hoped it would be the one that Baker would get on north of the city. As we neared the town where he was staying, my anxiety rose, and oblivious to the passing scenery, I kept glancing at the empty seat next to me. My whole journey was a rash decision, booked the day before. What if Baker had a ticket for a different bus? My trip would be for nothing, a foolish pursuit of a last-minute interview. But the curiosity that had compelled me to take the chance had not gone away.

The feeling had seized me days earlier, at a fundraising event, when I heard Baker speak. He was a humanitarian doctor who had received the Order of Merit, yet he was little known in New Zealand except by members of the Church Missionary Society. The Christchurch branch had done an impressive job of rounding up an audience, including university students of Christian faith, like me. The church was full. When the room hushed and Baker began speaking about his life's work, his energy, incongruous with his slight build and white hair, was contagious. Everyone was listening.

In the Bangladeshi village of Kailakuri, one of the world's forgotten corners, Baker had established a centre where he trained local people to provide healthcare. His workers had little schooling and no formal medical training. They worked in mud huts with no running water, minimal equipment and only occasional electricity. Yet these 'paramedics' were filling a void in primary healthcare. According to Baker, his team achieved results that Western doctors would envy, and they did so on a shoestring. Baker explained that for an average cost of $NZ1.40 ($US1.10) per outpatient visit his workers assisted thousands of people.

I was no health student, but I could do maths. Healthcare was expensive. In my city of Christchurch, a doctor's consultation cost each patient between 50 and 60 dollars, and that was after significant subsidies from the government. How did Baker provide care so cheaply?

After his talk, emboldened by curiosity, I cornered Baker and bombarded him with questions: 'Could his project be replicated? Had anyone ever tried?' I was 24; Baker, bright, animated, charismatic, seemed to me an elderly man. I asked if anyone had ever written an account of the development of his project in Kailakuri. He answered no, and tapped his forehead: the lessons were stored in his mind. To me this seemed a perilous place for such valuable information. Someday soon, perhaps, this doctor would die. The lessons of this clinic needed to be documented while its founder was still alive. Although no one knew it then, the task turned out to be urgent as Baker was terminally ill.

This feeling nagged at me, too persistent to ignore. A few days later I tracked down the doctor in Paraparaumu, north of Wellington, and phoned him to request an interview. Baker apologised saying his schedule was too tight before his return to Bangladesh. But then he paused. 'Except, I have to take a bus ride the length of the North Island, tomorrow. If you can get on the bus you can interview me.' I flew to Wellington immediately and the next morning boarded a bus, hoping it was the right one.

One hour into the drive, we came to Paraparaumu. Baker was waiting on the curb. He climbed aboard and took the seat next to me. In close proximity he was unremarkable – average height and clean-shaven, with blue eyes that appeared gentle and inquisitive through reading glasses. Once he had greeted me, he laid out ground rules for our conversation. He wanted 10 minutes rest after every 50 minutes of interview, and added as justification, 'I am an old man!' I obliged, and then from the North Island coastline to the Desert Road to Auckland motorways, he told me about his clinic. For just one stretch he requested complete silence: as we skirted the foot of Ruapehu. When he spoke again he said, 'I have not seen that mountain for a long time.'

Had I known this 10-hour journey would become so important, I would have noted Baker's posture and gestures, his clothing and the bag he carried. Was he out of place in

New Zealand, a foreigner in his own country? I noted none of that. I only recall that he spoke in old-fashioned, deliberate English. He was courteous. He asked about my interests before he let me turn to his. Throughout the long conversation he appeared to be enjoying my questions and gave thoughtful, sometimes humorous answers.

We said goodbye in Auckland, Baker's throat hoarse from talking and my audio recorder full. I don't remember if I shook his hand. I flew home; he continued his jam-packed schedule. That was the last time we met. I wrote up the interview, sent it to him and returned to my political science studies and ordinary routine. Baker emailed to thank me for the transcript, which was put on a website and read occasionally by prospective volunteers. For the next four years I had little contact with his organisation. I moved overseas. It was there, with sadness, I heard of Baker's death in 2015. I did not expect this to affect my life.

Then God, with a chuckle, threw me back into Baker's story. In 2016, I made a New Year's resolution to develop my writing skills. I was thinking along the lines of poetry – maybe limericks. That was on 1 January. On 2 January, out of the blue, Baker's organisation emailed to ask if I would write his biography. When they had floated the idea with Baker, he had mentioned me.

I took a long time to give my answer. I had no qualifications or desire to write a book. While many writers long for a project with wages, travel and a guaranteed audience, I had no such aspiration. In fact, in those early months I applied for numerous jobs in other fields but was declined for all of them.

At first, I agreed only to conduct the research. On a visit back to New Zealand I interviewed dozens of Baker's associates, intending to pass on my findings to the biographer. But the story sucked me in. By the time I had interviewed his mother, aged 100; a former girlfriend; and a man who had been imprisoned with him in Vietnam, I was intrigued. Then I was invited to Bangladesh and I could not say no. I travelled to Baker's clinic and for four weeks interviewed his trainees and friends. Their hospitality during that time was incredibly attentive. Days before our arrival, terrorists had attacked Dhaka and security across the country had been ramped up; our kind hosts merely adapted plans. When I met Baker's people, I knew I had to continue the project. His team were saving lives, despite many of them having less than a high school education. En route home I traced Baker's earlier movements in Vietnam. After all that, I was won over.

Had I known I would write Baker's biography I would have asked him tougher questions. What had sustained him for 30 years in Bangladesh? How exactly did he unite people of diverse religions and win their loyalty? What was the solution to the root problem that drove him: the lack of healthcare for the poor? And what about Baker's personal life? He had chosen not to marry and sacrificed proximity to his immediate family back home in New Zealand and nearly every material comfort for his work. Was he happy? How did he view God, who inspired his care for the poor, yet seemed to allow their suffering? Did Baker himself feel peaceful about dying? Had he done enough?

This book is my attempt to answer these questions. The 5-year project has included research trips through Bangladesh, Vietnam and New Zealand, speaking with 150 of his associates and reading hundreds of his letters. I have discussed Baker and public health in the mud-brick homes of Bengali villagers and in the offices of their Prime Minister. I have touched a lock of his baby hair in his mother's diary and visited his grave.

In doing so I have learned that I am a perfect candidate to write his biography. Baker had a knack for selecting workers with no formal qualifications and little confidence. Sometimes he chased and charmed recruits who needed the job more than he needed them. Ill-qualified and reluctant, I now see that I am exactly the sort of biographer Baker would choose.

This book is therefore my response to an unexpected task. From the outset my partiality is clear; it is because I consider Baker a great man that his story has taken over my life. But even great people are human. I have done my best to depict his flaws, for true portraits include shadow.

As it happens, Baker himself was hijacked by a story. In childhood he read the biography of Doctor Albert Schweitzer, who received the Nobel Peace Prize for founding a hospital in French Equatorial Africa. That book captured Baker's imagination and inspired him to become a missionary doctor himself. Since his death, people have compared Baker to Schweitzer. In fact, these two doctors are alike in more ways than one. They were not merely great physicians: they gave boldness to others and transformed their lives. Perhaps your life will be next? Baker's story grabbed me and engulfed me. I hope it grabs you.

1

The simple idea

In the dry season of 2003, a father watched his daughter lose her sight. There was no specific day when it happened. Shilpi's blindness crept up slowly. It arrived like the dry season, when the paddies shrink until they are empty and colour fades until it is gone. Although this father could see it coming – at first he could see his daughter straining to see, then straining less and less, conceding – he could feel his own stomach sinking but could do nothing. He could no more heal his daughter than save the rice paddies from the scorching sun.

Place is everything in this story, because Shilpi may not have gone blind if she had lived down the street from you or me. Shilpi was born in Panchbibi, a remote area in the northwest of Bangladesh. Her country struggles to provide healthcare for its people. Although the government has rebuilt after war and lifted millions of people from poverty, millions more remain poor. Shilpi and her neighbours felt life's blows acutely. Their families counted every cup of rice – one illness could grind them to the ground; one flood could sink them into debt. They could not afford healthcare. Meanwhile, the government's health funds were like a dash of water on a fire. Some officials fell to greed or desperation and stole even those meagre funds away.

The result was that when Shilpi went blind, her country had one third of the doctors it needed. The World Health Organisation described the shortage as 'staggering': in 2007, Bangladesh had 40,000 doctors and needed 90,000 more.[1] Existing doctors clustered in cities which had electricity, good schools for children and patients who could pay. But two thirds of Bangladeshis, like Shilpi, lived in the countryside. In cities there were 18 qualified doctors per 10,000 people. In rural areas, there was only one.[2]

In Shilpi's town there was no one who could identify her mystery illness. Aged 16, while preparing for her final exams, she had collapsed. Her teacher rushed her to the nearest clinic but the staff could not tell them what was wrong. Desperate, Shilpi's family took her to a hospital in a faraway city. The staff diagnosed her with diabetes. No one in Shilpi's family

---

[1] World Health Organization Regional Office for the Western Pacific, *Bangladesh Health System Review* (Manila: WHO Regional Office for the Western Pacific, 2015), pp. 95, https://apps.who.int/iris/handle/10665/208214.

[2] Masud Ahmed, Md Awlad Hossain, Ahmed Mushtaque Raja Chowdhury and Abbas Uddin Bhuiya, 'The Health Workforce Crisis in Bangladesh: Shortage, Inappropriate Skill-mix and Inequitable Distribution', *Human Resources for Health 9* (January 2011): Table 2, www.human-resources-health.com/content/9/1/3.

had heard of the disease. Even the hospital staff lacked sufficient knowledge and sold Shilpi tablets that could not solve her problem. Her father spent extra hours at work so that he could afford her medicine as well as the family's rice. He did not know that the tablets were useless, and that rice played a part in keeping his daughter sick.

Like all diabetics, Shilpi's body had a problem with sugar: there was too much in her blood, and too little in her cells that needed it. As Shilpi ate, her body broke rice down to sugar to be used as energy. But because of her Type 1 diabetes, her body lacked insulin, a hormone that enables the sugar to be delivered to the cells. The results were disastrous. Without insulin, sugar accumulated in her blood while her cells were starved.

What Shilpi needed were insulin injections and training to manage her diet and exercise. But even if she had known that, her situation would have remained perilous. In her country of nearly 160 million people, most of them in rural villages, diabetes treatment was only available in the capital and largest cities. Even there, it existed only in a fledgling state, and at a price. For Shilpi, it may as well have been on the moon.

As her blood sugars fluctuated out of control, Shilpi's weight dropped to 28 kilograms. Cataracts grew in her eyes, shrouding her world in white. By the time she was 18, she was blind and could not walk. Day by day she lay alone on the verandah of her home. It seemed that Shilpi would surely die. But if she did not, might that be worse? She would never marry. She could only remain lying on that verandah, a burden on her family, unable to ward off despair. Her father worked longer and longer hours, so he could keep the family afloat, and so he wouldn't have to look at his beautiful daughter who was too weak even to weep. The family prayed to Hindu gods, invited healers and stayed home from school or work to care for her. For a year they bought the medicine. But it became clear the tablets were doing nothing. They gave up.

Shilpi had no reason to hope, yet even as her family lost heart, she held on. One day, into her world of sound and touch came the voice of her uncle who had stopped by for a visit. Shilpi broke. She begged him to take her to a first-class hospital. She was asking the impossible; her family could not afford the transport let alone the fee. Yet her uncle paused. He had one friend in Mymensingh city who knew foreigners – members of Taizé, an ecumenical Christian community. Could they do anything for the girl?

After one look at Shilpi, the foreigners took her to Mymensingh Medical – a more modern hospital than she had ever experienced – and bought her one vial of precious insulin. The impossible had happened! She held the key to wellness in her hand! Shilpi began to take the insulin. But that vial cost the foreigners 415 *taka* ($NZ9; $US6 at that time) and it would last her 50 days – a price of 8 *taka* per day. Shilpi's family scraped by on her father's daily wage of 200 *taka*. They could not afford this regular expense. Shilpi had come so close to what she needed only to crash back into despair.

What happened next was so improbable it is the subject of this entire book. By a chance connection, the Taizé brothers introduced Shilpi to a New Zealand doctor called Edric Baker. Two hundred kilometres from Shilpi's home, he lived in the village of Kailakuri, where locals knew him as 'the crazy foreigner.' Doctor Baker was indeed unique. In that remote place, he ran a healthcare project for the poor. His clinic would accept Shilpi even though she could pay nothing. What was more unlikely still, and what brought a sob of joy to Shilpi's throat, was that the project specialised in diabetes care.

Shilpi became a patient at the Kailakuri Healthcare Project for the next year. For the first time, staff explained her illness: her body could not regulate blood sugar, but she could learn to do this herself. They helped Shilpi to measure her sugar levels, to monitor her food intake and inject insulin. Her blood sugar steadied and she began to recover.

The clinic provided no luxuries but many reassurances. All patients slept on a mud floor as they did at home. The buildings were dotted among trees; Shilpi could hear their branches above her and feel their shade. In time, Shilpi relearned how to walk. She rediscovered the forgotten feelings of deep ease and sound sleep. Slowly another sensation returned: the delight of being well. Shilpi joined in meals with the other patients and staff and sometimes heard the doctor eat with them, speaking Bangla with his strange accent. One day he asked Shilpi how she was. She replied, 'So much better, but I still cannot see.'

Eight weeks after Shilpi arrived, the Kailakuri staff sent her back to Mymensingh for a cataract operation. As soon as the bandages were removed, Shilpi could see. When she returned to Kailakuri and for the first time saw the clinic appear among the trees, she was surprised to also see a row of people. The staff, whom Shilpi had known only by voice, were greeting her with a game. Could she guess who was who? The doctor stood out plainly, though he was skinnier and shabbier than Shilpi had imagined, not like foreigners on TV. The other workers were silent and grinning, not wanting to give their identities away. Then Shilpi spotted one person in the middle: her father! His face was strained, almost crumbling from hope that Shilpi would recognise him, that she could truly see. The girl was transformed by health almost beyond his recognition, but her father knew her from her squeal and sobs as she hugged him even as his own eyes were blinded with tears.

Shilpi went on to work as a health educator with the Kailakuri diabetes programme. By the time I met her in 2016, Shilpi and her colleagues were replicating her transformation in the lives of many others, driven by a simple idea: that healthcare should be available for every person, rich or poor. Their belief will take time to be realised. In 2019 there are an estimated 8 million Bangladeshis with diabetes – a number projected to rise to 15 million by 2045 – and most cannot access treatment. Shilpi and her colleagues work to change that reality.

This book is the backstory to Shilpi's story, and to the tales of many others whose lives have taken dramatic turns. It is about the New Zealand doctor who came from half a world away with the view that every person should have access to healthcare. He believed it so fiercely that the idea shaped most of his major decisions. Edric Baker refused to accept that healthcare would remain out of reach of the poor and devoted himself to living out an alternative.

This is the story of his radical and adventurous life.

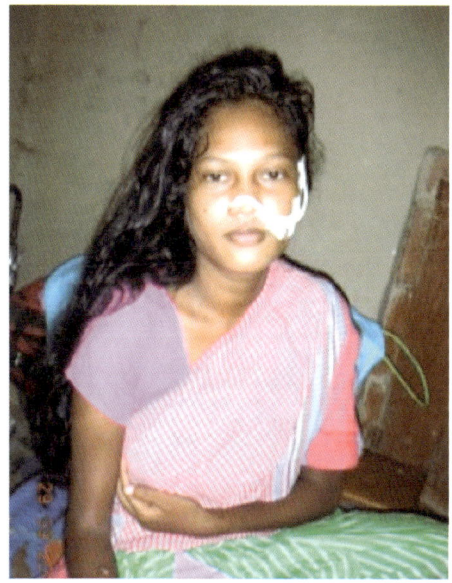

Shilpi during her recovery. Photo from the Kailakuri Healthcare Project.

Shilpi as a health educator, speaking in front of 300 diabetes patients in 2016. Photo from the Kailakuri Healthcare Project.

A self-portrait by Edric Baker, year unknown.
From the Baker family collection.

2

A gentle soul

Edric Baker's journey to Bangladesh began with a decision he made as a young boy. Perhaps it was more like a discovery. In 2012 he reflected to a Radio New Zealand reporter,

'I was about seven when I realised that I had to be a doctor.'

'*Had* to be?'

'I knew that was what I wanted to do.'

This conviction seized Edric during his childhood in Wellington, New Zealand. He was born in 1941 and was learning to crawl as World War II spread into the Pacific. But Edric was too young to fear a Japanese invasion or to notice his father's work with the Home Guard. On the whole, his early life felt safe and carefree; he liked to explore the bare hills behind his house and watch farmers driving sheep along an unsealed road below. He spent his days with his blonde hair wild and ears full of the whipping Wellington wind.

The idea to become a doctor was most likely not Edric's own. His mother, Betty, had seen many people out of work during the depression and aspired for her children to gain reputable jobs. In Edric, her second son, she saw intelligence and a caring nature, so she encouraged him towards medicine. During his primary years she pressed Edric to learn first aid. She bought a poster of human anatomy and put it behind the toilet door. Betty's father may have reinforced her efforts – he knew the value of health and hygiene: he was proud to have raised his children safely through polio epidemics. Whether Edric's mother or grandfather was the source, Edric soon took on the aspiration as his own.

When I began to research Edric's life, I visited Betty Baker in her retirement home in the town of Whakatāne. Betty had had time to reflect on her son's life; she was aged 100. Among a row of greeting cards in her room there was one from the Queen and another from the Prime Minister John Key. I was excited to hear Betty's insights. What had taken her son from comfortable Wellington to Bangladesh to serve others? Could she trace the origins of his character, not just his career? Before I could ask my questions, Betty wondered aloud, 'How do you grow a conscience in a child?' She mused as if such a thing were impossible, as if her son's conscience had blossomed before her eyes while she and his father simply watched. Even if Betty was right – and the seeds of Edric's character were a gift from God or nature – the nurture of his parents certainly ensured that they would flourish.

Edric's parents Betty Sargisson and John Victor Tuwhaka-hewa Baker were descendents of English settlers. Betty's ancestors had sailed to New Zealand in the mid-nineteenth-century; John's parents arrived in about 1911 and gave him a Māori middle name after interacting with indigenous people in their new land.

Betty and John met in the State Advances Department where they both worked. Following an office picnic, John gave Betty a ride home on his motorbike and proposed to her. The pair married in 1938, when Betty was 23, then moved to a state house in the suburb of Ngaio. Edric's older brother Leslie was born there in 1940 and Edric Sargisson Baker on 12 August 1941. The distinctive name 'Edric' was a twist on 'Eric', which appeared in both his parents' families.

Betty could see her sons' personalities emerging at a young age. She told me, 'Les would always be building; I could tell he would be an engineer. Edric was always into colours and flowers and nature. ... I just knew that he would become a gentle soul.' Betty kept journals of her children's early years. She noted that at age three, Edric regularly picked bouquets for her and his nose was often yellow with pollen. He had discovered a joy in flowers that would last his lifetime. Edric was also methodical, bordering on perfectionist. Aged two, he had insisted on returning matches to their box with all the heads the same way, to his grandfather's surprise. Weeding the garden with young Edric exasperated Betty. He weeded only tiny sections but made them immaculate.

Betty developed a deep fondness for her gentle son. This may be in part because she nearly lost him: aged five or six, Edric caught pneumonia and had to be hospitalised. He grew

The Baker children in about 1955. From left, Edric, Hilary, Bruce, Hilda, John and Les. Photo from the Baker family collection.

to be artistic, enjoying sketching and water colours. Betty noted in her journal that Edric was 'a charming boy when good!' and he employed a disarming humour to evade trouble. Yet he was also sensitive and had that endearing quality in a son: needing his mother. Betty told me: 'Edric once offered to take part in a play. The teacher told him, "You'll never be any good." Edric came home in tears. He said, "Mother, I'm not any good at anything," and I said, "Yes you are."' Betty in her retirement room reflected, 'I think he probably had the right mother, and I had the right son.'

Although Betty was her son's greatest supporter, Edric inherited many traits from his father. John Baker was a scholar and statesman who possessed what Betty called 'a determined streak that runs through the Baker family'. He rose through the Civil Service to become Government Statistician – New Zealand's highest position in statistics. He lectured at university and gained ardent fans among students and staff: when it came to the census, a few in jest recorded their religion as 'Bakerite'. John had a light humour to accompany his heavy intellect and was known to many as J.V.T.

John and Betty were resourceful in providing for their growing family. By 1945, they had bought a hillside plot in the suburb of Raroa, and John built them a home out of old railway huts. Though sturdy, the house was no palace: it had only cold water; outside was a long drop toilet and a big copper for boiling the laundry. Betty reflected, 'A railway-hut house for seven years! The place had one tap, and no sink, bath or washing machine.' Three new babies arrived in that house: Hilda, Bruce and Hilary. The challenge of parenting five children was one that Betty rose to with ingenuity. She told me she took the train to her parents' place to do the laundry: 'I used to go every week with my pram, and all the washing, with the baby sitting on top. ... My parents knew the children very well.'

Betty used other skills to stretch the family finances. While John tended the vegetable garden, Betty was renowned for keeping beehives. She sewed clothes. Her children recalled 'pants made from sacking and underclothes from sugar bags.' She also cooked all the staple economical meals of the era: sheep's brain, ox tail, brawn and junket. Yet Betty's zeal for economising surpassed other parents of her generation. 'She was a master at making do,' Edric's sister Hilda told me. 'In the wet weather, Mother didn't want our shoes ruined in the rain, so it was "Go barefoot thanks" and we took our shoes in our bag. I remember getting to the classroom one winter's day … and everyone asking me, "Aren't your feet cold?"'

With Edric's father now in a government job, such economy was not essential, but the Bakers' sacrifices paid off. In 1953, when Edric was 11, the family shifted to a bigger home in the suburb of Khandallah. Their sixth and final child, John, was born there.

I visited this former home with John, Edric's youngest brother, in 2016. We peered through the holly hedges at a homely and dignified villa. Before the Bakers' time it had been two flats: Edric's father had torn down a dividing wall to make one house for their large family, and consequently it had two of everything – two kitchens, dining rooms and entertaining rooms. As a baby, John had slept in the 'spare' bathroom in a cot.

John remembered the house as a wonderful home for children. It was perfect for playing hide and seek. In one narrow hallway, 'you could walk up the wall with hands on one side and feet on the other, and people wouldn't find you because they didn't look up.' The playroom fitted a full-sized table tennis table and there was still space for children to ride bikes around the edge of the room. Near the house were the church, primary school and swimming pool and above them stood Mt Kaukau, its labyrinth of bush tracks waiting to be explored.

By the time they lived in Khandallah, the children could not have missed the prestige of their father's job. As a senior civil servant, he sometimes hosted guests in the Baker family lounge. The children were paraded for introductions, but otherwise banned. Later, their father published a book – the 660-page academic epic *War Economy*. Yet, even though J.V.T. was at the top of his game, he never grew too removed to have fun with his children. The family spent evenings playing cards or singing songs around the piano. In breaks from writing, J.V.T. jogged with daughter Hilary and played golf with younger son Bruce. He involved the children in home improvement projects and he poked fun. Hilda told me that at the breakfast table, he used to say, 'Look at that spider,' then grab your toast. He and Betty presided over a happy, healthy household.

One important factor in Edric's formation was a beach house. This was the crowning achievement of Betty's frugality and saving: a quarter-acre section at Paraparaumu, 50 kilometres north of Wellington, bought when Edric was about 13. The family took the train there most weekends. At first, they stayed in tents on an empty section. John later constructed a shed and eventually a three-bedroom house. The children were sent out with sacks to stuff with pine needles: those were their mattresses.

At the beach the family lived rough and made do, and they loved it. The children explored the estuary to their hearts' content, built forts, hunted for blackberries and caught fish. Edric also carried brushes and painted landscapes. His sisters, who were four and eight years younger, remember him creating 'all the games imaginable.' There were stilt races; hide-and-seek through the lupins; and races atop kerosene drums, running to roll the drums along. Their brother Edric 'was the leader in all those activities that children just love. He could think of them and make them magic for us.' These holidays deepened family relationships; they also instilled in Edric a love of nature and living simply. 'Camping, sleeping rough and making do was something we grew up with,' Hilda reflected.

The Baker family at Paraparaumu beach in 1958. From left Hilda, Les, John, their father J.V.T., Hilary and Edric. Photo from the Baker family collection.

Edric would embrace simple living for the majority of his life.

Over these years that he was falling in love with the natural world, a far deeper personal formation was also taking place. The Bakers went to an Anglican church most Sundays, as many New Zealanders did. To some children, services could be tedious. One childhood friend of the Bakers told me, 'We called the minister Thunder Guts. You weren't allowed to laugh or talk in the house of God.' Yet Edric felt drawn to the church, which sat diagonally opposite the Bakers' home. On Sundays he would arrive 10 minutes early. In the quiet of the building and his own heart, it felt like God was there with him. The young man pondered the words of Jesus: 'Blessed are the poor, for theirs is the kingdom of heaven.' 'Love your neighbours, even your enemies.' 'Those who seek to gain their own life will lose it, but those who lose their life for my sake will gain it.' Edric was captivated by these ideas, and the God who spoke them seemed both mysterious and approachable. Before long, Jesus' invitation came like a whisper in Edric's ear, gentle and compelling, 'Come, follow me!'

Aged 13, or thereabouts, Edric resolved to follow Jesus with his whole life. Friends and family noticed the change. After taking communion, Edric now paused to pray. Christian themes crept into his artwork. A childhood friend reflected, 'Edric had seen the light. ... His shift to missionary work came as no surprise.' Both parents encouraged Edric's faith and several siblings shared it. An event in 1959 sealed Edric's commitment: the evangelist Billy Graham visited Wellington. Edric, then 17, went with Hilda. 'We were both fired up and buzzing afterwards,' she told me, 'I don't think that ever left him.'

At a similar time, a book changed Edric's life. His mother gave him the biography of Albert Schweitzer, a French-German theologian who diverted from an elite academic career to become a doctor among the poor in French Equatorial Africa. Schweitzer had established a hospital so remote it could be accessed only by canoe. The author wrote that surrounding it 'is the forest, huge, black and mysterious. A few native trails ... rife with peril, penetrate the jungle.' The doctor stared out of photographs from under a pith helmet and thick moustache. Here was a role model Edric wanted to emulate! Schweitzer was someone who took seriously Jesus' challenge to lay down one's life for others. Could there be a path more noble or full of adventure? Edric promised himself that he too would help the helpless. Aged 18, he announced to his family that he wanted to be a missionary doctor.

These aspirations gave Edric a sense of direction during his schooling. In education he was fortunate to be the son of J.V.T. Edric had inherited his father's studious nature; he also saw in his career the value of academic pursuits. Edric was therefore a naturally motivated student, and, according to Betty, the highest achieving boy in his year when he finished Khandallah Primary.

Wellington College, where Edric studied from 1955 to 1959, put his mind to the test. It was a boys' high school with a reputation for rugby, and for one other famous offering, which a classmate described for me: 'An observatory! On a hill facing Wellington East Girls' College! So the observatory was used much more during daytime than night-time … though I'm sure neither Edric nor I ever used it.' Edric was in the top stream, where he and his classmates enjoyed the teachers' respect but also bore the burden of their high expectations.

Just as Edric's mother had noticed a 'gentle soul' in her very young son, his classmates also remarked on this quality. They described Edric as quiet and sensitive: fellow student Ross Buddle told me, 'At that stage he had a gentle spirit. … He was a very nice guy to have in your class.' Others noticed humility in Edric. Classmate Alistair Gooch told me, 'Right from the first year in 1955, Ed sort of stood out. Everyone else wanted to make a name for themselves. Ed stood out as one slightly shy and retiring: he didn't seem at all interested in being kingpin in anything. But you could talk to him about anything and you felt that he was interested.' Other class-

Onslow Rugby Club Midget A team in 1953. Edric is the second child from left in the back row. Photo from the Baker family collection.

Scholarship form at Wellington College 1959. Edric is in the front row, far right. Photo from the Baker family collection.

mates agreed that Edric never pressed to the front and was never self-promoting.

Along with these qualities, friends noticed strength in Edric. Alistair continued, 'He wasn't afraid of arguing his point of view – ever. If Ed had a point, he would make it. … He was comfortable in his own skin.' What was unusual was his manner: 'He had a disarming way of putting his view across. Disarming, but clear. You'd think, "Oh I can crawl over this guy." Then you'd find quickly he was a very easy speaker, but his standard or idea was very firm. He was not afraid to let you know where he stood.'

One incident pitched Edric's gentleness against his firm ideals. In the schoolyard it was common for boys to taunt each other. One day a boy provoked Edric but he didn't respond. Ross Buddle described this as typical of Edric: 'He ignored the provocation multiple times. Then, all of a sudden, Edric had had enough. He said, "Leave me alone!" and the two of them fought.' Ross felt that even though Edric gave in to provocation, 'mentally, Edric had the upper hand.' That was the only incident his classmates recalled in which Edric was violent. Though he had a quiet spirit, he was no pushover, and as Ross put it, 'was not willing to put up with injustice indefinitely.'

By the senior years, many boys had left school, and Edric's class had shrunk to only a dozen students. Those remaining felt pressure to win scholarships, although only one of Edric's classmates did. Edric passed his best subjects, Chemistry and French, with credit. He was among the top four students in his class and his name was added to the Honours Board in the assembly hall.

For someone who had not pushed himself forward, Edric had done admirably. He finished school a good-humoured, bright young man – the product of a happy, healthy home; of freedom in beautiful New Zealand spaces; and of high expectations and encouragement from both parents and school. He also had a calling, from a seed planted by his mother that found roots in a deepening Christian faith. Whether or not his conscience had been with him from birth, his childhood had helped it grow strong.

Edric had one trait that would amplify all others: his father's fierce determination. Betty told me, 'When Edric made his mind up to do something, that was it, he did it. I could have told him to change his mind, but I didn't.' Betty got her wish; Edric would become a doctor. While her son's choice of profession was always a source of pride for Betty, it was also bittersweet. Edric's vocation would consume his life, and call him to live far away from his mother for the majority of his adult life.

Edric and classmates as fifth year medical school students in 1964.
Edric is in the front row, far right. Photo from Tony Baird.

3

New Zealand
is full of doctors

In 1961, Edric travelled down the South Island to Dunedin, a university city enlivened by students and dashed by ocean breeze. He was 19. The previous year he had completed his introduction to Health Science at Victoria University of Wellington. According to his sister Hilda, Edric had 'worked like he had blinkers on' and come sixth in his class. He was therefore accepted into the further five years of the medical degree, which took place at Otago Medical School, Dunedin.

Edric's arrival must have felt both exhilarating and intimidating. He wrote home that he felt 'awestruck by the keen-looking students all around.' As he sat down to his first lectures, except for the 12 females in the class, he and 120 classmates were all in suits and ties. His heart must have pounded with excitement but also anxiety. The workload was formidable. One of Edric's classmates, Alister Rhodes, told me, 'I foolishly tried to learn everything that was dished up and only in retrospect realised that was impossible.' Edric survived by retreating to his hall of residence, Knox College, and burying himself in his books. He was relieved to find his studies confirmed that he was fascinated with medicine.

Anatomy was one difficult subject, and students employed a type of learning aid no longer used today. Peter Strang, one of Edric's classmates, told me that it was common to see, 'a student's bike go past with a femur (thigh bone) poking out of a pannier bag.' These were real human leg bones that students had to purchase for anatomy study: 'Most of us had a skeleton in our flats! Not necessarily complete, but with the main bones or examples of them, including a skull and pelvis. Femurs didn't quite fit in a satchel, and one end stuck out through the zipper.'

I do not know whether Edric carried human bones around campus, but he did ride a bicycle, and in his first year in Dunedin he suffered a life-threatening accident. He and two friends were racing from Knox College down Opoho Hill when a trolley bus turned and Edric barrelled into it; he was thrown from his cycle and crashed, rupturing his spleen. He was lucky to survive – helped, no doubt, by the company of medical students trained in how to respond. Edric required surgery to remove his spleen. He saw the inside of a hospital ward far sooner than he was intended to do in his course, and he also received an official warning from the police. The accident was the talk of the anatomy room and an education for all that a person can live without a spleen.

Edric's recovery took several weeks followed by an arduous period catching up on lecture notes. Then he was back into the normal gruelling workload. His fellow students endured this in timeless ways. Many subdued their stress with alcohol; others threw themselves into sport to chase endorphins as a natural stress relief. Edric chose different methods to escape. Classmate John Bonifant told me, 'He was not a boozing medical student. ... I don't remember him going to class bashes.' Edric went on occasional tramps with friends or rested in the quiet sanctuary of his church.

Edric attended All Saints Anglican Church in north Dunedin, where he helped with Sunday School. He also joined the Student Christian Movement. In addition, at Knox College, where Edric boarded, most other students were training to become Presbyterian ministers. These home and church environments were perfect territory for theological discussions and Edric engaged in many debates. After his trip home to Wellington in the summer of 1961, his mother noted in her diary, 'Edric is very cooperative with children in the Sunday School but far too engrossed in religious problems.' This habit may have cost him some friendships. Classmate John Bonifant also went to All Saints church and remembered Edric as 'a bit of a loner, very intense but well read about his faith.' To medical school classmate Robin Briant, Edric was 'quiet, reserved and Christian.' Other students recalled him as someone who earned their respect, and enjoyed a joke, but did not suffer fools gladly. Christopher Evans described him as 'a gentleman in the truest sense of the word,' another, Grahame Pohlen, remembered him as 'a sensitive and enigmatic ... distancing human being who was friendly, conscientious and shy.' Some classmates felt that Edric was so remote that they did not know him at all. Robin Briant continued, 'Despite being in the same big study group I have to say I didn't know Eddie well. Looking back he was quite likely unknowable! He was not "one of the boys" nor one of the girls.' He did not have any serious girlfriends in those years, according to siblings and friends. A classmate, David Kitchen, recalled, 'He was generally quite friendly with girls but I cannot remember any significant friendships. I did step in for him on one date because he was unable to make it, but it was a very casual situation!'

In the students' first year in Dunedin came a major milestone: the dissection room. Here the students discovered the feel of a human cadaver and the secrets under its skin. The event was sobering but professionally exciting – every system they had studied was now before their eyes, offered there in the flesh. Classmate Peter Strang recalled being filled with wonder 'that this cadaver that I was dissecting ... was once alive, and someone's loved one, a father or mother of a family.'

That their subject now had form and depth must have given the students satisfaction. But for Edric, the next two years, 1962 and 1963, were years of academic struggle. In September 1962, he failed his first professional examination in medicine. Betty wrote in her diary, 'It's been a long time since I felt so upset about things. ... John and I feel that [Edric's] attention has been diverted to solving religious problems. Maybe he'd be better with private board than staying at Knox College where the pressure of Presbyterianism is strong and antagonistic.' In the November exams, Edric failed again. For the next two months he exhausted himself with study, while the February 1963 exams loomed large. Betty wrote, 'I am very worried about Edric. … He does not think he will pass. I do hope God in his mercy will see him through. It seems to me Edric is at the crossroads.'

There is no record of his February 1963 results or what changed for Edric afterwards. However, by November he had better news. Betty wrote, 'Glad tiding and rejoicings for dear Edric has passed everything! Telegram today.' His marks sat about the middle of his class. In the summer that followed, Edric could relax from study, although Hilary remembered seeing Betty teaching Edric to darn socks, so he could learn to use a needle for surgery. In his spare hours, Edric worked at a meatworks in Masterton. There he joined the union and acquired what Betty called 'very pro-worker ideas.'

Edric's fourth and fifth years of study, 1964 and 1965, were clinical years, when students saw patients for the first time. 'We traipsed around the wards, surrounding the patients, in the wake of the mighty specialist,' classmate Tony Baird remembered. Later, students examined patients for themselves and their awareness of their responsibility grew. The students were now wearing white coats. A stethoscope became a heavy weight against their chest. Edric noted this transition in a letter to his parents from an internship at Grey Hospital: 'My official title is "clinical reliever" but everyone refers to me as "doctor". It takes a bit of getting used to.'

Edric must have felt great satisfaction to be seeing patients, and once again keeping pace with his peers. Yet, by his clinical years he was eager to go overseas. This pull was so strong that he even considered giving up study. His sister Hilary told me, 'Edric came home part way through the medical training and said he wanted to go out to the mission field now.' Their father convinced Edric that he would be more useful when fully trained, so he returned to his study. However, Edric remained committed to using his skills abroad. Betty told me, 'He said New Zealand was full of doctors; the doctors here could cope with the patients who were here.'

Edric graduated with his Bachelor of Medicine and Bachelor of Surgery in 1965 and returned to Wellington. There he took a job at Wellington Hospital for three years, 1966 to 1968, to complete the work experience he needed to register as a doctor. A colleague there remembered him as, 'a charming eccentric. He certainly was not … out to impress people. In some ways he was a slower, more methodical worker and may have been ribbed by his peers.' Edric developed a reputation for his meticulous examination of patients, which exasperated his colleagues. Bridget Hodgkinson, who was a student nurse at the time, told me by email, 'While Edric was on duty in Casualty [Accident and Emergency] another doctor arrived and was alarmed to find a large backlog of patients. … The queue had arisen because Doctor Baker was examining all patients from top to toe and not just what they came in to Casualty for.'

Here again was Edric's childhood trait of perfectionism: his lining up matchsticks or weeding a tiny area until not one weed remained. Perhaps too, he wished to consider all the factors affecting that patient's condition. Methodical examinations would later become one of Edric's signature traits. The emergency room, however, was no place for this behaviour and he needed to adjust.

Edric was also known for speaking his mind. 'Some of us say that Edric was saintly, but saints are difficult to live with,' recalled John Bonifant who also worked at Wellington Hospital. 'Edric could be very determined and quite direct. When we were still juniors, he challenged medical registrars and consultant staff if he didn't think things were right. One … registrar got quite annoyed with Edric!'

It was at Wellington Hospital that Edric decided on his first overseas destination – Vietnam. Several of his colleagues had left to work there, and once Edric registered as a doctor, he could join them. He received his registration in 1968, a year that stands out in New Zealand history. On 10 April, in a fierce storm, the *Wahine* ferry ran onto a reef in Wellington Harbour. Hundreds of passengers abandoned ship and 53 died. Wellington doctors played a key role assisting survivors. There is no record of whether Edric was involved; nonetheless, I am sure that this tragic event would have sealed his commitment to work somewhere he was needed. New Zealand had enough doctors, even to cope with a disaster. Edric was young, qualified and hungry for adventure. A few months later, he got his ticket to Vietnam.

Edric in 1969. Photo from the Baker family collection.

4

Vietnam

Vietnam in 1969 was a formidable landing place for a new doctor. North and South Vietnam had spent nearly 15 years at war and the Americans were nearing the height of their involvement. When Edric arrived in Saigon in January, there were soldiers it seemed on every street corner. Shanties crowded the streets and buildings had protective sandbags piled against their walls. These sights fascinated Edric as he was driven across the city. Aged 27, he had three years' work experience in an efficient New Zealand hospital. He was now embracing a new continent, climate and language, having left behind a peaceful country for a war zone.

Edric headed for the city of Qui Nhon, where he was the newest member of the New Zealand Surgical Team. This was a group sent by the government to treat civilians. Members had rotated in and out since 1963, two years before New Zealand began sending combat troops. When Edric arrived, the team was made up of 14 Kiwis: doctors, nurses, lab technicians, radiographers and mechanics. They were stationed in Binh Dinh Provincial Hospital to support the southern Vietnamese whose co-workers had been called away to the military hospitals. The New Zealanders worked day shifts and stayed on call to support Vietnamese colleagues at night.

In Qui Nhon, Edric saw fewer army trucks and less visible war damage than in Saigon. Instead, the war was manifest in refugee shacks with their ragged inhabitants, in destitute people holding begging bowls, and – Edric would later learn – in occasional night-time flashes of gunfire in the surrounding hills. Fighting was close, and the hospital treated war injuries continually, yet the city saw little of the conflict that was experienced in the surrounding Binh Dinh province. Qui Nhon was one haven where life carried on.

That 'normal life' was far from salubrious. In his first letter home, Edric wrote, 'Think of the most ramshackle, decrepit living conditions you can, and that is Qui Nhon.' But the streets were mesmerising. Motorbikes zigzagged round potholes, dodging three-wheeled Lambretta vans and yielding to larger trucks that ruled the road. Edric saw one motorbike balancing six passengers. Women wearing long, split dresses rode bicycles. Edric wrote home, 'The girls hitch the front half of their *ao dai* around the handlebars and the back half in the carrier.' In markets, customers bobbed and bustled under conical hats. Edric had taken Vietnamese lessons before leaving New Zealand, but the language was too fast and unfamiliar; it flowed over and around him like a conversation among birds.

Edric's enchantment turned to dismay when he came to the hospital where the New Zealand team was stationed. Binh Dinh Provincial Hospital was a stark contrast to the New Zealand hospitals he had left. Edric wrote home, 'If Saigon depresses me, and Qui Nhon more so, the hospital is just about the limit. The place is filthy, crowding is appalling, sterile theatre technique is just about impossible, and, in any case, flies come and settle in the wounds and on the instruments.'

Edric's colleagues told me that the hospital had an atmosphere and hygiene standard comparable to a crowded railway station. Skinny children leaned along the fence. Families crouched in the dust. The hospital comprised several two-storey buildings and perhaps 200 beds, but that was a useless measurement. The wards were always as full as creative use of space allowed. Patients lay two or three to a bed, on a piece of plastic or a bamboo mat. Stretchers covered the floor and sometimes the hallways.

Family members hovered to keep their loved ones fed and bathed and to take them to the toilet. These tasks were easier said than done. Water often ran out. While the taps were flowing, nurses would rush to fill up containers. Patients traipsed mud inside from the grounds, but staff lacked enough soap and mops to clean up after them. Rats sometimes ran through the wards. The stench from the buildings extended out into the grounds, where there were too few lavatories, and behind them, an incinerator burning medical waste. A nurse, Barbara Meier, remembered, 'the smell was so strong it would make your eyes water'.

The four main ward blocks of Binh Dinh Provincial Hospital where the New Zealand Surgical Team was stationed. Photo by Peter Eccles-Smith.

Ward 8 for lower limb injuries. Note the crowding and the number of stretchers in the middle of the room. Photo by Peter Eccles-Smith.

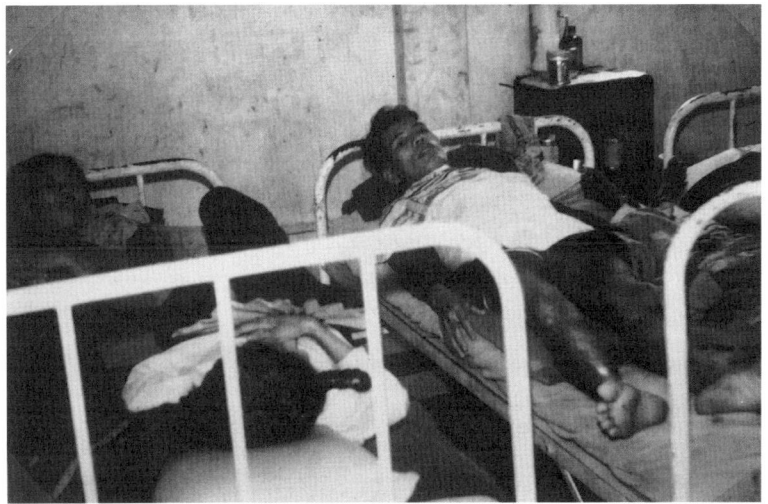

Ward 5 for surgical patients. There are two patients in each bed and both men and women share the ward. Photo by Peter Eccles-Smith.

In that hectic context, Edric was thrust into surgery within days. He later wrote, 'I was not a qualified surgeon. I was what was called the "third surgeon", that is someone who was beginning in surgery, but we had the advice of senior surgeons. And we had to cope with whatever came.' Edric and senior colleagues Graham Power and Jack Enwright took turns managing all surgeries over a 24-hour period. A curfew kept nights relatively quiet, but there would be a flood of new patients at seven o'clock every morning.

If Edric felt intimidated, he did not show it. In early letters he wrote home: 'I am thoroughly sold on the life here. There is just so much worthwhile work to get your teeth into, and the patients are so appreciative! I find that I always have a child or adult, patient or relative holding my hand. And I have been kissed twice now, once by a Buddhist monk!'

He also noted many frustrations:

For a start, the day is far too short. … There is a two-and-a-half hour siesta and except for life and death procedures the hospital comes to a stop. Outside work hours I have no interpreter, and even if I did have one, in most of the wards there would be no nurses. It is very difficult when you are unable to communicate not only with the patients but also with the nurses. … I have decided that I must learn Vietnamese.

Edric worked hard to master the difficult tonal language. His frustration and curiosity motivated him, as did the example of Jack Enwright, the senior surgeon, who was a capable Vietnamese speaker. Edric also remembered the words of an elderly Greek patient he had treated in Wellington: 'If you want to be happy in a new country you have to learn the language and take the people to heart.' Edric worked hard to follow this advice. By the end of April he was able to do ward rounds without an interpreter.

The stories of Edric's patients revealed the cruelty of war. One patient was a young girl who had been riding a buffalo that stepped on a mine. She lost her left arm and leg. She arrived by a Lambretta 'ambulance' nearly a day after her injury. Another case was a boy who lost both eyes to gunshot wounds. The hospital had no artificial eyes to give him. Edric doubted there were any in Vietnam.

These first operations turned the stomach; they made a doctor's blood boil at the horrors and the waste of war. One team member, David Morris, told me, 'You'd just shake your

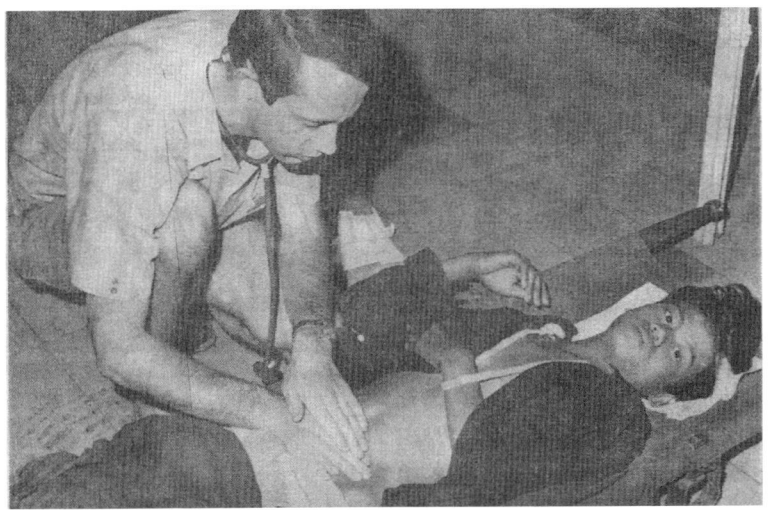

Edric examines a patient at the Binh Dinh Provincial Hospital's emergency admission ward - often the waiting room floor. Photo originally taken by a Vietnamese newspaper, republished in *The Times* Hamilton in 1975.

An airstrike near Qui Nhon in 1970. Photo by Dennis Montgomery.

head and think holy hell, this is dreadful. You treated what was in front of you.'

When it came to the technical aspects of surgery, Edric was on a rapid learning curve. With Jack as a mentor, he learned to improvise with basic equipment and to manage a whole new variety of injuries. This was surgery such as Edric had never encountered in New Zealand. There, patients would arrive at hospital quickly, with injuries that were clean, and survival was expected. In Vietnam it was the opposite. Patients could arrive a day or more after injury. Infection was expected; survival was not. This was no context for the meticulous examinations that had backed up the Wellington Hospital emergency department. In Qui Nhon Edric learned to compromise to keep up with the injury toll.

While the war injuries were horrific, Edric also noticed the ailments that resulted from poverty. Accidents on pot-holed roads were common, as were burns from fires in thatched huts, all adding to surgery queues. Then there were patients at risk of death from malnutrition, cholera or other preventable disease. 'Poverty is a state of emergency,' Edric realised, and would later write, 'Just as in a time of war a state of emergency is declared ... so extreme poverty is a state of emergency.' When Edric was not conducting operations, he would assist his colleague Margaret Neave in the children's department or help Jack to run an outpatient clinic. Patients would come from afar. There was always someone desperate to be seen.

At the end of his long days, Edric would go back to the house he shared with other team members and flop, exhausted, onto his bed, oblivious to the clunking electric fan. But on a deep level, he was energised. On 20 May he wrote home,

'Do you ever have that feeling that you're doing what you've always wanted to do? Well, that's how I feel now, but the work is often horribly frustrating and one feels so dreadfully ignorant.'

There were many challenges: constant heat, regular sickness and the ever-present threat of war. It was sometimes impossible to give patients proper care, a situation maddening for medical professionals. One nurse, Bev Collins, told me about a boy whose broken leg refused to heal. She discovered he had been removing his leg from traction, which aligned his bones correctly, and limping to the toilet because there were too few nurses to help him. Behind all these difficulties, the war risk hovered, with occasional small-scale attacks in the city.

Against this backdrop Edric learned significant lessons. His first came from one needless death. It was a man who needed complex surgery. Edric operated on him for hours, seeking advice from senior colleagues and poring over the surgical textbook as the team worked. The operation was a success and the man lived. The patient's expression, weak with relief, was one positive image that Edric kept in his mind. Three months later, the man came back to the hospital. He was once again unwell, but this time with dysentery, a common disease contracted from drinking contaminated water. Dysentery was preventable simply by boiling water and washing hands – straightforward steps anywhere except the homes of the poor. The condition was also treatable if caught early. But this man's illness was advanced and he was severely weakened by dehydration. Despite the labours of Edric's colleagues, the man died.

The lesson was so weighty it stung. Edric's team had spent hours on complex surgery, requiring expensive equipment and skilled staff, and this man had died for lack of clean water and soap! The inference was clear: simple interventions were what mattered most. To address the emergency of poverty, Edric must focus on primary healthcare: preventing disease and improving access to basic treatments. Edric would always have said that those mattered, yet after the dysentery patient the lesson was linked to a human face. This revelation of the importance of primary healthcare would transform Edric's future practice.

Edric's second major lesson came from Margaret Neave, whom he assisted in the children's department. Margaret was a respected pediatrician who had previously worked in Tokelau and Samoa. She knew how to save young lives using few resources. She was also a Christian, and renowned for her devotion to patients. Team member David Morris told me, 'Margaret was a saint. She was tireless and caring and she gave everything to other people.' Margaret took Edric under her wing. As she frowned over malnourished babies or told off mothers for wiping children's faces with dirty cloths, she explained everything to Edric. The younger doctor must have had numerous questions for Margaret, a senior doctor who shared his faith. While the pair treated patients or walked together to the Catholic Church, no doubt Margaret was a sounding board for Edric's developing philosophies. Margaret believed that it was interventions during childhood that brought the greatest gains. Her life choices testified to this conviction: she poured all her vast energy into improving the health of mothers and children. She would certainly have

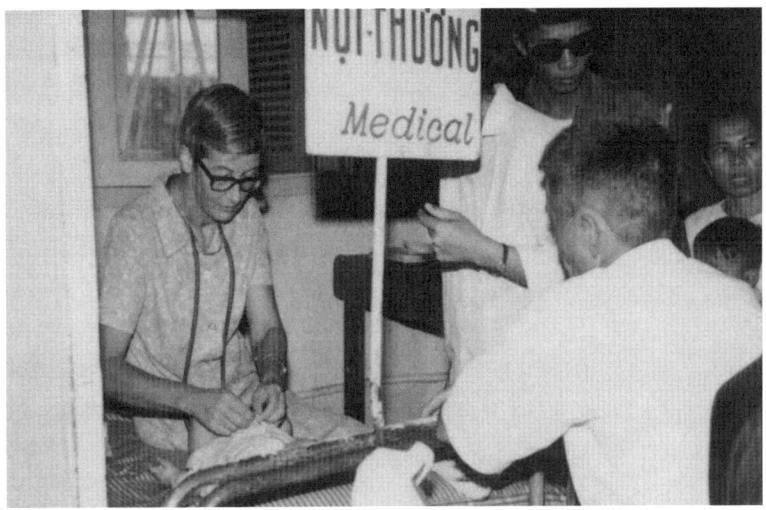

Dr Margaret Neave examines a patient at one of her clinics.
Photo by Dennis Montgomery.

emphasised to Edric that there was nothing more important, nowhere else to invest more energy! Margaret became a long-term mentor for Edric, and her passion rubbed off. Alongside primary healthcare, a second pillar of Edric's lifelong work would be mother and child health.

Within months of arriving in Vietnam, therefore, Edric's experiences had shaped his life direction. Meanwhile, when he could take his mind off patients, there were people to enjoy and fun to be had. Outside hospital work the New Zealanders enjoyed the social life and hospitality offered by the American military. The Kiwis were welcome at American social events and the Officer's Club. They could always get a coffee from the huge urns that appeared wherever there were Americans. New Zealanders were allowed to take American military air transport, and, if no seats were available, could even take the seats from lower-ranking Americans.

The team had access to the American Post Exchange, a department store that, according to nurse Bev Collins, sold 'literally anything.' There was one short-term crisis when New Zealand nurses were barred entry to the store: American officers claimed their jandals – the Kiwi term for flip-flops or rubber sandals – did not meet the dress code. Such an accusation was affronting. 'Without delay, the problem was escalated to the US Provincial Command office,' the team mechanic Dennis Montgomery remembered. 'It was agreed the jandal was part of the Kiwi work "uniform" and we were given dispensation to shop wearing jandals.'

The New Zealanders also made their own social life. Many team members lived at the 'Pink Palace', a sprawling bungalow, which was the team's social centre. That house was home to many parties, to a fridge that worked and to a little dog. The team also enjoyed swimming at an isolated beach near a Catholic leprosarium. The beach was welcome relief from the hospital and the heat. It was so peaceful one could almost forget there was a war, except for the warships out on the horizon.

Edric joined swimming trips but was otherwise absent from the New Zealand social circuit. A colleague Rob Meier told me,

> *The young single guys were a bit boisterous, but Edric didn't partake in a lot of that. He was quiet, ... a very gentle man, and kind. Yeah, that was one of the things. When I first met him I thought, 'You're either going to survive all this or you're going to be hurt by these rough-*

Le Van Duyet, a Qui Nhon street where the Pink Palace was situated.
Photo by Dennis Montgomery.

A family traveling in a buffalo-drawn cart outside Qui Nhon.
Photo by Dennis Montgomery.

ies giving you a hard time.' They'd say, 'Are you going to come down to the club?' He'd politely say, 'No thanks.'

Instead, Edric went out on his scooter visiting Vietnamese friends. He accepted social invitations from local colleagues long before his language was strong. There were memorable first encounters. He found himself guest of honour at a dinner party for a colleague's entire extended family, as he described in a letter home, 'I had already had a big dinner, and they had turned on a magnificent five course meal! You can imagine how I was bursting at the seams at the end.' A few days later, he was amused to have to decline an offer of a Vietnamese bride.

When the security situation allowed, Edric's Vietnamese friends took him out into the countryside. He wrote home in November, 'Yesterday I had a magnificent day driving out in the country with one of my patients and three Buddhist monks. The country is just beautiful: lush green rice paddies and tall coconut palms. … I have obtained a black pajama suit and coolie hat, which I wore. I suppose you could say we did a pagoda crawl. We had lunch at a tiny little pagoda well off the road, all sitting crosslegged on a mat.' These friendships opened up new worlds for Edric, showing him rich details of Vietnam that he could never have found on his own.

They also showed him the poverty that underpinned so many of his hospital cases. Writing home, Edric described one friend's house: 'It looks as if it would fall down if you touched it.' Another family lived 'in a small upstairs shack of a room, probably about as big as Dad's study at Khandallah.' Access was by a rickety outdoor ladder. Just like the patient who had died from dysentery, these families also risked death from

Refugee houses in Qui Nhon about one year before Edric's arrival.
Photo by Peter Eccles-Smith.

Refugee huts at An Khe. Photo by Dennis Montgomery.

squalid living conditions. Such visits made Edric more determined to prevent disease and improve access to healthcare.

Outside Qui Nhon, the conditions were even more bleak. With two colleagues, Edric visited the highlands town of An Khe, a large refugee resettlement area where the New Zealand Red Cross team worked. The journey involved a dangerous drive up the An Khe pass, a common spot for ambushes. At the top they met Peter Wilson, an agriculture expert who would later play a major role in Edric's story. Peter and his teammates worked as jacks of all trades, facilitating the resettlement process. Many refugees were members of Vietnam's indigenous group, the Montagnards. The men dressed in loincloths and women wore elaborate rings about their necks and ankles. Their health was particularly poor.

These realities were challenging. Edric wrote to his sister Hilda, 'I think that when I return to New Zealand I shall be absolutely over-awed by the wealth and standard of living. … It is no exaggeration to say that the worst homes in the poorest of New Zealand city suburbs would correspond to very wealthy homes here.' To his other sister, Hilary, he wrote,

I didn't answer your birthday present question. I must confess I feel a little uncomfortable having so many possessions when so many people around about have nothing. Would it offend your sense of the birthday spirit to combine a birthday and Christmas present and send over some baby bottles and teats? We have a desperate shortage of these at the hospital. Be sure that when you send them we will not give them away but that they will be stolen – but what does it matter? The people who need them will get them!

Vietnamese friends also brought Edric closer to their experience of the war. Some of the saddest times were when friends were drafted away into the army. Edric's Vietnamese teacher had been married only three months before he was called to Saigon for infantry training. Edric also said farewell to the senior laboratory technician, another close friend. The goodbyes were heartrending for those who knew the danger these people faced. As the Greek patient in New Zealand had encouraged him, Edric had indeed 'taken the people to heart', with all the accompanying joy and pain.

Because Edric ventured into Vietnamese social circles, it is unsurprising that the New Zealand team found him remote. Nurse Bev Collins shared with me that 'he was always separate. ... He was doing his own thing, which was getting out in the community with the Vietnamese families. I really admired him and liked him as a person, but couldn't say that I ever got to know him. ... He joked with the Vietnamese in the times we went visiting, but since my language was so terrible, I couldn't understand. They loved him. The Vietnamese really loved him.'

There was one particular friendship. Theresa Le Thi Ngoc Lan was an interpreter, the daughter of a French teacher in Saigon. She spoke beautiful English and French. The two met soon after Edric's arrival, when Theresa worked at the hospital during a short visit to Qui Nhon. They discovered a shared admiration for Albert Schweitzer. Theresa helped Edric find a Vietnamese name, calling him Anh Hoa – 'Anh' a term for an older male, and 'Hoa' meaning peace. As she assisted him with ward rounds, she noticed how sweet he was, and how wonderfully idealistic. She was soon accompanying Edric on outings to visit friends or to offer medical care at the local prison. Theresa balanced on the back of his Vespa, her arm about his waist, the only touch Vietnamese culture allowed. Edric wrote home to his parents, 'I thought you might like to receive some photographs of the one who is claiming my attentions these days. Her Vietnamese name is Ngoc Lan (pronounced Ngock Larn), which means "magnolia". Don't you think she looks like a magnolia flower?'

Although Theresa returned to Saigon, the pair stayed in contact. As this relationship blossomed, it became clear to Edric that he wanted to be in Vietnam long term. But first, there was more he wanted to learn. Inspired by Margaret Neave, he wished to pursue specialties in tropical and child health. When his one-year term in Qui Nhon approached its end, he registered for training in Australia and New Zealand. His farewell to Theresa and her country was reluctant, but not final. The question was not if he would return, but when.

5

Separations

Edric's next two years passed in writing study notes and love letters. He moved to Sydney for six months to study tropical medicine, then to Auckland for six months to study gynaecology and obstetrics. The hospitals seemed like palaces, and how easy it was to work in English! Edric soaked up every drop of knowledge and wrote to Theresa daily.

In the following year, 1971, Edric spent 10 months as a registrar at Christchurch Hospital. I spoke with one of his junior colleagues, Bill Sugrue, by phone. He reflected that in Christchurch, Edric dressed differently from local doctors, had a deep gentleness and seemed without ego, providing opportunities to his juniors. 'Most doctors were trying to impress their bosses. He wasn't. ... I just knew he was a deep Christian. He had that kind of faith that speaks from action.'

Edric's mind remained on Vietnam, or more specifically, Theresa. Letters in her tidy writing stacked up on Edric's desk. Her photo hung on his wall. Edric wrote to his parents, 'Theresa sent me two portrait photographs of herself recently. Do you know, she is the most beautiful girl I've ever seen!' He later wrote, 'Please Mother, do not be annoyed if I write letters to Saigon more frequently than to Wellington! After all in the Bible … we are told that in due course a man leaves his father and mother for someone his own age.'

Edric's life as a registrar sometimes topped 100 hours a week. Nonetheless, he managed to throw himself into the Vietnamese community in Christchurch, making fond friends. Even on his busiest days, he had time to write to Theresa.

Finally, their separation was over. In March 1972, Edric returned to Vietnam. Two years of war had made Saigon appear rougher, but to Edric, the tree-lined streets still felt familiar. He stayed with Theresa's family, and the pair were soon zipping out on the Vespa to reconnect with old friends and visit favourite places, including the only Anglican Church in the country. Edric's plan was to stay in Saigon until early April, then leave for Kontum, the provincial capital of the Central Highlands.

This period in Saigon with Theresa seemed a joyful reconnection, but something must have changed in Edric's thinking because their courtship did not lead to marriage.

As I researched Edric's story more than 40 years later, I emailed Theresa, now living in the United States, to ask how their relationship had ended. All these years on, she recalled it with tears. Edric had simply told her he was not ready to be married. He felt a duty to go to Kontum; that was all there was to it. Heartbroken, she had grabbed back her letters – treasures Edric had carried with him across the world in his suitcase. When he left Saigon, Theresa was too upset to say goodbye. From Kontum, Edric wrote her one final letter that confirmed the relationship was over. From then on, her letters to him were returned, unopened.

Edric's choice to end his three-year relationship with Theresa was a decision never to marry. Edric was 30. He had no further girlfriends, nor do his writings hint of possible relationships. In later life, Edric commented to a friend Peter Wilson that he had chosen not to marry because it would not have been fair to ask a wife to share the type of conditions he knew he wanted to live in. Among Edric's circles of overseas workers, his choice to remain single was not unusual. He was prioritising vocation. Jack Enwright and Margaret Neave never married; they were independent and devoted to patients. Singleness and single-mindedness characterised Edric's role models.

Edric's arrival in Kontum and the Central Highlands felt like setting foot in a new country. The air was cooler than Saigon, and the landscape was rolling hills. The population included many ethnic Vietnamese, but the region was the heartland of the indigenous Montagnards – a group Edric had encountered only once, when visiting the New Zealand Red Cross team at An Khe. Each tribe had its own customs and languages. The highland area was a new slice of Vietnam waiting to be explored.

Edric joined a project he had long admired, based on stories that had reached Qui Nhon – the Minh Quy Hospital run by American doctor Pat Smith. Pat was a scotch-drink-

Edric at Minh Quy. Photo by Kerry Heubeck. ©

A street in Kontum. Photo by Kerry Heubeck. ©

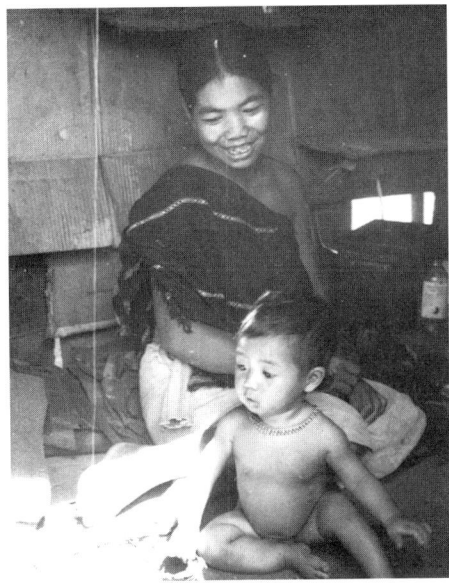

As described by Edric, 'A happy Madonna and child scene from Minh Quy. Note the IV bottle in background and cardboard living quarters.' Photo from Edric Baker's collection.

A Montagnard man in traditional dress for a festive occasion. Photo from Edric Baker's collection.

ing, straight-talking Catholic. Thirteen years earlier she had made her home among the Montagnards, and, learning that they were not welcome in existing health services, she had built up a new hospital for them. Pat emphasised teaching and had soon trained up Catholic sisters and other local people as staff. By 1972, when Edric arrived, a handful of foreigners supported her otherwise Montagnard team.

Edric warmed to many aspects of Pat's hospital. He agreed with their priorities of preventing disease, offering simple treatments and promoting health of mothers and children. One further characteristic appealed to Edric: at Minh Quy Hospital, poor patients were not required to pay for their care, just to bring their own food if they could. Edric was thrilled to join Pat's team. Finally he could apply his recent study and learn more from a brilliant mentor.

It was fortunate that the hospital offered these appeals, because Kontum was not safe. Artillery fire could often be heard all night. The South Vietnamese held the city but it was vulnerable to attack. In the western hills were the Ho Chi Minh trails along which the North Vietnamese Army moved. According to Hilary Smith, an American nurse at the hospital, Pat claimed the army was close enough to spread a northern form of cholera among the Montagnard population. Kontum was the largest city in the region and a strategic prize: if the North Vietnamese could capture the city and control the Central Highlands, they could cut South Vietnam in two. Both armies recognised this significance. The South Vietnamese had placed cannons around the perimeter and fired out rockets as often as every 20 seconds. The North Vietnamese sent shells back. This tussle, though varying in intensity, was a constant backdrop to life in Kontum.

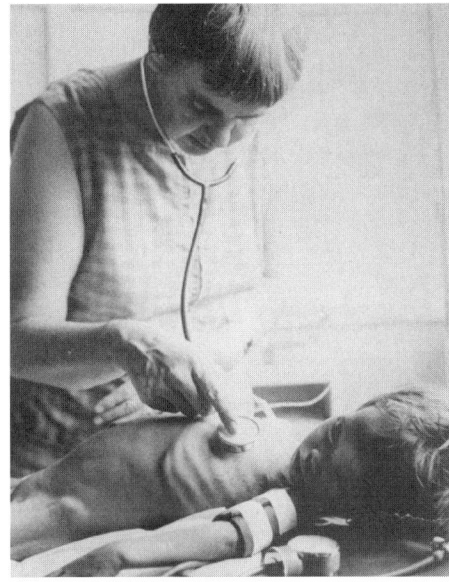

Pat Smith examining a child.
Photo by Rita Lampart.

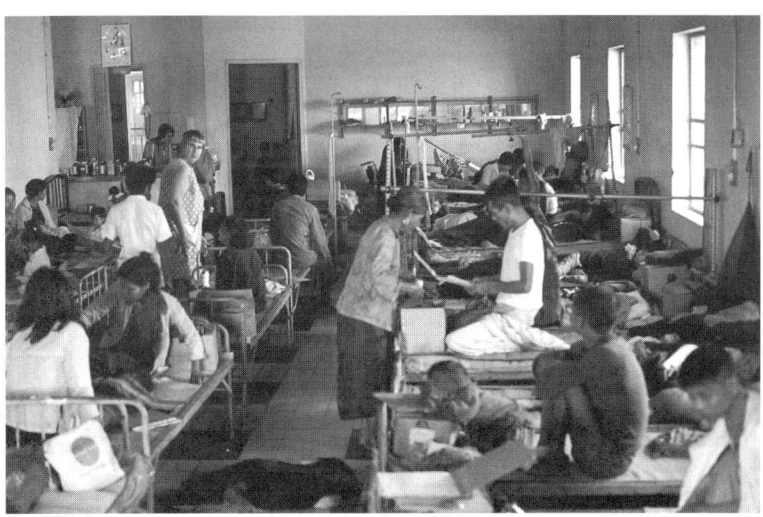

Pat Smith (top left) in the main ward. Photo by Kerry Heubeck. ©

Tents housing patients who cannot fit inside the main buildings of Minh Quy Hospital during its 'temporary' operation out of the Catholic School.
Photo by James Tuohy. ©

Because the city had long been insecure, Minh Quy Hospital was forced to work from an unusual site: a Catholic school. Hilary Smith told the dramatic backstory in the book *Pat Smith and the Minh Quy Experience*. The original site of the hospital was north of the city. In 1968, the North Vietnamese Army attacked; several people at the hospital lost their lives and the army took one German nurse prisoner. Within hours, Pat and her team had to relocate the hospital. The school welcomed them and the sister in charge instructed schoolgirls to sleep in classrooms so patients could have the beds. By the time Edric arrived, this 'temporary' arrangement had lasted four years. Edric described the setup in a letter to his family:

> *Minh Quy, although probably one of the best hospitals in South Vietnam is no plush job. You can smell it when you walk down the street – rather like a pigsty. This is not because it is any dirtier than it should be; it is the inevitable consequence of housing a large number of people in a small area. We have about 200 patients and ... relatives as well. The less acutely sick (often still pretty sick) are in the tents at the front, side and back. ... We have two large wards joined end to end and another large wing which contains store and operating theatre. Outpatients' clinic (80 – 140 per afternoon) is conducted in a shed at the front. Our power supply comes from the Bishop's generator, which means lights from six to ten o'clock at night and about six to eight in the morning. ... [Outside those hours] we try if possible to do emergency surgery by torch light!*

These were difficult conditions, yet Pat and her team had already overcome far greater challenges. As Smith's account describes, when Pat arrived in 1959, she estimated that the lifespan for Montagnards was less than 30 years. Many parents would delay naming their children to see if they would survive. Montagnards had no trust in hospital medicine, preferring to consult traditional healers who 'treated' by offering sacrifices. Through years of patience, Pat and her team won their trust. In time, Minh Quy staff no longer had to persuade people to accept treatment; they sought it themselves, the traditional healers among them. Health improved dramatically. In 1972, the local bishop blamed Pat for over-enrolment in the local schools. Child mortality had dropped to near zero in the areas the hospital served.

Unsurprisingly, Pat was loved by the Montagnards; they gave her the respected 'Ya' title in the local Bahnar language and named her Ya Tih Po-gang, 'The Big Grandmother of Medicine.' However, her legacy came not only from her personal dedication, but her commitment to teaching. She had built up a team by training her 'nurses' to administer medicine and intravenous fluids and perform numerous other procedures. She taught illiterate aides to run errands, clean beds and transport patients. Few of her team had received more than primary education. Besides the foreigners who came to support, no staff had any formal medical qualifications.

To Edric, this was groundbreaking. He had never realised the power of a doctor teaching others. In Qui Nhon, Edric had seen a 1960s book *Medical Care in Developing Countries*, which advocated that doctors train other people to do the majority of jobs in order to maximise their own impact, but he had never seen this concept in action.

Edric noted that the low education level of his Minh Quy colleagues sometimes created difficulties. 'Arithmetic is not their forte,' he wrote, which became a problem when staff needed to calculate a fraction of a dose. However, errors were rare. Smith quotes Pat saying, 'You know, the staff find their own level. We've had auto mechanics who transformed themselves into nurses and nurses who became construction workers. They find the job that fits them.'

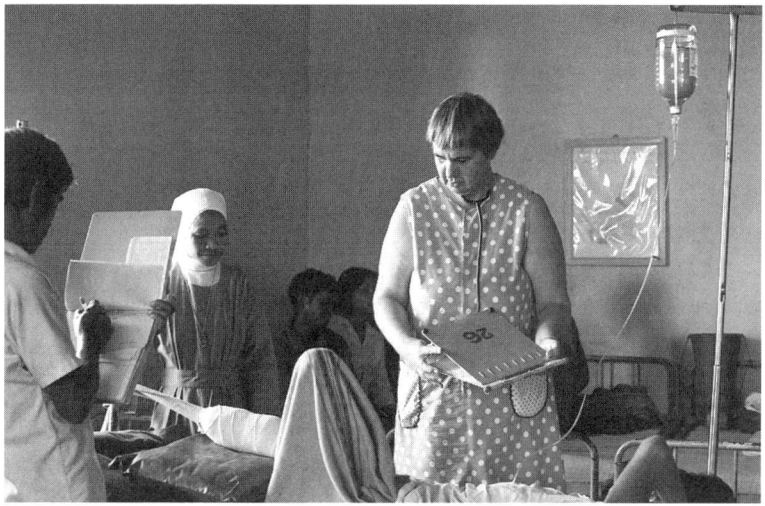

Pat, Ya Gabrielle and a colleague examine a patient.
Photo by Kerry Heubeck. ©

For staff who excelled, Pat arranged specialist training. She sent two sisters to the New Zealand Surgical Team in Qui Nhon to train in anaesthetics and x-ray. Donors funded another of her workers to gain pediatrics expertise in New York. All this training was informal, but these were dedicated people who would not let the lack of formal opportunities stop them helping their own.

Many team members won Edric's deep respect. Lung did physiotherapy for survivors of war injuries. Hiao, aged about 33, did all the minor surgery and served as Edric's surgical assistant. Ya Gabrielle, aged about 37, did medical work, supervised other nurses and ran outpatient clinics. Edric would later describe her as 'a tiny Montagnard who is

Minh Quy's own version of Mother Teresa.' In 2016, I met Ya Gabrielle in Kontum. The petite woman, whose head barely reached my chin, was in her seventies. She was still leading a daily clinic and a midwife training programme, and caring for over 75 children who stayed in her compound in order to attend local schools.

At the time of Edric's arrival, Pat's team were poised to step up their teaching even more by launching a village health programme. Staff would be trained to deliver health education in people's homes, and to treat common conditions without patients needing to come back to the hospital. The team practised by interviewing hospital patients before Pat did, then compared their own diagnoses with hers. Edric must have been delighted to learn of these plans. He had not forgotten his lesson from the dysentery patient in Qui Nhon: if only that man's village had known more about sanitation and diarrhea treatment, he may not have died. Edric was eager to become involved in the village health programme, making up for his lack of Bahnar language with his Vietnamese, English and French.

Edric's start at the hospital was thwarted, however, by a new chapter of the war. Soon after he arrived in Kontum, the 1972 Easter Offensive brought Minh Quy to its knees. This was a ferocious push for territory by the North Vietnamese on a scale the war had not yet seen. Kontum was one of the three fronts of attack. On 12 April, the army took two towns to the north. Kontum was next in line. On 24 April, only three weeks after Edric's arrival, he found himself gathering with the other foreign staff to discuss evacuation. In Edric's words, this is how things unfolded: 'I've never been so bloody scared in my life. ... All the exit roads from Kontum were blocked. You could only get out by air. ... Both the American military and the French bishop considered the fall of Kontum inevitable and possible at any time. We must get out urgently because our presence just increased the risk to the Montagnards and South Vietnamese who must remain behind! So we decided to desert.'

They planned to leave at noon the next day. Edric describes the implications: 'We had no alternative but to just leave the patients – about 200: 120 in the hospital and 80 in the tents outside. We just left them. Some had intravenous going, some were in plaster, some convalescing from surgery, some with broken legs in traction. Only the Montagnard nurses were left to look after them.' Such a departure went against all a doctor's instincts – it was unthinkable to leave patients without one qualified doctor or nurse. Edric had never faced such a predicament. The Montagnard sisters were capable, but they had never run the hospital! How many patients would die for lack of appropriate care? I wonder whether another thought, even more chilling, entered Edric's mind. If patients died, that would result not from a true lack of qualified people at the hospital, but from those people's *choice* to withdraw rather than sacrifice their own safety. Such a thought would have felt haunting to Edric. How many people would die because he was saving himself?

The following morning, each and every thought was drowned by sound, as rockets poured into Kontum. In the flurry of terror there seemed no choice but to follow the momentum of foreign colleagues and head into the bunker. The 10 people gathered could hear rocket fire from the airport

– their escape route – whenever a plane tried to land. No doubt Edric and others said fervent prayers. In the nearby town of Dak To, 10 people had died while attempting to evacuate, and just hours earlier a rocket had killed a seminary student at Kontum airport. Edric later recalled,

> As we sat there in that dark room, we had [those deaths] upon which to meditate... Then even while we were in our bunker, a rocket landed in the bishop's compound, just over the road ... outside his door, but no one was hurt. Rockets arrived about every half hour.
>
> The time for our plane departure came and went. ... Then Glen, our magnificent administration officer, came back from the airport and told us that the plane came, was loaded, then just took off without even closing the hold because the rockets started coming in. There were great holes in the airstrip and a truck and a plane were in flames!

Plan B was evacuation by two helicopters from the other side of the city. After a hair-raising truck ride, Pat boarded the first chopper, Edric the second. Hearts pounded as they gained height, knowing a rocket could strike at any moment. Only when Kontum was a distant dot could the team relax somewhat, and their prayers ease from 'please, please' to 'thank you', then, thinking of the Montagnards, back to 'please'. The team arrived in Pleiku still jittery and flew on to the peaceful town of Nha Trang. There, dazed, they heard the news of Kontum's fall. Each felt sick to imagine what this meant for the patients they had left behind.

Minh Quy staff on the evacuation plane from Pleiku to Nha Trang in April 1972. Edric second from right. Photo from Rita Lampart.

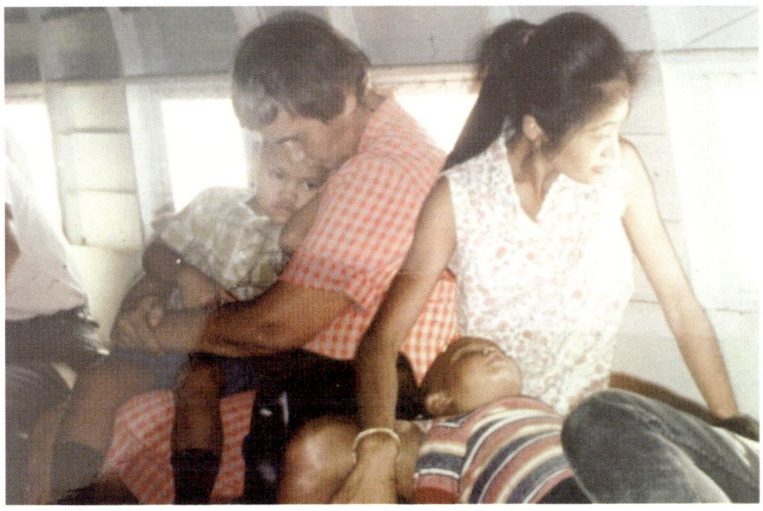

Pat Smith with Det and Wir (her two adopted boys) and a colleague on the same evacuation plane. Photo by Rita Lampart.

Ya Gabrielle (centre) talks to Dr Pat Smith in front of the hospital during a celebration. From Edric Baker's collection.

6

The lesson from the Montagnards

Although shaken, Edric was determined to stay in Vietnam. By mid-May 1972, two weeks after the evacuation, he had learned that the New Zealand Surgical Team was short of doctors and he therefore returned to Qui Nhon. But the communist advance had also transformed that once familiar city. Fearing invasion, more than half the population had evacuated south. They left behind a ghost town. Shops were closed. Tension was visible in the remaining residents. The hospital's medical wards were quiet, but Viet Cong activity in the province kept surgeries as busy as ever.

Meanwhile, Pat Smith had moved to the city of Pleiku, near Kontum, and had begun to bring a disused hospital back into operation. Edric decided to stay in Qui Nhon six months, then join Pat in Kontum if she could go back there. The weeks passed, people drifted back and Qui Nhon was restored to the place Edric knew. As routines returned, so did familiar frustrations, particularly as the hot season reached its height. In July, when Edric was waking to morning temperatures of 32 degrees, he wrote: 'I find I lose my temper very easily – and not very wisely. The other day I told the police director of the reform centre where to get off in no uncertain terms. I was furious. He hands us sick prisoners and then removes them from hospital before treatment is completed.'

A few days later he wrote, 'I think the heat and work are addling my brain … I thumped a policeman today.' The officer had grabbed the arm of a woman who was bruised from head to toe; Edric believed she had been tortured at the hands of police. Such encounters lowered Edric's opinions of the South Vietnamese authorities. He wrote home, 'My political leanings are becoming markedly leftist!' In August he wrote, 'How I wish the rainy season would come.' The temperatures did not drop until September, calming tempers, but the new season also brought rains that covered the potholed streets with lakes.

Despite Edric's occasional outbursts, he must have been an asset to the Surgical Team. In New Zealand, his mother received a phone call from Doctor Doug Kennedy, Director-General of the New Zealand Health Department, who visited Vietnam in June. He told her Edric was the best linguist on the team, 'even better in Vietnamese than Doctor Jack Enwright himself.' Edric was also putting into practice his tropical medicine study in a role overseeing the hospital's tuberculosis programme. Tuberculosis was potentially deadly and it was a challenge to treat because patients had to take medication at home for over six months. Unless patients were supervised, most gave up; they therefore relapsed and continued to infect others. This programme was Edric's first taste of management responsibility. Otherwise, his life was back to the 'wartime normal'. The province bustled with close to 100,000 refugees. There were occasional scares, although nothing compared with the insecurity in Kontum.

Edric heard no news of the Montagnards, though no doubt he regularly thought of them. He must have been desperate to know – how was Minh Quy Hospital faring? He knew the Montagnard staff would not be prepared to manage a hospital under fire. They could have been bombed or looted. The sisters might have lost patients, or even their own lives.

In fact, Kontum had not been attacked immediately after the foreigners' evacuation. An eerie calm extended there into early May, and, concerned for their Montagnard colleagues, two of Pat's foreign staff, John Taylor and Tom Coles, managed to catch a helicopter ride to check on those left behind. They were astounded by what they found. Under the leadership of the nurse Ya Gabrielle the hospital was humming. Hilary Smith quotes John's description:

This is [Minh Quy's] finest hour. Care was almost as if the Western staff were still there. Ya Gabrielle and Hiao were in charge and competent, though lacking confidence. A child with meningitis presented while we were there and Ya Gabrielle asked me to see him. When I turned the responsibility to her she examined him, decided he needed a spinal tap, did the tap, and started treatment all on her own. Not bad for less than a sixth-grade education...

The Montagnard staff had received years of training from Pat. Now, in her absence, they had stepped up to fill the empty roles!

The Battle for Kontum began on 13 May. North Vietnamese troops occupied part of the city and three weeks of intense fighting followed – including in the streets around the hospital. According to Hilary Smith in another account of Minh Quy, *Lighting Candles*, Ya Gabrielle smuggled the following note to John in Pleiku on 31 May: 'From 25 to 30 May we thought every one of us was going to die. We were afraid all the time: afraid of the Viet Cong, afraid of the planes. We saw the Viet Cong kill two people outside the gates of the hospital.' Edric later recounted the Montagnards' story: 'The nurses and patients spent two days hiding under the beds with nothing to eat or drink.' Rockets hit the house where Edric had lived as well as the Cathedral next door. But remarkably, the hospital came through unscathed. By early June, the South Vietnamese Army regained control of Kontum, though skirmishes continued in the city's outskirts. The Montagnards continued to lead the hospital in the absence of Pat and other foreigners. Hiao even conducted successful amputations, which was extraordinary for someone with no formal training in surgery.

In September 1972, Kontum was finally considered secure enough for Pat to return. Edric also visited for a relieved reunion, and he received a transformative lesson. Before his eyes, the hospital was running smoothly under Montagnard leadership. His colleagues Ya Gabrielle, Ya Vincent and Hiao were performing at a level Edric had not imagined possible, considering the limits of their informal training. The sight brought an epiphany: people did not need six years of formal training to provide medical care. These Montagnards were delivering healthcare that they had learned and observed on the job, and their informal training had been tested in adversity.

This was another turning point for Edric. In Qui Nhon, Edric had learned *where* his focus should lie – on simple primary healthcare and mother and child health. Here in the Montagnards' hospital, Edric realised *how* to deliver it – by training local people. His next steps flowed naturally. He later wrote, 'It became obvious to Pat and me that the thing to do was to prepare the local people to run the hospital better.'

In 2008, Edric reflected on the Montagnards' success in an interview with Radio New Zealand: 'They had a lot of spontaneous initiative. Most peoples have spontaneous initiative to cope with emergencies when they arise.' But the Montagnards' success was more than a disaster response. Their people had not always had access to healthcare, which made Minh Quy unique and precious. Edric reflected, 'The Montagnards saw it as *their* hospital: they had a sense of ownership. That is absolutely key.'

In November 1972 Edric shifted back to Kontum. At last, he had a chance to settle into the rhythms of Minh Quy. The supposed 'security' felt tentative – there were frequent outgoing rockets and a few incoming shells – but these were not considered a major threat. He and Pat merged into the reunited team, being mindful to support, not relieve, the Montagnards who had stepped up in their absence. The pair focused more on their teaching role.

Edric, Ya Gabrielle and a colleague visiting a refugee site near Dak To.
Photo by Kerry Heubeck. ©

But once again, Edric's time with Pat would be brief. The
same month as his return, Pat flew home to the United States
to undergo a scheduled operation to remove her gall bladder.
The only other foreigner at the hospital was a Swiss nurse.
Edric was the only qualified doctor at Minh Quy until April
1973 and he took over Pat's role of Medical Superintendent
for over four months.

This was the most significant management responsibility
Edric had held. The task was both humbling and daunting:
Pat was trusting him to oversee a hospital of 200 beds and
the same number of outpatients. Adopting her routine, Edric
began his days with rounds of the wards. This included those
in the tent city in the grounds, where there were dozens of
patients too well for beds, but too unwell to return home. In

the midday heat there was occasionally time to nap or write a letter. Then the afternoon clinic brought another 100 or more patients and staff scurried to clear beds for those needing to be admitted. Emergencies and urgent surgeries punctuated the day as patients' needs did not conform to business hours; Edric would be lucky to get through the night without an emergency to attend.

Although the pace of work was gruelling, Edric found time to get a feel for Kontum. It was a beautiful city of French-style architecture amid fields and jungle-covered hills. The sounds of cicadas and cowbells mixed with the distant thud of rockets. Evidence of April's battle remained: two large planes lay wrecked in the airport, providing, as Edric wrote, 'an encouraging sight for the newcomer.' Yet nature provided a returning normality. 'Rice has been harvested again,' he continued. 'Livestock is again present, houses rebuilt, and even the bomb craters in due course merge in somewhat with the landscape.'

Edric gained an understanding of, and warmth towards, the Montagnards. When he ventured by bike to explore the villages, he found people curious, direct, and full of good humour. Along the roads, some carried possessions in baskets worn like backpacks. Despite owning little, they were hospitable. When Edric visited people's homes, it was difficult to avoid getting tipsy from their offers of rice wine. The Montagnards had distinctive houses – families lived in one-room huts on stilts with woven walls and thatched roofs. Each village had a 'long house' for the teenage boys. The tall roofs of those buildings appeared like oversized hats, and their stilts like feet put down to escape floods. Edric wrote of his excursions, 'You

A Montagnard home. Photo by Kerry Heubeck. ©

A Montagnard long house. Photo by the author.

can find the most beautiful scenery. ... I also feel it is very helpful to get an understanding of the living conditions and the social problems of the people we work with.'

Montagnard customs formed the basis of the Minh Quy social life. Many of the staff members were Christians, and on Sundays they held Catholic Mass in the ward, with staff and patients singing loudly in the Bahnar language. Christmas and New Year involved lively parties with women dancing in lines and men playing gongs. A key pastime was 'drinking the jar' – a tall vessel filled with fermented rice wine – and everyone sat up late, passing around the long straws. (This hygiene risk was not lost on Edric.) Altogether with its traditions and close-knit team, Minh Quy was unique. Edric wrote home, 'Kontum is about the most fabulous place on earth – who having once come here could ever be persuaded to leave?'

Edric had found a hospital with colleagues he admired, priorities that matched his own and even the opportunity to lead during Pat's absence. This context would prove Edric's ideal, but it would not last forever. Edric did not know it then, but the wheels of war were already in motion that would bring this unmatchable time to an end and leave him struggling to recreate it for years afterwards.

As celebrations ended the year and 1973 began, a significant moment was approaching. The North and South Vietnamese were to sign a ceasefire in the Paris Peace Accords. Conversation buzzed throughout the town: could this conclude the war or would it in fact spark another battle for Kontum? Locals feared that the North Vietnamese would try to seize the strategic city before the ceasefire took effect. As the event loomed, anxiety hovered. As medical leader of the

Montagnard nurses at a rice wine party. Photo from Edric Baker's collection.

Minh Quy Hospital front entrance. Photo by Kerry Heubeck. ©

hospital Edric must have felt this acutely.

These fears of another battle were not realised, but neither were the hopes of peace. The agreement ended American involvement in the war, but otherwise brought only a pause in hostilities. In Kontum, where outgoing rockets had been firing every 20 seconds, the sky grew temporarily calm. Edric wrote, 'Sometimes it is hard to sleep at night it is so quiet.'

The sounds of war would soon return. In April, so too did Pat, just as the hot season was drying out the Kontum fields. For Edric, it must have been a relief to hand back responsibility, but he remained busy. Pat and the team seized the moment of the calm in hostilities and prepared to move back into the old Minh Quy site, a few kilometres north of the town. This move was no small effort. The buildings had sat empty for five years. Parts of the complex were damaged and the South Vietnamese had planted mines in surrounding fields. The Minh Quy team started minesweeping and repairs, completing these in time for the hospital to shift back to its old site on 5 July 1973.

Back in the purpose-built buildings and grounds, the staff and patients could breathe more freely. The space was larger and more scenic; the rainy season turned the fields and foliage a deep green. But the pressure would return for Edric. Soon after the team settled at the old site, Pat took an extended visit to the United States. Again, she left Edric in charge of the hospital, this time for one year.

Edric and Dr Pat Smith. Photo by Kerry Heubeck. ©

7

Brushes with death

Pat Smith was showing enormous trust in Edric by leaving him in charge. It was July 1973. Edric had worked as a doctor for just over seven years, two and a half of these in Vietnam. To lead a hospital for an extended period was a step up in responsibility. In preparation for longer workdays, Edric set up a bed in a small converted trailer so that he could live full time on the hospital grounds.

Edric took to the new role with great energy. One of his first activities was to improve the tuberculosis programme, drawing on his experience from Qui Nhon. More than 800 patients had defaulted on treatment, so Edric sent staff members to follow up those patients to prevent them from spreading the disease.

Meanwhile, day-to-day tasks remained a just-managed chaos. Edric wrote home:

I am just about driven up the wall by crazy young men! I have two psychotic youths, tied down to their beds ... who every time they wake up from their last tranquiliser injection start singing lovely religious songs. This would be okay, except that the volume is too loud and the record is not turned over, not to speak of being turned off! Into this mad hubbub we get patients comatose with cerebral malaria who won't stop fitting ...

One night a psychotic patient disappeared from the hospital. Wandering into a neighbouring village, the man attempted to steal a chicken, then was shot in the leg by guards who mistook him for the Viet Cong. Edric wrote home that the patient 'plus gun-shot-wound fractured femur and dead chicken were delivered to the hospital ...' Edric arrived the next morning to find the patient in traction with the chicken strung up next to the intravenous bottle!

The risk of belligerent or careless fire was as unpredictable as the patients' behaviour. In September 1973, 'friendly forces' began firing old ammunition into fields near the hospital. Edric wrote, 'Two days ago they got their aim wrong and we rescued a large piece of outer shell about the size of a pudding plate which fell from the sky and landed in the garden 50 yards from the hospital kitchen!! I really threw a cranky! You wouldn't believe how coarse I've been getting since working here. My language is just terrible!'

Edric worked to the point of exhaustion managing these challenges. During his first six months of leadership, he had

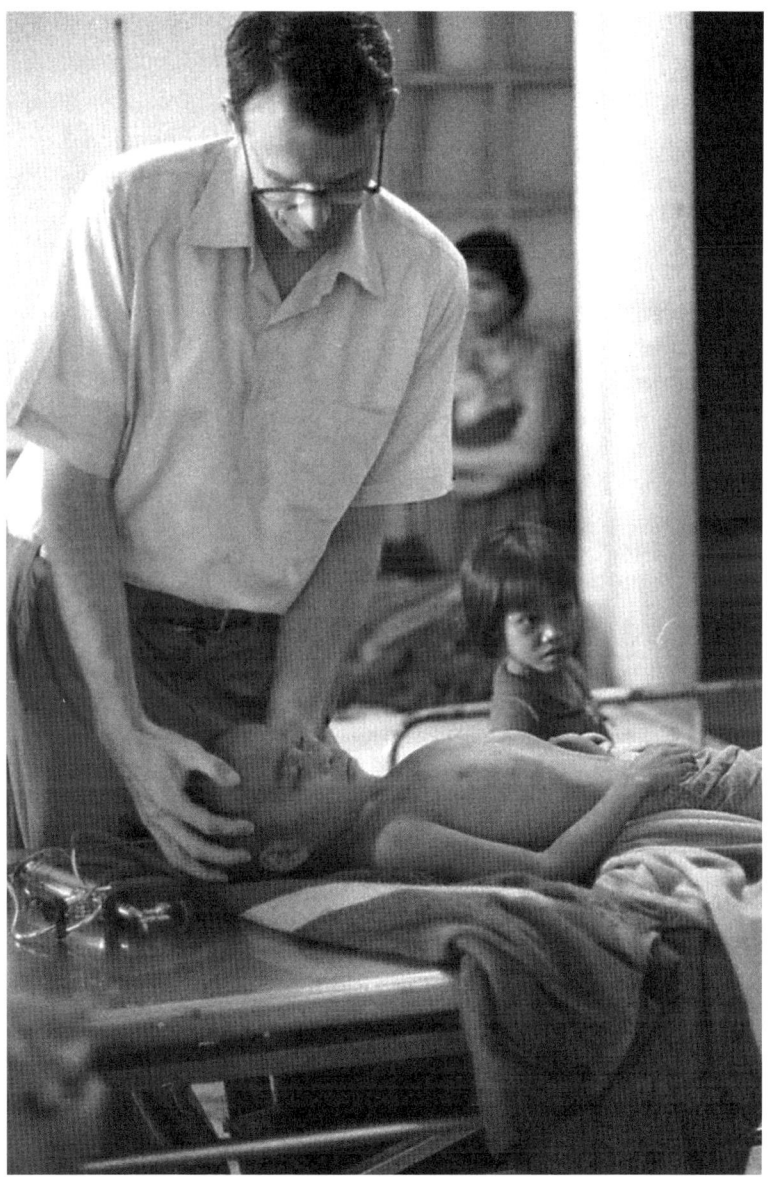

Dr George Christian attends a patient. Photo by Kerry Heubeck. ©

the help of an Indian doctor, George Pradhan. At the start of 1974, midway through Pat's absence, a third doctor arrived. It was an American, George Christian, an affable man in his forties who would undergo several ordeals alongside Edric. The presence of these two doctors reduced Edric's workload but not the weight of responsibility. He would not get a holiday until Pat returned in July.

In such tiring conditions, Edric could have been forgiven for flagging in his commitment to patients. Yet the opposite occurred: his courage and dedication were about to be tested. In March, Edric wrote to his parents of a remarkable event, 'A young Montagnard man was brought to hospital with an apparently unexploded M79 round buried in his buttock! You could see it beautifully on the x-ray and we were all terrified it would explode on the least movement. The M79 is a horrible thing that is primed by rotation and then explodes on contact. … It is impossible to tell how many more rotations are needed before explosion!'

I imagine that cold fear must have fallen over the staff with this discovery. Who would risk operating to remove such a dangerous object? Each doctor must have weighed in their mind the likelihood of success, against the risks of losing their own hands or lives to an explosion! Edric, as doctor in charge, must have felt responsibility heavily. He decided the surgery would proceed: three doctors would take part and Edric would put his own life on the line as one of this team. In a field behind the hospital, Edric and colleagues spent half a day building a bunker of sandbags surrounding the patient. The operation would be performed through a small hole between the sandbags. Should the device explode, the surgeons would be shielded, at least partially, from the explosion.

The doctor who led the surgery was a visiting Vietnamese man. Edric assisted him and George Christian gave the anaesthetic. From a safe distance, a crowd of spectators stood watching, transfixed. Even the Province Chief came to witness the spectacle. The suspense must have sparked furtive prayers from the crowd as the operation commenced. Should they look? Or look away? Everyone awaited an explosion.

I wonder what filled Edric's mind as he assisted in this surgery. Operating within inches of an explosive, *touching* the device in order to remove it, was among the greatest risks Edric had ever taken. This was a natural extension of his choices to return to Vietnam and Kontum – both moves that put his life at risk. Yet, as leader of the hospital, he was allowing other surgeons to endanger themselves too. Was that responsible? Most likely, Edric believed that doctors had a duty to put aside their own safety for patients, and was choosing to demonstrate that in action.

As the crowd watched the field surgery, captivated and ready for horror, no explosion came. The Vietnamese doctor, Edric and George completed the operation, causing the crowd to erupt in cheers and then laughter in relief. Edric described how the event concluded: 'The three of us received the [South Vietnam] Cross of Gallantry, the patient did very well, and the round turned out not to be an unexploded M79, but rather an already exploded Viet Cong B40!'

In July 1974, Pat returned to the hospital and an exhausted Edric handed back the reins. He must have felt relieved but also proud. 'Minh Quy continues as always to be a shambles,' he wrote, 'but it is a much more orderly shambles than it was

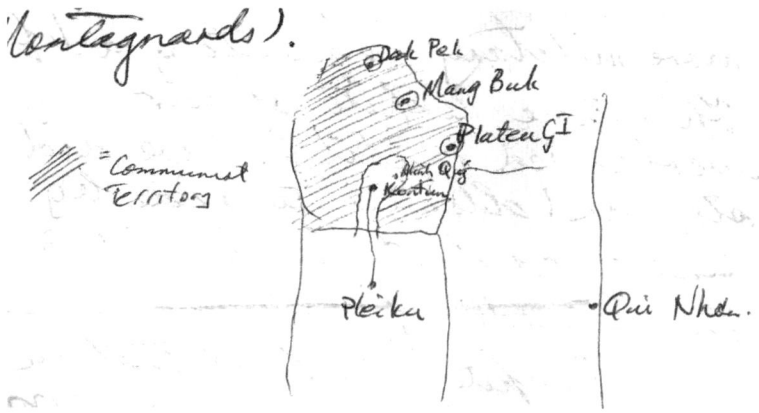

A sketch by Edric showing Kontum surrounded by area held by the North Vietnamese Army. From a letter to Betty Baker, 9 June 1974.

a year ago.' The security situation in Kontum remained tense. The hospital was bursting with patients because of incoming refugees and the North Vietnamese now surrounded the city on three sides.

Within days of Pat's return, the threat of attack became reality. To the horror of hospital staff, the South Vietnamese set up guns just south of the Minh Quy compound. It appeared they intended to use the hospital as a shield! Sure enough, they soon lobbed artillery over Minh Quy towards the North Vietnamese in the hills. Several returning rockets landed in the hospital grounds, killing two Montagnard workers and one patient. Pat had experienced a similar incident in 1968. She ordered an immediate evacuation to town, where, this time, the staff and patients found refuge in the Provincial Hospital. (Several Montagnard staff bravely stayed on at Minh Quy to deter looters.) Edric operated on a groundsman who later died from his wounds. The only person to be found whose blood matched was Pat. She gave one bag of blood, and then another. 'After giving her third bag of blood Pat had to go and lie down,' Edric later wrote. 'This is the woman who inspired us.' The team spent one uncomfortable night in the Provincial Hospital, but was able to return to Minh Quy the next day.

After this incident, Edric finally took a holiday. He had now been in Vietnam continuously for nearly two and a half years, and in two stints, he had spent 16 months in charge of Minh Quy. For much of that time, he had longed for a break. But even now that he could take one, he ruled out returning to New Zealand owing to the 'exorbitant' cost:

> *The return airfare to New Zealand is about $US1200 or put in more practical terms, it would employ eight Montagnards for a year at Minh Quy, or … would be equivalent to about 1800 bed days and 1200 outpatient consults. When one considers also that there is still plenty of malnutrition around and lots of people are in rags it becomes difficult to justify such an expensive holiday. To do so virtually destroys the meaning of one's being here.*

Edric's financial frame of reference, and the place he belonged, had become Vietnam. He chose to take a less expensive break, staying for one month at a swimming spot near Qui Nhon.

By the turn of 1975, Minh Quy had much to celebrate. New projects were about to launch, and Edric was studying the Bahnar language – an investment for long-term work at Minh Quy. Yet even as excitement for these projects grew, a cloud was gathering. In late January, several attack scares set patients screaming and staff scrambling to bring all patients inside the concrete walls. By late February, the threats had become real. Rockets showered down on Kontum in greater numbers. Several times the staff huddled in the bunker, their bodies and minds rocked by the sound of explosions. This was disruption the staff could not afford. The hospital had 340 patients, a record number, much higher than the usual 250.

By March, supply roads were being cut one after another. The staff could see the South Vietnamese Army aiming guns over the hospital towards the North Vietnamese positions on the opposite hills. The foreigners packed evacuation bags. Then on 10 March came dreadful news. The North Vietnamese Army was attacking Ban Me Thuot, a town 140 miles south. The army now surrounded Kontum on all sides. An invasion of the city was imminent.

Five days later, a messenger delivered a grim note to the hospital: foreigners who wished to evacuate must be at the airfield in one hour. There was a flurry as Pat and others said hasty goodbyes. Questions echoed down hospital halls in French, Vietnamese and Bahnar: The foreigners were leaving? What did this mean? But Edric and George Christian had other plans. They had no family responsibilities that obliged them to return home. They predicted that if communists seized the city they would be allowed to continue work. The pair also made a simpler calculation – where else could a doctor do more good? Although the Montagnards had managed the hospital alone, it was clear they could use assistance. Pat may have guessed what the doctors were considering, because years later George recalled her remark: 'You're not going to do something stupid, are you?' She had no time to persuade them, however. The moment for evacuation came and Ya Gabrielle and the Montagnard staff lined the driveway as Pat and other foreigners waved farewells. Peggy Braile, an American nurse, recalled her last glimpse of Edric amid her rushed goodbyes: he was in the operating room, head down, carrying on.

NZ Doctor Elects To Remain In Sth Vietnam

A NEW ZEALAND doctor has elected to remain in a South Vietnamese hospital taken over by communist forces.

Dr Edric Baker, whose parents live in Paraparaumu, has remained behind at the Minh Quy Hospital in the Central Highlands province of Kontum, which was swept up in the North Vietnamese advance two weeks ago.

Refused

Although he knew of the impending takeover, Dr Baker refused to join the flood of refugees heading to the coast and the south.

His mother, Mrs J V T Baker, said today: "He made the choice and stayed on for the benefit of people who may have become refugees and patients.

"We have had just the one letter from him — dated March 13 — which he gave to one of the evacuees. We have not heard since.

Dr Edric Baker, who has remained in South Vietnam.

him. Food may not be getting through. You can imagine the

Kiwi doctor won't budge

N.Z.P.A.-REUTER

SAIGON, Tuesday. — A New Zealand doctor is refusing to budge from a hospital at the Central Highlands town of Minh Quy.

Though the rest of the staff were moved out, Dr Eric Baker, and American doctor George Christian, stayed with the patients.

And at Dalat, 145 miles north-east of Saigon, 15 missionaries were among the dozens of hospital staff in the highlands who have left for safer areas.

Nurses Praise Courage Of N.Z. Doctor

10.4.75
Daily Teleg
(48)

From
NIGEL PARSONS
Herald Staff Reporter
Singapore

When the Communist forces in Vietnam moved in to occupy the Highlands province of Kontum last month, a New Zealand doctor stayed to do what he could for the people under his care.

"The last I saw of Dr Ed Baker was in the hospital operating room; we have not heard of him since," said Miss Marion Brown, a New Zealand nurse.

Miss Brown

Miss O'Neill

same circumstances, but they will pull through."

Miss Brown and Miss O'Neill had been surprised by the speed of the recent Communist advance.

She had been in Vietnam since 1968 with the New Zealand surgical team and was working in Qui Nhon in Binh Dinh province. The situation there had been "normal," she said, until 48 hours before the evacuation.

Vietnamese civilians to whom she spoke had been terrified of the Communists. Both nurses favoured the evacuation of orphans.

Commitment

"It is justified, and I hope

N.Z. medic missing in Vietnam

NOTHING has been heard of New Zealander Dr Edric Baker since Communist forces over-ran the South Vietnamese hospital in which he was working almost two weeks ago.

Dr Baker was working in Minh Quy Hospital in the Central Highlands province of Kontum.

Though he was apparently aware of the impending Viet

Articles in New Zealand newspapers *Kāpiti Observer* (top left), *The Daily Telegraph* (bottom left) and *The Dominion* (top and bottom right) in March – April 1975.

8

Eat with, work with, live with the people

For the next few days, the hospital team must have run on adrenalin. Work continued for the remaining staff, but the tension was palpable. Edric and George Christian tactfully destroyed the decorations they had received from the South Vietnamese Army. Huge fires lit the sky as the army burned munitions and began their retreat. Vietnamese civilians poured out of Kontum on foot to escape the coming siege. When Edric drove into town to collect patients he found the streets in disarray – doors were ajar, belongings dropped in the street.

As Kontum was undefended, the North Vietnamese Army took it easily in their victorious sweep towards Saigon. At first, the hospital continued to run as normal, though with reduced patient numbers. After about 10 days the new authorities made their first visit to Minh Quy: an officer and three armed soldiers asked the doctors to remove certain maps and pictures from the walls and informed them that education sessions would soon begin. The soldiers did not, however, request the doctors to stop work. Edric and George wondered – would they be left alone?

The answer came a few days later. More soldiers arrived in a jeep and requested that the two foreigners go with them at once. Edric protested – he was in the middle of ward rounds – but the messengers assured him he could soon return. Edric and George went with them; that was the last they ever saw of the hospital.

The front page of Wellington newspaper *The Dominion* on 21 March 1975.

The following account is based on separate summaries written by Edric and George. In 2016, I contacted George, then in the United States, and he generously emailed to me his memories. The pair were taken out of Kontum in an open truck supervised by armed guards. They were driven north then east into the jungle, before being forced to walk three hours on foot. The end of their journey was no welcome sight: a large wooden stockade with guard towers, surrounded by a dozen thatched huts. From one building emerged a young man in a black outfit who barked, 'Viet Cong number one.' George recalled, 'In Vietnam "number one" means very good … so naturally, we agreed.' Guards locked Edric and George into a hut, 7 by 10 feet, with an old ammunition case in the corner for relieving themselves. There they lay sleepless on the dirt floor beneath wooden barred windows.

In the morning guards unlocked the door and Edric and George could take stock of their surroundings. They were in a Viet Cong prison camp. Music and propaganda played from a loudspeaker. Forest canopy covered the site, disguising it from the air. Near their hut was the main stockade, which Edric and George were not allowed to enter. It stretched 200 feet across with four guard towers and walls of upright timber too high to scale. Edric estimated there were about 100 prisoners beside themselves. Prisoners and Viet Cong personnel came and went between the stockade and fields, huts and open latrines.

For Edric, these sights must have been at once fascinating and terrifying. Here were the Viet Cong who had sat hidden on the Qui Nhon and Kontum hills. He had heard much about them, but seen little. What were they like? At the same time, Edric must have felt unease if not dread. What was the purpose of their captivity? He could not predict how this encounter would end.

Edric and George quickly learned the rules and routines of confinement. During daytimes they could walk freely, within bounds. Unlike other prisoners, they were not made to go to re-education sessions. Neither were they forced to work the fields, where lines of prisoners bent in long lines, supervised by guards. The doctors could wash in a small river daily, a guard watching. They were barred from practising medicine, even to assist the camp personnel, and their requests to return to Minh Quy were denied. They were also forbidden from speaking to other prisoners, though Edric stole conversations at the latrines. He learned that he and George were the only foreign prisoners; the others were all Vietnamese with perceived links to the former government. George spoke little Vietnamese and relied on Edric for explanation.

Each day they ate three meals of rice and vegetables. The occasional meat was unappetising – fish, porcupine, rat and bat ('which I do not recommend', George wrote, 'they are bitter'). Edric and George ate the same food as the guards, but never enough. They began to feel the weakness and dizziness of malnutrition.

They also felt the toll of boredom. Some days they helped to clean the grounds, or crushed peanuts for meals, but most days passed without occupation. They thought of the hospital. How were Ya Gabrielle, Hiao and the others? Was Minh Quy still in operation? What a reckless waste it felt to be sitting idle on hands trained for surgery! The days became weeks. To pass the time, Edric wrote out the Lord's Prayer in Vietnamese inside a piece of split bamboo. He and George recounted their pasts and mused on their futures. Edric's future vision was clear. He had a list of four places he would like to visit: Papua New Guinea, Zambia, India and Bangladesh. If he could not stay in Vietnam, perhaps he might work in one of those places. But any future for the doctors was uncertain. Would they ever be released? Each night, when guards locked them back in the hut, Edric poured out his frustration and fears in his prayers.

Outside the camp, there was no word of Edric or George. Certainly, no news came to New Zealand where Betty, John and family waited desperate for word of Edric's where-abouts. As the communists established their administration in Vietnam, Betty posted one food parcel after another into a communication black hole. More than 40 letters for Edric either returned to their sender or vanished. For Betty and John the worry mounted – had Edric been killed? Hope did not fade, however. One of Edric's former colleagues commented to a New Zealand newspaper: 'Edric speaks and writes Vietnamese perfectly, and if anyone can make it, he will … He could live off the smell of an oily rag.' In July there was a glimmer of hope when the South Vietnamese embassy reported a sighting of Edric in Kontum. But this news was false, bringing disappointment greater than the hope it aroused.

For Edric and George, more weeks passed in boredom, hunger and unease. Though they never heard or witnessed violence at the camp, they remained prisoners with an uncertain fate. Twice they feared the worst. One morning the guards did not unlock their door. Through the barred window George could see guards digging a hole nearby. He and Edric froze. This was it! They had refused evacuation only to be buried in a jungle camp! But their fears were misplaced. The guards were simply digging a foundation, unlocking the doctors' door a forgotten chore. A second hair-raising incident was a policeman visiting to question them. His inquiries implied that Minh Quy had served the South Vietnamese Army. But nothing came of this interrogation. As Edric reflected, 'I expect they didn't quite know what to do with us.'

In spite of their imprisonment, the doctors came to appreciate the ingenuity of the Viet Cong. These jungle dwellers channelled water to the camp in open, overlapping pipes of bamboo. They built huts without nails. At the nearby river, they fashioned a bridge entirely from bamboo and vine. When conditions allowed, some were friendly. On one occasion the camp commander invited Edric and George to his office and shared his brandy.

Edric also came to admire some of his captors' ideals. Although he could not forget the Viet Cong's atrocities that had brought patients to the hospital, in the camp Edric saw them as idealists acting on their principles. These were people with few resources surviving in harsh jungle for what they believed, and their prisoners – at least Edric and George – ate the same food as the guards! Edric was given communist magazines and a children's book to read, and the content struck him. '[It was] about the suffering and potential of the people,' George recalled. 'Revolutionary heroes, that sort of thing … There were slogans like "People united to solve their own problems".' One slogan lodged deep in Edric's mind: 'Eat with, work with, live with the people.' This idea would resurface in his work in years to come.

After three and a half months in captivity came Edric and George's gravest challenge. George, wasted from malnutrition, developed back pain so severe he could not walk. A medic offered to take him for treatment, but George opted to remain at the camp. Their captivity had no end in sight. With only aspirin for relief, painful days rolled on.

One day, 11 August 1975, without prior warning, Edric and George were told they were leaving the camp. They had spent four and a half months in captivity. Guards escorted them out that evening, carrying George in a hammock beneath a pole. It was a tortuous journey. The dirt road was no longer passable in the heavy rains, so Edric and the guards waded through mud for hours, trudging 30 kilometres of jungle towards the main road. Sometime in the night they reached a river too swollen to cross, and slept a few hours on the bank, exhausted and miserable. In the morning they found the main road and made it to Kontum. There an officer told them they were being expelled as enemies of the state. George later said, 'That was fine by me.'

The pair were driven via Cam Ranh Bay to Saigon, then flown to Bangkok on a French chartered plane evacuating foreigners. Once they landed, Edric and George went their separate ways. Both were too physically and emotionally shattered to celebrate. They never knew what political wind changed to enable their release, except that other foreigners were released at a similar time. It is possible their captivity was the length of time it took the new regime to decide to expel foreigners, and then to carry it out. In parting, George took with him a gift from Edric, the split bamboo on which Edric had written the Lord's Prayer in Vietnamese. When the pair reconnected many years later, George recalled this gift, and when he wrote to me in 2016, he still had it.

From Bangkok, on about 17 August, Edric phoned his family for the first time since captivity. He spent a few days recuperating at the home of the New Zealand ambassador, a friend of his father, and from there he poured out a long letter home, joking about 'four and a half months of zero social life'. But beneath his humour was sincerity: 'Confinement is not a wonderful experience but one can discover thrilling things about Christ.' He asked his family to pray for the Vietnamese, 'the most important people in the world'.

Edric had been ripped away from Vietnam and would never return. He could not have imagined such a reality, and the weight of it would not settle on him for some time. In the moment, Edric's mind remained on healthcare. Instead of returning directly to New Zealand to see his family, he spent three weeks of his newfound freedom visiting health initiatives in Thailand, Papua New Guinea and the Solomon Islands. He wrote to his parents, 'Please forgive the delay in arriving home but this is important work!' Somewhere he picked up an illness, perhaps malaria. He arrived in New Zealand nearly collapsing from exhaustion. His body and emotions would take time to recover, but his resolve was intact. It had just withstood fire.

9

The wanders

Edric took time to recuperate in the care of his family. By 1975 his parents had moved to Paraparaumu, north of Wellington. Their new garden was filled with familiar flowers and out to sea was Kāpiti Island, the backdrop of Edric's childhood holidays. Betty stripped her lemon tree making hot drinks for him. Soon the Bakers were reunited for the first time in more than three years. Edric had missed many significant moments in the life of his family. He had nieces, nephews and in-laws to meet.

But Edric did not really want to be back. One of his colleagues from the New Zealand Surgical Team, David Morris, told me, 'I assumed he was one of those people who would have stayed in Vietnam forever.' Edric's thoughts remained on Kontum. The drama of war had bonded him with his colleagues and it was impossible not to imagine them in the turmoil of the war's end. He later learned that Ya Gabrielle was being held in captivity. Minh Quy, as a hospital for Montagnards, had been shut down for good. Edric was powerless: the country was closed. It felt like being separated from family.

One comfort for Edric during this time was Margaret Neave, his mentor from the New Zealand Surgical Team. Margaret had returned to Wellington. As Edric recovered his health, she visited several times. The two were 'like minds', sharing opinions on faith, vocation and healthcare priorities; no doubt they reflected at length on Vietnam and discussed future plans. I can imagine they also had lively conversations about the four destinations Edric had listed in the Viet Cong camp: Zambia, Papua New Guinea, India and Bangladesh.

Staying still must have felt unbearable for Edric, because within a few weeks of returning to New Zealand, he had decided to leave again, this time for Papua New Guinea. His brief stop there on his return from Vietnam had piqued his interest. Margaret also found the country intriguing; she would soon shift there herself, albeit to a different region.

Edric was perhaps busying himself, moving quickly to escape the fact that his chosen life had been cut short. He was not the only one to return restless from Vietnam. A friend of Betty's who had served there wrote from Western Samoa, 'As you can see, those of us forced to leave our people have all got "the wanders". I am not surprised Edric is in Papua New Guinea.'

Edric's parents must have been crestfallen when he announced his departure, so soon after he had relieved them of worry. Perhaps his mother tried to persuade him to stay; perhaps she knew that such an attempt would be fruitless.

Either way, Edric said his goodbyes. His 'wanders' would take him to three continents and away from his family for the next five years.

In November 1975, Edric arrived in Papua New Guinea, one of the four places he had wished to visit while in the Viet Cong camp. He was eager to learn more about medicine for the poor. Edric settled in the town of Goroka, the provincial capital of the Eastern Highlands. It had a climate he described as 'perpetual spring' – cold at night and hot in the afternoons. His stay in Papua New Guinea would last only nine months, however, as he felt unable to deliver healthcare in line with his ideals.

Edric's new role had two parts: he was to lead the children's ward in Goroka Hospital and oversee a rural health centre. It felt like he was moving between worlds. Goroka residents were urbanised and wore western dress. The people in surrounding villages were subsistence farmers. Women had grass skirts and bare chests – save for elaborate necklaces – and men wore pig tusks through pierced noses.

In both contexts, Edric's key battle was with malnutrition. Four in five children were malnourished, he estimated, and wrote, 'These figures must be among the highest in the world.' The response was to track children's growth against weight charts. Health centres had started to roll out this programme but supply shortages limited its success. Edric put his own money towards printing 10,000 more health books. He also asked Betty to gather donations in New Zealand, which she did with enthusiasm.

Edric enjoyed the work on prevention and community health. Yet Papua New Guinea did not captivate him as

Vietnam had done. He must have realised this on arrival, for he did not invest in learning the language, instead spending his time reading about anthropology and communism.

Furthermore, at Goroka Hospital he found he did not have freedom to lead as he chose. When he encouraged nurses to upskill beyond their qualification, as he had done at Minh Quy, his superiors at Goroka Hospital did not approve. He wrote in a letter,

> *I can see we are heading for a conflict with the hospital matron over what is the role of nurses. On the pediatric ward we hold very strongly that the sisters have to do the work of doctors ... because this is a poor underdeveloped country and with emergence from Australian colonisation there just aren't going to be enough doctors to go around. The matron ... rests everything on the Australian model and is very upset when sisters are asked to do things for which they haven't been trained!*

The matron would soon be relieved of her concerns: when Edric's nine months were over in August 1976 he did not extend his stay. Meanwhile the focus on pediatrics had sparked his interest in further study, so he left for Liverpool to do a six-month course in Tropical Child Health.

On his way to the United Kingdom, Edric had the chance to visit two more places he had thought about in the Viet Cong camp. He spent one week in India and another in Bangladesh. The latter immediately appealed. In 2012, he told Radio New Zealand, 'When I got down out of the plane in Bangladesh, I could just tell by the feel of it that it was going to be the right place. ... It was maybe three years later that I finally came to work [there].' How did he know? I wondered. Was it the climate, the people or the healthcare needs? Of all the questions I wish I had asked Edric, this ranks highly among them. Perhaps what Edric felt was one of God's rare but significant nudges of direction, describable only as a peaceful certainty, a knowing that sits in the gut.

In that significant week in Bangladesh, Edric visited five healthcare projects, spending hours travelling along highways that cut through shining, flooded fields. One programme that impressed him was the Savar Rural Health Project, where doctors had trained 40 paramedics to provide health services. All Bengali, they lived together in a commune. Each member of staff – even the doctors – helped to maintain the gardens, a practice that disrupted typical hierarchy. Edric stored these ideas away. He departed from Bangladesh feeling certain that he would be back.

Edric's week in India was different. He felt no comparable excitement or pull in him to return. He did, however, learn valuable lessons. Edric was searching for ways to serve the poorest people. Observing an Anglican hospital in Delhi, Edric identified stumbling blocks to avoid:

This must be one of the few mission hospitals in the country which is [financially] self-supporting. This is achieved by graded charges according to [patients'] affluence, but as I think must be almost universal for mission hospitals in this country, it means that you get very few of the really poor, although plenty of moderately poor. The hospital has just had a new block built costing $150 million [contributed by overseas aid] ... However this massive new palace will only do a little more than double *the patient capacity, but will multiply running costs by ten! So I do not see how they will be able to accept any but very rich patients!*

Edric was more impressed by the priorities of Mother Teresa's projects in Calcutta. He wrote, 'They really do get the very, very, very poor, by going out with the van and picking them up off the street – and charging nothing. As an act of love their work cannot be overestimated, and to visit their centre for the dying destitute is a deeply moving and purging experience.' However, he noted their limitations: 'They also do slum and rural clinics, but I was not very impressed by the standard of their medical work – how could one be? In one of the clinics they do, three sisters (religious not nursing) plus about three helpers go out and in about half a day see 1500 patients! With no doctors!' Edric remembered these lessons, along with all the other observations from his travels, and journeyed on to the United Kingdom.

His course in Liverpool was a six-month breather in a cooler climate. Edric arrived at the time of year when the trees along the River Mersey reddened and their leaves fell. His course was on Tropical Child Health: he spent his days reading about the world's warmest countries, while frost began to form outside his windows. By mid-winter, the Cathedral 'evening' service was at three thirty in the afternoon before the sun set half an hour later. It was impossible to recall tropical sunshine when fog was 'turning to ice inside your nostrils', as Edric put it. By the time the weather warmed, he had passed his exams and was ready to move on.

His next destination was the peaceful country of Zambia, east Africa. In April 1977 he settled in the rural town of Katete, his starting point for a one-year stay. Zambia was the fourth and final country he had listed in the Viet Cong camp. Edric had set out to explore work opportunities in each of these places, and with dogged determination seen this through.

His workplace in Katete was Saint Francis, an Anglican mission hospital built from red bricks rising out of red earth. It had over 300 patients. Edric oversaw the pediatric ward and also practised obstetrics. Both units had a high death rate. As in Papua New Guinea, the main battle was with malnutrition, although in Zambia, Edric felt the main cause was parents' lack of knowledge about nutrition, not food being unavailable.

Edric warmed to the work, but once again, his philosophy clashed with that of the hospital. He wrote, 'Hardest of all [when starting at a new hospital] is that your boss and colleagues have different expectations about what you should do. Their idea and your idea of your role may be quite different!' Edric perhaps wanted to expand the role of the nurses, or explore new programmes, as he had done at Minh Quy. Edric also felt frustrated by the hospital's priorities: 'Like so many mission hospitals Saint Francis is geared in the wrong direction, focusing around surgery and doing cancer research(!) when the main emphasis should be on kids.' In Edric's mind, by funding expensive treatments, the hospital was not doing all it could to help the poorest people access care.

At least in the pediatric ward Edric led in his own way. Within two months of arriving, he had instituted what he called 'revolutionary changes' in the treatment of malnutrition. He wrote home, 'We are trying out a new milk formula for our severely malnourished children. This is made by mixing skim

Saint Francis Hospital in Katete, Zambia, in 2014. Photo used courtesy of the Friends of St Francis Katete Charitable Trust.

milk powder, sugar and oil, which creates a mixture that is high in both protein and calories and tastes like a very sweet milk shake. I hope the children like it.'

To Edric's seniors, this change was an affront. Saint Francis Hospital had been treating malnutrition for decades! Yet Edric showed no deference to tradition or to the hierarchy of the medical profession. In fact, he made the changes expecting his boss to disapprove: 'The big boss comes back from the United Kingdom any day now. ... I know he is going to object to [my new treatments], but if he tries to make me change I will offer to leave and he is very short of doctors! Am I being unkind? When I really believe in what I'm doing I'm prepared to stick to my guns!' One month later, the issue was unresolved. Edric wrote, 'Unfortunately the boss is reluctant to accept change and so I am still waiting to hear what his verdict will be.'

If this conflict came to a head, Edric did not record it in his letters, but he moved hospitals within months of the confrontation, perhaps weeks. However, he must have parted from his St Francis colleagues as a friend, because he later visited them on a holiday. By October 1977, he had shifted to the town of Monze, 700 kilometres southwest, where he took another pediatric post. At Monze Hospital, Edric encountered new peculiarities of Zambian life. With the rainy season came swarms of insects and his colleagues caught and roasted them with salt. When a young man arrived with a terrible leg injury it turned out to be a bite from a hippopotamus. Malnutrition was rife, as it had been elsewhere. Building on another lesson from Minh Quy, Edric and his colleagues dug a vegetable garden to teach patients about nutrition.

Meanwhile, the lure of Bangladesh had not worn off. Edric's hopes of working there had begun to creep into his letters as early as July 1977, soon after his arrival in Zambia. He set the date of the following April, 1978, to make his move. By then, the frequent shifting was getting to him: 'You know each time you leave a country ... you leave all your friends, knowing that almost certainly you will never meet again! That is why I hate moving around like this, and hope to stick in Bangladesh.'

Yet his much-awaited departure did not go smoothly. Just before leaving Zambia, Edric fell ill with hepatitis. He spent days in bed. He wrote home, 'Usually hepatitis is not very serious, but it makes you feel very weak. I will probably be off work for two or three months.' By the end of April

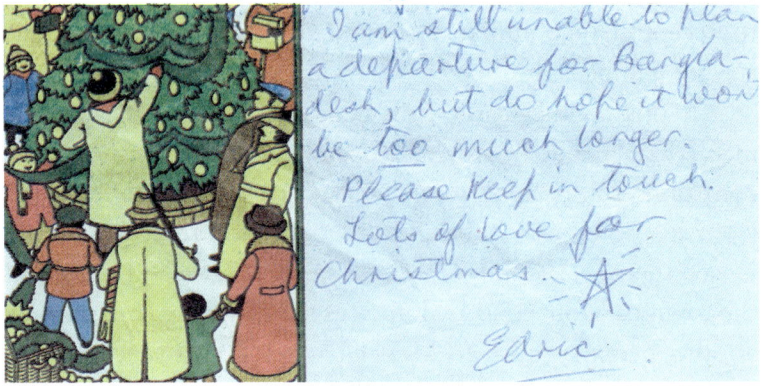

Part of a letter from Edric to his sister Hilda in December 1978.

1978, he was well enough to travel to the United Kingdom but the illness persisted. So began months of marking time. Edric stayed in Birmingham with a relative, David Handford, also a doctor. David reflected that when Edric arrived he was debilitated with exhaustion, muscular weakness and depression, symptoms that may now be diagnosed as chronic fatigue. Some days he barely had strength to walk downstairs; other days he could manage a walk of a few miles into the city. Again and again, Edric had to delay the date of his departure. His goal of getting to Bangladesh edged further and further out of reach.

I wonder what crossed Edric's mind through these discouraging months? Did his resolution to go to Bangladesh waver? Did he regret his move to Zambia where he contracted the disease? Perhaps he felt disappointed with God, or filled with doubt: why was God keeping Edric from Bangladesh, if he had even called him there at all?

When six months had passed and Edric was still unwell, David suggested that he be admitted to hospital. Tests concluded that he would recover with time; however, the months crawled and Edric's hopes were repeatedly dashed. He wrote in October, 'It will be really cold here for Christmas! I hope I am in Bangladesh by then!' But he was not. Edric allayed his frustration by using his available energy to study Bangla, the language of Bangladesh. He also enrolled at Selly Oak Mission College, where the Church Missionary Society offered training courses.

At last, after nearly a year in the United Kingdom, he was fit enough. He booked to leave for Bangladesh. For his remaining month, Edric moved from Liverpool to what he called 'the real slums of London' – Spitalfields – where half the population was Bengali. He practised speaking Bangla there. Then his time of waiting was finally over. On 27 April 1979, at long last, he boarded the plane, nearly two years after he had begun to make arrangements. But the destination would be worth the wait. Edric was starting an adventure that would last the rest of his life.

A Dhaka street in 2016. Photo by Francisco Anzola,
shared under a Creative Commons license (CC BY 2.0).

10

Beautiful visions that no one else sees

Dhaka greeted Edric with all the noise, dust and heat he remembered from his short visit three years earlier. It seemed perfect. The contrast with London was total. Colours shone from the women's clothing. Three-wheeled cycle rickshaws ruled the roads, the drivers standing up to pedal while their passengers reclined in decorated thrones. The sticky humidity brought back memories of Saigon, but these street sounds were new – hawkers' calls mixed with rickshaw bells. From shop fronts, Bengali signs taunted Edric with their hidden meanings. Besides recognising the odd letter from his studies, he was illiterate again.

Edric was to join Bollobhpur Hospital, which lay one day's journey west, in Meherpur district on the border with India. The hospital was run by the Church of Bangladesh, a union of Anglican and Presbyterian churches. Their bishop, the Right Reverend Mondal, met Edric at Dhaka airport. He was a warm and wise Bengali, who, despite his busy schedule, was delighted to make Edric feel welcome. At long last, Bollobhpur would get a doctor. They had not had one for three years.

It was May 1979, and as Edric drove the bumpy roads west, it was clear that the country was still in recovery. He had followed its history in newspapers. Back in 1971 a nine-month 'Liberation War' had brought about Bangladesh's violent birth. West Pakistan had invaded and that conflict became genocide. Political unrest hampered recovery, as did a flood and famine in 1974 that killed thousands. Then, in 1975, a coup clamped the country under martial law. Edric arrived only a few months after those restrictions had been lifted. As Edric drove past the farmers stooping in their fields, it is possible he shared how the country felt: uncertainty mixed with cautious hope.

Edric's timidity was justified. He was to lead a hospital he had never seen, in a country he had just entered. In addition to Bangladeshi staff, there were a few other foreigners on his team – some British nurses and an accountant sent by the Church Missionary Society. One of the nurses knew Edric's mother and she wrote to Betty of his arrival: 'To take over a hospital which has been without a doctor for three years must be quite disconcerting and I am conscious that we have been working at a sub-professional level. Nevertheless Edric is settling well, and hopefully, happily. He has quickly become popular with the young men on the staff and in the village, and obviously has a real love for the people. For us it is just wonderful to have a doctor.'

Edric must have felt delighted to be there. At last he was in Bangladesh, able to learn the language and customs in earnest. Bollobhpur Hospital was small, with remnants of grand British-style furnishings, but hospital work extended beyond the buildings. Edric was pleased to see that the staff were running a village health programme, teaching health, nutrition and family planning in people's homes. The quiet life of the remote town also appealed to Edric. Monkeys squabbled in the jackfruit trees. At certain hours, singing wafted from the Church of Bangladesh and the Roman Catholic Church. Edric went to services at both places daily – an unusual convenience in a Muslim country with a Christian population of less than one per cent.

Despite the comforts the location offered, Bollobhpur was not an easy posting for Edric. He wrote home, 'The setup really is very much more basic than what I've encountered anywhere else, and there having been no doctor for so long there is so much to get sorted.' Equipment broke down with almost comic frequency. Edric felt spread thin.

Complicating matters, the hospital was in what Edric called 'a bad area for brigands' – groups of armed bandits that regularly attacked and looted the village. Eventually they struck at the hospital, the police intervened and 20 officers set up a permanent camp 100 metres away. The attacks did not bother Edric. He wrote, 'Paradoxically it gives me a certain sense of security of the familiar, which I have been missing since 1975!' The attacks did worry Betty, however, causing Edric to write to his sister Hilda in defence, 'I think people in New Zealand get a rather distorted impression of dangers from violence in other countries – especially Mother.'

Nurses at Bollobhpur Hospital in 2011. Photo by Chantal Anderson for the Seattle Globalist. ©

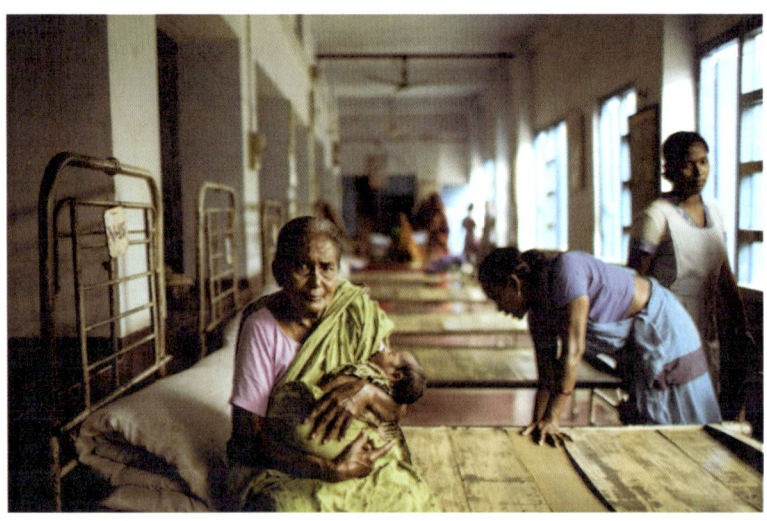

A woman holds her newborn grandchild in a ward at Bollobhpur Hospital in 2011. Photo by Chantal Anderson for the Seattle Globalist. ©

As usual, Edric's main concern was village health. There was reason for worry. Drought and famine had pushed up food prices. One kilogram of rice, enough to feed two adults for one day, cost seven *taka* in the local currency, when the daily wage was 10 *taka* (NZ 70 cents; US 67 cents at that time). Incomes did not stretch far to feed large families. People were starving.

In Edric's mind the hospital was not doing enough to respond. Poverty was an emergency! Yet the hospital still charged expensive fees. A five-day course of antibiotics cost 25 *taka* ($NZ1.75; $US1.65), more than two days' wages. What good was such medicine when patients bought it at the expense of food? Edric was emphatic: the hospital must waive fees for poor patients and pour all its resources into addressing malnutrition.

Edric was amazed to find, however, that staff resisted change. Bollobhpur had buildings to maintain, staff salaries to pay and better-off patients jostling for care. Their long-standing priorities did not yield easily to the newcomer's ideals. Edric wrote home, 'There are many things here that raise my revolutionary indignation, but I feel my role is to go slow, think it all out and then present the powers that be with a good plan for the future.' This presentation cannot have gone well, because he soon wrote home of a 'painful fallout with the local Church committee,' after which he travelled to Dhaka for a break, and returned 'refreshed in attitude', but the conflicts continued. Months later he wrote, 'Most of the other foreigners here do not agree with me at all!' Edric might have arrived in Bangladesh, but he had not found his 'fit' in the country yet.

At the same time as he faced these tensions, Edric also had major challenges with the Bangla language. The basics he had picked up were not enough. 'My work is crippled by language difficulties,' he wrote, and took one month off to study. This stint made his work much easier and his life more interesting and enjoyable.

Edric looked back on his first year in Bangladesh as 'a very bad year', but as 1980 began, things improved. In March he made plans to visit New Zealand for the first time since 1975. The trip was repeatedly delayed due to uncertainty over staffing at Bollobhpur. He finally left for New Zealand in November.

To go 'home' after a five-year absence was daunting. 'I sometimes get a bit worried,' Edric wrote, 'because I have been away from New Zealand and the family so long that there seem to be almost no emotional ties left.' He also felt the need to forestall criticism from Betty about his decision to work in Bangladesh because at times her concern for his safety edged on pressure to move 'home'. He wrote in a letter,

> *Please, when I come to New Zealand, do not try to get at me on my site of work location as it is certain to cause unhappiness. Mother, you have a huge admiration for Mother Teresa. So do I, but her life's work is a patching up of effects. I came to Bollobhpur because I came to the conclusion that the cause lies in rural poverty and hopelessness. Mother Teresa gives out a lifetime of love but the actual work she does in itself does nothing to prevent what she sees. ... Here it is not easy to see if one is achieving 'something beautiful for God' nor is there the same kind of dramatic satisfaction that we had in*

Kontum. Any results are very slow indeed, and it is necessary to keep reminding oneself what the aim is.

In a letter to his sister Hilda, he added: 'No doubt most people think my way of life is just madness but it is based on a conviction and a belief, and in its better moments on a love – and it's too late to change it now, despite Mother.'

Edric spent three months in New Zealand, reconnecting with family and refreshing himself in beautiful scenery. If he did have any disagreements with Betty, those did not deter him from returning to Bangladesh. But his time in Bollobhpur was done. In 18 months he had not been able to shift his colleagues' priorities. Edric chose to leave Bollobhpur, and in doing so also left the umbrella of the Church Missionary Society and the modest funding and administrative support it offered. By March 1981 he had begun working at Kumundini Hospital in Mirzapur, 70 kilometres northwest of Dhaka, run by a Hindu family who had mutual friends with Edric.

At Kumundini Hospital, in some ways, Edric was back in familiar territory. He was again in charge of the children's ward, as he had been in Papua New Guinea and Zambia, and his principal fight was against malnutrition. He was also now immersed in Bangladeshi culture to the greatest extent yet. Most staff members were Hindu and Edric missed Christian companionship. He was also communicating entirely in Bangla language – an achievement but also a strain. When an Australian couple came to volunteer at the hospital Edric wrote, 'I didn't realise how much I would appreciate having people with whom I can relax and talk to in English.'

Despite the divides of language and religion, Edric made Bangladeshi friends and was soon socially integrated enough to get himself into arguments. In January 1982, when Edric had been at the hospital nearly one year, he wrote home, 'Sometimes I feel I would do better by giving up all this and becoming a monk! I really do believe prayer is terribly important. The combination of prayer and active life is wonderful, but I find I get so caught up and entangled in disputes and emotional conflicts which wreck everything!' For Edric to be caught up in disagreements is evidence of his language proficiency. He was clearly capable of weighing in to disputes. It also shows that Edric had not chosen the typical manner of newcomers – polite or shy detachment. He could not help but speak his mind, even in a foreign language and context.

No one could tell me exactly why Edric left Kumundini after one year. An American friend recalled an incident that may have contributed: 'Edric was so thorough when examining patients, so concerned to get the real picture from patients, that he made some of the nurses who worked with him late for lunch. Someone complained to Mrs Poti, who was in charge. She told him not to upset the nurses' schedule. That could have been why he moved on.' Edric's methodical tendencies – the bane of the Wellington Hospital emergency department – had reappeared now that he was no longer in a war zone! If any person had suggested that Edric prioritise lunch breaks over quality of care, he would have fiercely objected.

Jenny Clarke, a Missionary Sister of the Society of Mary in Dhaka, suggested a simpler possibility, 'Edric had very high expectations about what people should do in the interests of the poor.' It is likely that Kumundini, like the hospitals before it, did not reach Edric's high expectations. 'Whatever the reason was, he moved on,' a Catholic Father, Robert McCa-

Edric in Bangladesh, December 1983. From the Baker family collection.

hill, put it philosophically. 'It was God's will that something detonated to get him out of there.'

By March 1982, Kumundini joined the long list of established hospitals from which Edric had moved on, dissatisfied. Since leaving Vietnam he had not found a good fit anywhere – not in Goroka in Papua New Guinea; Katete or Monze in Zambia or Bollobhpur or Mirzapur in Bangladesh. He had stayed nowhere longer than 18 months. Each hospital was in some way inaccessible to the poor, and as Bishop Mondol put it, Edric had been unable to 'bring them down to the level of ordinary people.' Brother Guillaume de Wolf, one of Edric's longstanding friends in Bangladesh, summarised the tension that was occurring on a deeper level: 'Edric had extreme visions which were beautiful. But when you have great ideas and nobody shares them, you have problems.' This was exactly what Edric was encountering. Since leaving Pat Smith's hospital he had carried his vision alone. In 2008, Edric told a Radio New Zealand reporter, 'I had come to the conclusion that established hospitals weren't really getting to the needs of the poorest people. I would say because of a Christian faith commitment and exposure to communism, I was absolutely convinced that it was essential to make the services available to the poorest people. Because of my experiences ... and training ... it was fairly clear what needed to be done. ... One had to go extremely grassroots.'

Edric had now spent 10 years in developing countries and he knew what he wanted: to work somewhere like Minh Quy, which prioritised the poorest people, emphasised prevention in the villages and gave Edric freedom to lead in line with his revolutionary ideals. Other hospitals did not share his vision and it was not something on which he would compromise. In order to make his 'beautiful visions' a reality, Edric would need to establish somewhere of his own.

Edric sits next to a colleague before morning prayers at Thanarbaid Clinic.
Photo by Judy Walter.

11

Call me Doctor Bhai

In March 1982, Edric set himself up in Jalchatra, Tangail district, a handful of buildings tucked into lush jungle. Along one dirt road were a *bazaar*, tea stall and post office, and a school and leprosy hospital run by a Catholic Mission. Beyond were scattered villages. To the southwest, the dense trees gave way to fields and plantations, and to the northeast the road ran deeper into the Madhupur Forest that stretched for miles. Edric did not know it then, but this region – 130 kilometres north of Dhaka and 40 kilometres from the nearest city of Mymensingh – was to become his permanent home.

Edric's connection with Jalchatra was Margaret Shield, an American teacher who lived at the Catholic Mission. Sister Margaret had met Edric on a visit to Bollobhpur Hospital. By email she recalled for me their brief conversation: 'I felt Edric was not feeling at home in the present established hospital, so I told him about the leprosarium in Jalchatra where some of our sisters were working.' One of those sisters was a medical doctor; the team also had registered nurses and a pharmacist. They provided inpatient and outpatient care for lepers and general patients, in separate wards, all free of charge. Sister Margaret told me, 'The team had a pickup truck which was used as an emergency service. Beds were arranged on the truck bed and the nurse would sit back there with the patients.' Her description stayed in Edric's mind. No doubt their free healthcare for the poor was one factor that attracted him to Jalchatra.

The leprosarium was just one project of the Catholic Mission, which was having a significant impact in the area. Father Eugene Homrich, an American priest, had founded the Mission in the 1960s and Christianity had spread. Schools and churches became part of the local landscape. Education and sanitation improved. By the time Edric arrived, Father Homrich was leading a small team of priests and sisters to run the leprosarium, schools and other development projects. Edric would add his medical skills to their team.

In 2016 I visited Bangladesh, and in Pirgacha village I met Father Homrich, seated in his office beneath a suspended bamboo fan. He was about to retire to the United States after 60 years in the area. He told me with pride about the progress he had witnessed over that period. Nowadays, almost all local children went to school. Almost everyone used toilets. All households had a tube well – a device that piped water from deep underground; these were far more sanitary than open wells. Thirty years earlier, when Edric had arrived in Jalchatra, such outcomes seemed a distant dream and he was joining the team which was working towards those goals.

As Edric settled into Jalchatra and explored the jungle paths around the area, he found villages of Muslims, Hindus, and also Mandi, an indigenous group he had not met elsewhere in Bangladesh. Mandi lived in the Madhupur Forest region as well as in hill areas of India. Edric noticed that Mandi were ethnically distinct from Bengali Hindus and Muslims, who made up the vast majority of Bangladesh. Mandi women wore skirts and tops in wide striped cloth of red or green, different from the saris and *salwar kameez* (baggy pants and long tops) of Hindu and Muslim women. Many Mandi had embraced Christianity instead of their traditional animism. Some attended Mass daily. Alongside one another, the three groups – Mandi Christians and Bengali Muslims and Hindus – lived peaceful if separate lives. Edric saw, however, that all three groups were suffering. Jalchatra was in famine, just as Bollobhpur had been, and no household was untouched. Many people were directly employed harvesting rice, wheat or fruit. Everyone else relied on the success of agriculture to ensure steady food prices and work opportunities.

At Bollobhpur hospital, Edric had been frustrated at the response to famine. In contrast, the Jalchatra Catholic Mission seemed to be doing all that it could to respond. The team offered advice on agriculture and helped people maximise their incomes by forming cooperatives. Edric's role was to teach people to get the best possible nutrition from their home gardens. He also taught people to treat diarrhoea with a mixture of salt, molasses and water so they could avoid needless deaths. These were some of the simplest possible health interventions. After five months with the Catholic team, Edric wrote home, 'There is a lot of challenging basic work which precedes even the things which I would have thought of a few years ago as being "revolutionarily" basic.' But this was just the focus Edric had longed for. He added in his letter, 'The simpler the work, the nearer to the gospel I feel.'

The team offered more specialised healthcare to individuals where they could. One Filipino priest, Father Alex Rabanel, took Edric on the back of his motorbike to visit patients at night. The motorbike was a rare luxury in an area where most people relied on pedal-powered rickshaw or bicycle transport. Father Alex and Edric bumped along the rough roads for hours to offer medical care. Sometimes they arrived too late and could offer only last rites.

As part of this Catholic team, Edric must have felt among 'like minds'. They all saw their work as an overflow of the love of God. They were living out Jesus' commands to love God and love their neighbour, sustained by Jesus who had given his life to end oppression and bring about a new society! The team understood that it was vital to work at the village level. They also saw, as Edric did, that health was inseparable from the wider social issues that they worked on. This was something Edric still needed to explain to Betty:

> Mother, you mentioned in your letter that you felt I was straying too far from medicine into social needs. I wonder if you would really want to say that. If Wilberforce had not strayed to look at social needs, Britain would have remained the world's worst slave trading country. ... After some years in developing countries ... my conclusion is that the most important factor in all this ill health

and premature death ... is a socially unhealthy community. Any action that does not recognise the basic cause is likely to have only limited effect.

The Catholic team also offered Edric a return to the sanctuary of Christian rhythms and company. Edric loved Mass and spent his evenings in prayer, bringing to God his joys and concerns and listening for the guidance and encouragement that followed. These routines left him cheerful. One of the team noted, 'He was more of a priest than we were.' Edric's place on this team seemed a perfect fit. Yet within one year of joining this team, a major change was in store.

At the end of 1982, the Church of Bangladesh offered Edric an opportunity: to restart and lead two rural clinics. The title 'clinic' was an overstatement. The sites had been dispensaries run by nurses, but they were now rundown, empty sheds. The larger site was in Thanarbaid village, and the smaller in Dhorati, distances of 8 and 16 kilometres from Jalchatra respectively. Although remote, the areas were well populated. The dispensaries' closure had left 1400 people without accessible healthcare. Jalchatra was at least two hours walk from Thanarbaid – or a rickshaw ride costing 20 *taka* ($NZ1.30, $US0.95 at that time) – even more if roads were muddy. Patients with serious conditions had to travel to Mymensingh, 40 kilometres away. The distance was too great. Patients struggled to afford the travel let alone the fees, and it was not uncommon for people to die en route. Meanwhile, in their own neighbourhoods, the two sites sat unused. It was a waste that cost lives.

Edric saw the potential in these rundown sites. Here at last was the chance to start a project in the way he believed best. Edric accepted the challenge and, as 1983 began, he started cycling daily to Thanarbaid and Dhorati, distances of 45 and 90 minutes on a rickety bicycle. The journeys were arduous, yet beautiful, as he described in a letter home: 'All the roads are of course dirt roads. Last week when cycling to Dhorati, I took a short cut and got terribly lost – the trip took me two hours. ... To cross a stream I walked across a piece of bamboo while carrying the bicycle! I continued through teak forest, rice paddies, dry moor and endless Muslim villages. It is such beautiful scenery that seems to stretch on forever.'

As Edric realised the scale of the challenge ahead, he chose to focus on Thanarbaid, the better resourced of the two sites and less remote. Edric described the village as 'beautiful with rice fields interspersed with clusters of forest-bush and fruit trees'. Cicadas sang and the trees sheltered birds. Villagers travelled past on bullock carts, bicycles or *vangaris* (rickshaws that, instead of a passenger seat, had a flat platform on the back) carrying rice, pineapples or people. Thanarbaid was home to about 100 families, most of them Mandi Christians, and there were several churches in the area. Muslims and Hindus lived in surrounding villages. For any of them, the arrival of a foreigner would have been a strange sight. I met one local who still remembered Edric's first ever visit there on his bicycle, his bag slung over his shoulder. These visits soon stopped turning heads as Edric spent day after day in the area.

Edric would have been both excited and dismayed by his minimal resources. He had four tin and mud sheds, the most basic structures that could be built around a mud floor, on a large but overgrown piece of land. He had four staff, none of whom had formal education beyond high school: three

The main building at Thanarbaid Clinic in about 1985. Komoni, a local birth attendant, is standing on the verandah. Photo by Judy Walter.

Edric with Thanarbaid colleagues in 1983. From left: Niponi Rema, Nissen Rema, Edric, and Sunit Chiran, Edric's first employee. Photo from the Baker family collection.

had basic healthcare skills and one served as both a gardener and cook. He also had a monthly budget of 10,000 *taka* ($NZ656; $US476 at that time). After salaries there was little left, but Edric was committed to making his resources go as far as possible. Because he could not afford to hire qualified staff, he would emulate how Pat Smith had run Minh Quy: he would train local people as paramedics to deliver simple treatments. However, Edric had only a fraction of Pat's resources. Through her foreign connections she had managed to secure funding, medical equipment and teaching staff. When I visited Thanarbaid I imagined Edric and his four staff crouching on the dirt in near-empty grounds, contemplating the vast gulf between their resources and the needs of the area. Where should they begin?

Edric's approach was systematic. His first move was to recruit Sunit Chiran, a Thanarbaid local, to help him survey the area. In Vietnam Edric had learned from the dysentery patient that simple, primary healthcare was paramount, and that was no doubt true at Thanarbaid. But what precisely were the needs of the area? To answer this question, Edric and Sunit spent weeks cycling to every local village. In 2016 when I met Sunit, clean-shaven and freckled, I heard how his work with Edric began: 'At that time he didn't speak Bangla fluently. I used to help him with some Bangla words. ... We went around the villages, doing a survey and writing a map of which road went where. ... All of the families were recorded, and how many families were in each village.' These dozens of conversations helped Edric to compile a rudimentary address book. At a local church I spoke to Binoy Kubi, a Mandi man who later worked at the clinic. He remembered Edric visiting his home and asking him questions. Binoy told me, 'After that survey, with any family in the Thanarbaid area, the doctor could just look at his map and he would know where to go.'

Most importantly, this survey helped Edric to understand the factors affecting health. The majority of conversations took place outside families' one-room homes built of mud or tin, positioned around courtyards shared with relatives. Their living conditions were plain for any visitor to see. No doubt Edric noted the state of their gardens, the energy levels of children, and how many people wore shoes or went barefoot. One theme was poor sanitation. Few families had toilets or tube wells, and people tended to relieve themselves in the forest, which could contaminate open wells. Crowded, unventilated housing was another common sight.

Malnutrition was one of the most pressing issues. The famine was ongoing. As Edric described in a letter, 'Rice has been so costly that many have switched to eating bread (about half the price). This is quite something for those who are rice eaters. One friend told me that they usually only eat once a day and sometimes not that!' Children were hardest hit, and weakened by malnutrition they were more likely to suffer other health problems. Edric also found other diseases typical of poverty. Diarrhoeal diseases spread easily because of the parasites and worms in dirty water. Hookworm, spread through contact with faeces, was widespread due to poor hand washing, outdoor defecation and walking barefoot. With families crowded in one-room homes, respiratory infections including tuberculosis and pneumonia thrived, as did skin conditions such as ringworm and scabies. Edric encountered *kala jor*, a 'black fever' spread by sandflies that was deadly if untreated. There were also ailments that would be found anywhere, such as cuts, burns and broken bones from accidents. Because people could not access health services, minor problems, left untended, were causing disastrous consequences. Edric saw that Vitamin A deficiency was leading to preventable blindness and ending people's working lives. Untreated hookworm was causing anaemia. Complications in pregnancy were resulting in needless deaths in mothers and babies. The scale of the problems was vast. The work ahead would have daunted even the most expert team.

The month that Edric and Sunit spent on this survey proved indispensable. The pair met nearly every family in the area; they also identified the key health needs and gathered evidence to show local leaders if necessary. Edric could now list with confidence the interventions to prioritise:

- Health and nutrition education
- Sanitation – toilets, tube wells and hand washing
- Treatments for potentially fatal diarrhoea, TB, pneumonia and black fever, and preventable blindness
- Mother and child health – in particular identifying high-risk births, and preventing malnutrition
- Treatment of skin conditions, cuts, burns and broken bones.

Edric then worked out low-cost 'standard treatments' and taught these to his staff.

Meanwhile, Edric faced another challenge: ensuring the poorest people could access the clinic. This is where established hospitals tended to fall short. As he told Radio New Zealand in 2008, 'If the people really are poor, that means they can't pay very much; you've got to cope with that.' At Thanarbaid, some patients arrived at the clinic in debt to their rickshaw driver. With the exception of Pat Smith's hospital and the Jalchatra leprosarium, Edric's past workplaces would not have served such patients. At Thanarbaid, he was determined to find a way.

The answer lay in simplifying medical work to the extreme. Edric told me on the bus trip in 2012, 'Because the poor people can pay almost nothing, that means that you have got to simplify medical work, in order to make it cheaper ... and understandable by the people to whom we're teaching it.' He started with the site. To minimise costs and overheads he upgraded nothing. The clinic remained tin and mud sheds. The grounds had no electricity or running water, only a tube well.

Equipment was similarly basic. The project would have no beds, just floor mats as the patients had in their own homes. Edric had one stethoscope and one blood pressure machine. There was no laboratory or x-ray. He accepted a donated opthalmascope for eye examinations, otherwise avoided electronic equipment. The 'pharmacy' was one cabinet containing antibiotics, paracetamol, aspirin, worm medications, vitamins, and government-supplied drugs for TB. One lotion, gentian violet, was used for all skin conditions – one staff member recalled, 'All children left Thanarbaid painted blue.'

Without a laboratory, Edric taught his staff to diagnose using only the patient's symptoms and history, or, if necessary, by sending lab specimens to Jalchatra. He taught them to set limbs without x-ray and to sew up minor cuts without anesthesia. He also trained his staff to identify patients with more advanced needs and to refer them to Mymensingh. By limiting his equipment and keeping treatments simple, Edric not only kept costs low, he also avoided breakdowns that could halt work. One donor recalled Edric saying as he declined a piece of equipment, 'Where am I going to get the batteries?' Most important of all, Edric was keeping his methods teachable. He made sure that his staff could learn to deliver the standard treatments.

One of Edric's decisions – seemingly extravagant – was to have a kitchen and a paid cook. All staff and patients at Thanarbaid received three meals per day; malnourished patients ate even more frequently. Edric was adamant that if patients did not eat regular healthy meals, they would not recover. In a context where malnutrition was rife, meals presented an opportunity to teach patients about nutrition and sanitation too. Cooks sterilised the dishes by boiling them and drying them in the sun.

This setup was the bare bones of a clinic, but it allowed Edric to use the budget effectively and save lives. In 1983, he and his first paramedics – Sunit Chiran, Nissen Rema, Niponi Rema and others – began seeing patients. They transported sick people from villages to the clinic and charged only what patients could afford, sometimes only 10 *taka* even if the treatment cost 1000. Edric wrote home about one patient whose life was saved for a medical bill of less than $NZ1:

> *One patient who had been having recurrent diarrhoea [potentially fatal if untreated] … spent a week on my floor. We did almost nothing for him except provide an easily accessible toilet, a supply for him to make up his rehydration fluid (water, salt, molasses), frequent meals*

A cook in the Thanarbaid Clinic kitchen in 1999. Photo by Peter Wilson.

A staff member washes dishes and leaves them to be sterilised by the sun. Photo by Peter Wilson.

and a friendly peaceful environment – but he was just so grateful. His medical bill for nine days was 16 taka, less than $NZ1. He was amazed, expecting three times that! In fact I think we overcharged him! He brought his own rice.

Here was a dysentery patient saved by the simplest possible of treatments. Years earlier, it had been the death of a dysentery patient in Vietnam that had shown Edric the importance of basic healthcare. Now, in Thanarbaid, he was putting that lesson into practice. The bare bones of his clinic were making a difference.

The minimal resources did mean, however, that the team had to know where to draw the line. Patients who needed surgery were one group the team had to refer to government hospitals, providing funds for transport, lodging and medical expenses if they could. The staff had to turn away cancer patients, usually to their death, as treatment costs anywhere were formidable. Another group they could do little to help was patients with more than 50 per cent burns. Their best chance of survival was referral to a burns unit in Dhaka, but that cost more than Edric could (or was willing to) pay for any individual. In those sad cases, Edric and his team could do nothing but provide the patient space to die. To some degree every health provider faces these decisions – which patients to prioritise with limited resources? Thanarbaid Clinic had to draw the line at a very low level. (An American doctor told me that she often spent more on a single patient than Edric had in his entire budget.) Although some decisions were heart-rending, Edric was committed to stretching every *taka* as far as possible to reduce suffering. That meant saying no to some patients who required costly treatment, to conserve resources for others.

Despite these limitations, Thanarbaid filled a void in basic healthcare and patient numbers soared. In the early months, the team welcomed one or two per day; by mid-year they were seeing up to 60. They soon began to run out of drugs, forcing Edric to take risks to replenish their supplies, as he described, 'Last Sunday I went buying medicines in Mymensingh and had to come through the forest by rickshaw in the night with 2000 *taka* worth of drugs, which I don't really like [owing to the risk of robbery]! The last stretch of "road" is too bad for rickshaws, but I managed to hire a [person to help me carry the load] in the dark.'

In July the clinic reached a milestone. Edric wrote to his parents, 'Our mighty "hospital" now boasts two inpatients! Unprecedented at Thanarbaid!' At first, these overnight patients had to move outside during the day to make space for others to be seen. Later the team divided one building in two so that inpatients could lie undisturbed. With patients now needing care around the clock, Edric packed up at Jalchatra and moved to the clinic grounds. One of the tiny tin sheds at the clinic became his home.

Living at Thanarbaid was the most remote posting Edric had ever experienced. He wrote home, 'Talk about being isolated! I find it impossible to keep up with what is going on in Bangladesh, let alone elsewhere in the world.' Thanarbaid was never lonely, as even rural areas of Bangladesh are densely populated, but gone was the companionship of other foreigners and comforts like running water, phones or electricity. Nights were particularly dark. Edric wrote, 'The rain really

Edric in his tin house at Thanarbaid Clinic. Photo by Judy Walter.

Edric's tin house at Thanarbaid Clinic, still standing in 2016.
Photo by the author.

crashes on the roof of my little tin house. The thing I miss most here is not having ... electric light at night. However I guess one gets used to hurricane lamps and torchlight.' As Edric lay down for sleep he heard the calls of jackals and knew that snakes might visit his hut at any time. No doubt, too, he missed his Catholic Mission friends. He wrote in June, 'I go into Jalchatra once every two weeks, that's the only time I ever speak English!' Yet these sacrifices allowed him to focus on clinic growth to a new level. He could now care for patients and supervise paramedics day and night.

As months passed and the clinic grew, not everyone shared Edric's excitement. As local customs required, he had a committee who oversaw his work. Edric was scathing about its efficacy, writing, 'Committees seem to be terribly important in this country but achieve almost nothing!' Worse, Edric found himself having to goad the committee to take interest. This pulled him away from patients and made him so frustrated that he threatened to leave. He wrote in September,

> *What I am trying to do here is to show that it is possible to treat most common illnesses at almost no cost – with community support. It is slow and extremely frustrating, especially the lack of interest of our committee and community and church leaders. They got quite a shock a few days ago when I told them I was going to leave in the next two or three days! I was ready to too. Then we had a committee meeting and sorted things out.*

In this instance, Edric had won their attention, if not enthusiasm. He had made it clear that to help the poor, he needed the community to back him.

As word of Thanarbaid spread, Edric faced one more problem of success. His new clinic attracted patients who were not poor. Such people could afford to travel elsewhere and treating them drew resources from patients who could not. Worse still, wealthier people questioned Edric's simple setup and pressured for a higher level of care – undermining the very model he had chosen to serve the greatest number. 'Whatever you do in this country the rich will take it over,' Edric later wrote, 'They can crush a project which is trying to help the vast majority.' For these reasons, Edric was adamant that his team must turn away non-poor patients: he believed that was the only way to use resources strategically and keep their focus on the poor. He began testing patients' means by sending staff to visit their houses, or by asking patients directly if they could afford to pay. As Binoy Kubi, a neighbour from Thanarbaid village, told me,

> *The patients didn't tell the truth. Someone might have been able to give 10,000* taka, *but they'd say 'I can only give 500', even if they were a rich person. ... Edric was also happy to accept that. Those that were poor, who worked for day labour, Edric knew who they were. From them he didn't take anything. Each patient brought an attendant with them, and the attendants could do some work while they were here. ... Later on Edric knew which people were rich or poor ... from going to people's homes.*

Edric was not rigid about his rules. When rich patients arrived at the clinic too ill to travel further, he accepted and treated them. Yet Edric took pains to protect his focus on

Edric and Roshid, a staff member, eat together in the kitchen/dining room at Thanarbaid Clinic. Photo by Judy Walter.

Edric collecting water from a tube well. Photo by Judy Walter.

the poorest. He wrote, 'We create an environment which is inhospitable to the rich, like bed-less wards. Meals are cooked by people who come from different religious groups from the rich. All the patients are flung together whatever their economic situation.' These decisions were strategic as well as an economic necessity.

As Edric established his life in Thanarbaid, he also went through a personal transformation. He adopted a lifestyle of utmost simplicity. He began dressing in a *lungi*, the sarong worn by Bangladeshi men. This was unusual for foreigners, and when Edric had meetings in Jalchatra or Dhaka, he would change into trousers en route. Bishop Mondol told me that Edric kept his hut spartan, containing only a few books and clothes. The Church of Bangladesh offered to buy Edric a motorbike, but he declined, content with his bicycle. A former volunteer, Nobine Chambugong, told me, 'His cycle never needed a bell; it made so many noises!'

In making these choices, Edric was assuming the lifestyle of his staff and patients. He wrote home, 'When I stay at Jalchatra Mission where living is quite luxurious, I pay about $NZ45 [$US32] per month. Here at Thanarbaid my living costs are about $NZ15 [$US11] per month. Mind you, we live extremely simply here – no electricity, water from the tube-well and we eat with our hands, sitting on the floor. For breakfast we eat puffed rice and molasses, for lunch and dinner, rice, lentils and greens and maybe fermented fish.'

Edric fiercely objected if kitchen staff showed him special treatment, for instance by trying to sneak extra pieces of fish onto his plate. His lifestyle had a protective effect, Nobine recollected, 'If a robber came they would not attack Edric because everyone knows he is the poor people's friend!' This was far from Edric's motivation, however. He was implementing the communist ideal he had admired since the Viet Cong camp – to live with, eat with and work with the people.

More than that, Edric was choosing to live in line with a 'revolution' inspired by Jesus. 'Christ's love and God's compassion reach to all,' he wrote. 'With that compassion and love we must move to the suffering poor.' It was Edric's belief that the love of Christ would transform society in a way that communism had not. He continued,

> *Lenin said that the condition of the poor will never change until the elite class are willing to declass themselves and identify with, motivate, lead the poor. Lenin could not identify sufficiently because of human weakness, and his revolution has now failed. Jesus, however, did [identify with the poor] perfectly and established a people's movement and a revolution that has continued. The Thanarbaid health programme is a part of this movement.*

As well as matching his neighbours' living standards, Edric's egalitarianism became apparent in one other respect too. Bangladesh is a hierarchical society, in which people use respectful titles to address people who are older or more qualified. As a doctor and western foreigner, Edric could have enjoyed high status. But he rejected any deferential treatment. Years before, at Christchurch Hospital, a colleague had noticed the same trait in Edric – he had shunned medical hierarchies by speaking his mind to seniors and deferring opportunities to his juniors. Edric showed similar disregard for hierarchy in Bangladesh. According to an early staff member, Leo Rema,

Betty and Edric riding to Thanarbaid Clinic and sitting in a jungle clearing.
Photos from the Baker family collection.

'he told the staff that he didn't like to be called "old boss", or "sir", because these were very official, formal words. If anybody is called "sir" it creates quite a distance from the other person. ... The doctor feels proud. He told all the staff they should call him "Doctor Bhai". He always used to say, "We are brothers."' The name stuck. Edric became known as Doctor Bhai, meaning Doctor Brother.

In December 1983, three years since Edric had last been to New Zealand, his mother Betty and sister Hilda visited Thanarbaid. Both were fascinated to see Edric's new home and to accompany him on bicycle rides around the area. The neighbours stared, especially at Hilda. Edric explained their curiosity: the local people thought the doctor's mother had come to deliver him a bride!

Betty and Hilda's short visit served as a window into his life. The pair found Edric leading a small but thriving health centre, his lifestyle indistinguishable from that of his staff and patients. He ate meals with his hands, sitting on the ground. He slept on a pile of straw, no doubt reminding Hilda of the pine-needle mattresses from their childhood holidays. He owned very few clothes. Indeed, when Betty met Father Homrich, she politely inquired if he could persuade her son to change his shirt from time to time – a request Father Homrich recounted with great pleasure.

Edric's mother and sister shared the simple conditions during their two-week stay. 'There were no other options available,' Hilda recalled. 'We slept on straw on the floor until mother was put onto a low table. One night a rat ate some of the straw I was sleeping on.' As Betty and Hilda adapted to the conditions, I imagine that Edric – with delight – would have explained what his lifestyle enabled: he could use every *taka* to save lives with the simplest treatments! His mother and sister would have been pleased and proud. Finally, Edric was in control of how he lived and worked. He was living his dream at last.

12

Competition
with the *kabiraj*

By the start of 1984, the tree-lined grounds of Thanarbaid saw a steady stream of patients. New Year was the time of the brief cold season and villagers came wearing socks, sweaters, knitted caps and shawls – if they had them. 'Winter was hard on toes and ears,' remembered Sister Margaret Shield, Edric's friend in Jalchatra. 'People used to ask for old newspapers to paper the inside of their homes so the wind could not blow through.' Edric woke each morning to find patients already waiting by the gate, some crouching holding babies, resting on a *vangari* or warming in patches of sun.

However, Edric was aware that certain sections of the community were not among his patients. He reflected to Radio New Zealand in 2012, 'I was pretty upset, because particularly our tribal Christian people weren't coming in.' There

The Thanarbaid site showing the main clinic building and a *vangari* in the foreground. Photo by the author in 2016.

were also Muslim and Hindu households, even whole villages, from which no patients ever came. A principal reason was one of faith. While many Mandi accepted Christian beliefs and education, their tradition was animist. They believed that health problems had a spiritual cause. Sunit Chiran, Edric's partner in surveying the area, expressed the problem simply: 'People thought the health problem is caused by a demon, and the doctor can't help with that.' Muslims and Hindus also sought healing through religious practices.

Instead of seeking modern healthcare, therefore, all three groups went to traditional healers known as *kabiraj*. For some conditions the *kabiraj* said prayers, made offerings to gods or worshipped statues. In other cases they blew air on the patient, gave them a cloth necklace to wear, or made them a medicine or ointment from plant or animal products. These treatments could cost hundreds or thousands of *taka*. But people trusted them. Father Donel, an assistant to Father Homrich at the Catholic Mission, reflected, 'It's a form of faith, this belief that the *kabiraj* can treat them.'

From Edric's perspective, *kabiraj* treatments were at best ineffective, at worst outright harmful, and they stopped people from accessing his clinic. Bishop Mondol shared his opinion, 'From traditional healers' treatment nothing happens. Only at the last minute would they come to Doctor Baker.' Some patients who trusted the *kabiraj* suffered disability or death. Staff member Leo Rema told me the sad story of a sick baby: 'Treatment from the traditional healer blinded one of the baby's eyes. The boy is now 14 or 15 and still blind in one eye.' Father Donel told me the story of a woman with breast cancer whom Edric referred to Mymensingh for surgery. Her family took her to a *kabiraj* instead; within months the cancer had spread and the woman died. Yet these sad cases did not dispel people's trust in the only healthcare they had ever known.

At the same time, locals were wary of modern healthcare. To them, Edric's methods seemed strange or even dangerous. Sunit told me, 'At the start, villagers wouldn't let paramedics weigh the babies. Some thought that when you weigh a baby, its life span would reduce.' Other rumours abounded: that treatments involved surgery and losing a part of the body or that a clinic was where patients went to die. Traditional healers encouraged such messages to spread to protect their customer base. Such rumours frustrated Edric. So too did the cases of patients who exhausted all other options then arrived at the clinic gate on the verge of death. Edric encouraged his team to persist and serve whichever patients came. He hoped that the clinic's results would speak for themselves in time.

For Muslims and Hindus, there was a cultural barrier as well: Edric's earliest staff members were Mandi Christians. In that area, Hindus, Muslims and Christians seldom mixed. From a distance, the three groups accepted each others' practices, but felt no pressure to change their own. Many Muslim and Hindu people therefore saw the clinic as a 'Mandi enterprise' and kept away.

Muslim women faced additional barriers. In the patriarchal culture of their villages, women were not permitted to leave the house unless a man accompanied them. Male relatives, however, were unlikely to take them to an unknown clinic, particularly one that appeared newfangled, perhaps dangerous and intended for Mandi. In some cases, disregard for women's health also played a part. One woman told me, 'Muslim women are often neglected by the community or by men. If a Muslim woman is ill … the family will not necessarily send her to the hospital.'

Each of these barriers distressed Edric. As he later put it, 'Something had to be done.' It was not enough to serve faithfully the patients who came; his team needed a new strategy to reach different groups. Edric needed to recruit more Hindus and Muslims to build trust in those communities. His team had to show that their methods were more effective than those of the *kabiraj*. Furthermore, they had to take healthcare to people's homes, so that patients unable to travel to the clinic would receive care.

Edric knew a way to achieve all three goals at once: they must start a village health programme. He had seen such ini-

Village health workers Fulmoti and Kanon Bala with the bicycles they use to visit patients. Photo by Christine Steiner.

tiatives at Bollobhpur and Minh Quy hospitals and he had tested similar methods nearby in Jalchatra while working with the Catholic team. Taking the best parts of those models, Edric began training Christian, Hindu and Muslim staff members to become health workers in their own communities. He explained to me in 2012, 'This is the key to success. People are working in among their own people. ... Because they are in and of the community, they are able to understand the community problems and make themselves understood when expressing what needs to be done.'

The workers' priorities were to educate villagers about sanitation, nutrition and common health issues, and to treat basic conditions. Mother and child health soon became a focus. In May 1984 Edric wrote to his parents, 'We are starting to do things in the villages! Hope springs eternal. I sent Niponi [a Mandi paramedic] for a one-week training course for birth attendants and she will be starting antenatal supervision in the village.'

When funding allowed, Edric recruited Hindu and Muslim staff to join the Mandi members of his team. He also made a point of recruiting female staff. Women had few other work opportunities. They connected easily with women and children, and found it easier than men did to build trust with communities. They were perfect ambassadors to spread knowledge to the people who needed it most.

One of Edric's first recruits was Mormiron Begum, a Muslim woman. When I met her in 2016, she was so stooped she barely came up to my shoulder, but under her pale blue sari she had a strong gaze and she spoke forcefully. She had lived in the area before Edric arrived, she told me, and came to the clinic when one of her seven sons fell ill and died. Edric saw that she was a single mother and destitute, so he invited her to live on site. This was the beginning of a long friendship. Mormiron told me, 'Doctor Bhai was like another son to me. He called me Ma.'

Mormiron began working as a cook and later trained as a village health worker. 'When Doctor Bhai went to the villages, he used to take several of us trainees with him and show us how to do the work,' she reflected. 'We saw difficulties like diarrhoea, dysentery and fever; we weighed babies; and we assisted Doctor Bhai with deliveries.' Their visits to people's homes were a spectacle, Mormiron remembered, because with the houses grouped around courtyards, every neighbour gathered to watch.

After Mormiron, Edric recruited another Muslim woman, Rejia Begum, in 1986. These appointments brought one challenge: Muslim women did not cycle. They never had; it was frowned upon. Yet on foot it would be exhausting to travel the distances the job required. Mormiron got around the restriction by sitting on the back of her colleagues' bicycles to be carried where she needed to go. Rejia, Edric's second female Muslim worker, began a revolution.

When I met Rejia in 2016, her nose and wrists were decorated with gold jewellery and she wore an orange sari over a green t-shirt. She told me that Edric had visited her house to seek her husband's permission for her to work. I later met her husband Mohammad Hanif, a smiling older man. He told me that, although it went against local norms for his wife to work, he gave her permission because 'caring for people is very important. If you want to love God, then you have to love other people.' His support made Rejia's employment possible, even though the neighbours grumbled.

Riding a bicycle, however, went to the next level in assaulting cultural norms. Rejia did it anyway. 'In my area, among the Muslim women, I was the first to ride a bicycle.' She remembers people staring, 'The first time I rode a bicycle I felt nervous. Gradually it became easier. Male staff helped me to learn, sitting behind me ... then I tried by myself.' Rejia felt thrilling independence as she zipped along the jungle roads. Mormiron told me that other women had muttered, 'Rejia is Muslim, why is she riding a bicycle? She shouldn't do that.' Rejia would reply, 'How would my job be possible without riding a bicycle?'

Rejia learned quickly, and before long, her health knowledge won her respect. Her only formal study was about four years at primary school. Despite this, Edric wrote in 1990, 'I think if Rejia was quizzed on common conditions, she would be the best in the staff.' Her community members overlooked her method of transport and allowed her to pass on her skills and experience to others.

After Rejia, more village health workers came who embraced their new knowledge. In 1988, Edric wrote, 'We have a 19-year-old Muslim, illiterate, diabetic girl. ... She and her brother-in-law have ... converted 1000 people from drinking open-well water to tube-well water. Every day from dawn to dusk they go house to house organising the treatment of diarrhoea and dysentery patients.' Such efforts saved many lives. Without patients needing to set foot in the clinic grounds, Rejia, Mormiron and the rest of Edric's team were now transforming the health of many families.

Mother and child health was a priority for the team alongside sanitation and basic treatments. Edric wrote in 2013, 'It was so obvious that the most important and cost-effective work was with mothers and children.' One aspect was preventing malnutrition. They did this by weighing infants and tracking their growth against standard weight charts, as Edric had seen done in Papua New Guinea. Underweight children and their mothers were referred to the clinic for an intensive feeding programme. Later, staff taught parents to grow vegetables such as beans, cucumbers and squashes to supplement children's meagre diets of rice.

Another vital aspect of village health work was antenatal care – teaching and monitoring the health of pregnant women.

Village health worker Lakhoni Hagidok weighing a baby. Photo from the Kailakuri Healthcare Project.

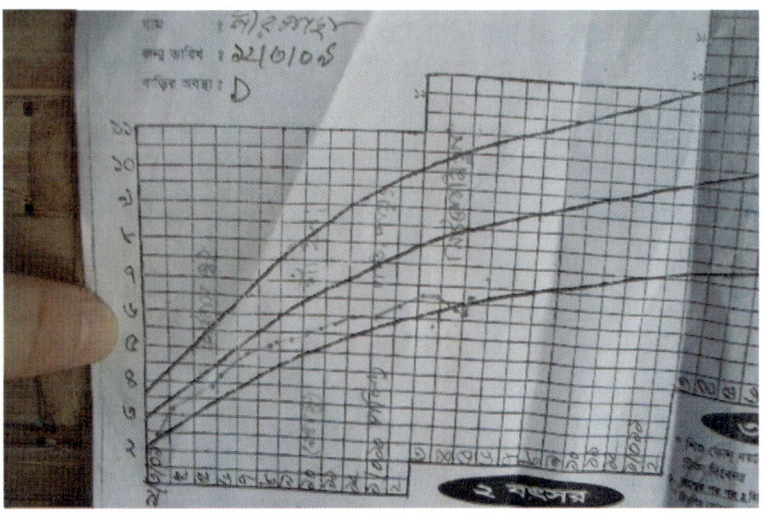

A chart showing a baby's weight gain compared with expected growth rates. Photo by Christine Steiner.

Such a service was rare in that region. As Judy Walter, a nurse who volunteered at Thanarbaid, told me by email, Muslims believed that 'Everything was "*Insha Allah*", or God's will. ... To prepare for the birth of your baby was failing to trust that whatever outcome Allah permitted was the Holy Will.' Without antenatal education, harmful beliefs thrived. For instance, Judy told me, 'People believed pregnant women should not eat much, so that the baby would be small and easy to deliver.' This belief caused malnutrition. Edric taught his staff to correct misinformation and fill knowledge gaps.

Assisting with childbirth was one area in which the team made significant impact. Deliveries were high risk: it was not unusual for mothers and babies to suffer injuries or die even if traditional birth attendants were present. Judy listed for me practices that were common during labour: 'Feeding the woman cow-dung to make her vomit, believed to increase the strength of her contractions; pulling the baby out with rope; or after the birth, stepping on the woman's stomach to hasten the delivery of the placenta.'

Edric's team worked to change such beliefs and provide safe assistance. Other organisations ran short courses on midwifery and antenatal care so Edric sent his staff to them for training. His team learned to identify complicated pregnancies and bring these mothers to the clinic for their labour. They monitored the health of mothers and babies during early weeks and supported them with breastfeeding. These efforts improved the wellbeing of countless women and babies.

Gradually, success stories bolstered trust in the clinic and wore down the popular myths and faith in *kabiraj*. At the same time, patients and their families were becoming advocates for the clinic. Binoy Kubi, the Mandi man I met inside Thanarbaid church, was one such proponent. He and his wife had been on their way to a *kabiraj* to treat his wife's finger, when along the road they saw Edric and he treated her on the spot. Her recovery strengthened their faith in Edric's methods. Later, Binoy's son fell ill. The family could not afford to pay anything for his treatment at the clinic, so Binoy volunteered to cook, transport patients and take their temperatures. When his son recovered, Binoy became such a passionate advocate that Edric called on him to fetch reluctant patients. Binoy and I sat just a short walk from the clinic site where his son had recovered, and he told me, 'I would say to people, "My son got well; Edric could make your son well too."'

In one instance, Binoy helped save the life of his neighbour's son. The boy had been ill with diarrhoea, but despite Binoy's pleas, the family was determined to take him to a *kabiraj* instead of the clinic. Binoy told me that he and a friend effectively kidnapped the boy to save his life, 'We took the boy forcefully at night to the clinic. He was nearly dead. Doctor Bhai gave him saline and he recovered. ... I went back to the family and said, "Look, this boy would have died. Doctor Bhai saved his life."' Advocates like Binoy challenged rumours and strengthened people's faith in the clinic's style of medicine.

Edric also won people's trust through his own lifestyle. People were intrigued by this 'crazy foreigner' who ate with, worked with and lived among them. Not only did he cycle through the night to assist patients, he also cared about people beyond their medical needs, accepting invitations to social and community events. Staff member Kanon Bala Bormon was touched that Doctor Bhai attended Hindu celebrations, and that he allowed Hindu staff to take Thursdays as their day off so they could visit the temple. 'He understood our religion, celebrations and history,' she said.

Because of his workload, Edric was strategic in his social engagement. He befriended teachers and religious leaders who could refer their charges to the clinic. He also worked out ways to maintain some control over his time. With a smile, Binoy told me how Edric managed Mandi celebrations, 'Doctor Bhai was busy. He would say, "Plan a specific time for me to come. … I'll come and eat, then I'll leave." That was a teaching point for us: Westerners don't like to waste their time. I passed on this observation to other Mandi people.'

Gradually, through the efforts of Edric's team and the relationships he formed, people's trust in the clinic grew. More patients ventured to Thanarbaid instead of traditional healers. Edric wrote home in October 1983, 'I have been feeling just a little bit victorious the last few days. A young man with schizophrenia whose parents refused my treatment about six months ago in favour of traditional healer, other methods failing, is now coming back to me! Is this a non-virtuous sentiment?'

There were more and more such cases. However, the numbers through the clinic gates were just one measure of impact. As health workers prevented problems in the villages, less treatment was needed. Edric later reflected that providing healthcare for women and children had brought 'a dramatic change in the health of a whole village over a period of 18 months to two years'.

By 2016 when I visited the area, the long-term impacts of village health work could be seen. Leo told me that educating

Edric sitting with a Muslim family. Photo from a Thanarbaid newsletter in 2000.

Edric giving flowers to local friends. Photo by Christine Steiner in about 2013.

The team of village health workers, year unknown.
Photo from the Kailakuri Healthcare Project.

people about sanitation had lowered disease rates, in particular the rate of dysentery. 'Now you rarely see blood dysentery at all.' I asked him how this change had occurred. 'Through lots of advice: repeating it and repeating it,' he told me. 'Most changes took about three years.' Another staff member told me, 'Now, when any patient has diarrhoea, they start giving them saline straight away.' Before, people had not known about this basic, lifesaving response.

Many people described the programme's impact on women. Pregnant women, who used to deliver their babies at home, now knew to come to the clinic if they had problems. 'Their minds are now changed … because workers went to the villages,' Mena, a neighbour, told me. The village health programme also benefited the workers themselves. Another

Mandi woman told me how earning an income as a health worker meant she could afford to buy food and medication.

But what happened to the *kabiraj*, I wondered? How did the clinic impact upon traditional medicine? In Thanarbaid village, I met a teacher, Mironi Hagidok, who gave me my answer: 'Now, in our area, there is no animist worship any more, and very few traditional healers. Their practices are nearly all gone because of Doctor Baker.' The clinic had interrupted centuries of tradition for the sake of better health. I asked her, 'Were they angry, the traditional healers?' I assumed the growth of the project would have undermined their reputation and livelihoods. Mironi was surprised at my question. 'Angry? No, they didn't get angry. They began coming to the clinic.'

Staff member Mohammad Masudur Rahaman Khan teaches diabetic patients to measure insulin by counting the 'big ticks' and 'little ticks' on the syringe. Photo from the Kailakuri Facebook page.

13

The diabetes programme begins

In 1984, when the clinic at Thanarbaid was making its first strides in village health, a patient stumbled in with a condition the staff had not yet seen. The disease was common in the developed world, but one that Edric had encountered seldom, if ever, in the developing countries where he had worked. His response to this patient's case broke new ground for the clinic and for the region – likely for all of Bangladesh – and sparked a programme that would become the flagship of his work.

The patient, Sultan Ahmed, should have been in his prime. He was 26, with a wife and two young children. But something was deeply wrong. Sultan was thirsty and hungry all the time. As much as the family's meagre income would allow, he ate; yet each day he grew thinner and weaker. Work was impossible. His legs became puffy and he needed to pass urine often. Worst of all, he would sometimes get lost in confusion and behave as if drunk. This was unacceptable for a Muslim man.

At Thanarbaid, Edric took one look at Sultan's wasted arms and sunken cheeks and insisted that he stay at the clinic. Edric knew that this was no ordinary case of malnutrition: Sultan had Type 1 diabetes. Without urgent help, he would die. What Sultan needed was insulin, but Edric had not seen it offered at any Bangladesh hospital let alone a rural clinic, and Sultan would need regular supplies for the rest of his life. His predicament seemed hopeless. I imagine Edric must have paused at this point, thinking of the line he already drew in the sand for patients with cancer or severe burns. Was Type 1 diabetes another condition that Thanarbaid could not treat? Perhaps the best they could do for Sultan was refer him elsewhere? Unknown to Edric, not only Sultan's life, but the lives of countless others hinged on his response.

Edric set off immediately to search for insulin, starting at the leprosy hospital at Jalchatra. They did not have any, neither did the Mymensingh government hospital, reported the Catholic sisters who volunteered there. Nowhere in the region had insulin. To Edric this must have seemed a dead end, and he could have felt justified conceding defeat. But he did not. As Sultan described later, 'Doctor Bhai worried about me so much that he did not eat or sleep.' Because of stubborn persistence or a nudge from God, Edric continued to search for a solution.

He set off alone for Dhaka. This was a day's travel thrown on a wild gamble: there is no record of why he hoped to find treatment in the capital. It was the days before cellphones and a traveler was isolated, so for two days the clinic staff heard nothing from their doctor. When he finally returned, it was late at night. Sultan remembers that from the Thanarbaid gate Edric called for him to get up: 'Sultan! I have found your treatment!' I met Sultan in 2016. A full beard covered the cheeks that had once been hollow caves. He was now an expert at living with diabetes; he declined Bangladesh's famous sweet tea. Sultan told me what had happened next. Despite heavy rain, he and Edric had set off right away in the dark, Edric supporting him to walk until they could catch a rickshaw then a bus.

Once in the capital, Edric showed Sultan his discovery. It was a makeshift clinic where a doctor, Mohammad Ibrahim, was pioneering the first diabetes care in the country. Under Doctor Ibrahim's care, Sultan received nutritious food, and – that liquid gold – insulin. His progress was dramatic. Having arrived weighing 35 kilograms, within a week he gained 10 more. Sitting across from me, Sultan laughed as he remembered his transformation. 'When I looked in a mirror, I thought I was somebody else. ... Then, when I returned to Thanarbaid, no one else recognised me!' He weighed 60 kilograms by then and his mind was sharp. 'When my family saw me they were amazed and so grateful to Doctor Bhai. It was like he had brought someone who was dead back to life.' But this recovery was only part of the miracle Sultan needed. In order to stay well he would need regular injections of insulin, and Edric knew of no supplies outside Dhaka. I can imagine Edric negotiating with Doctor Ibrahim, who no doubt recognised in Edric a fellow pioneer. He agreed to supply insulin for Sultan and other Thanarbaid patients, so long as someone collected it from Dhaka each month.

Insulin supplies, however, were only part of the solution. Sultan also needed to learn how to manage his diabetes, hour by hour, for the rest of his life. To study these skills, Sultan moved to Thanarbaid Clinic for an extended period. Edric taught him how diabetes works. As a Type 1 diabetic, his body failed to produce insulin – the hormone that enabled his body to process the energy in food. (Sultan would later learn about Type 2 diabetes, and how those patients did produce insulin, but in too small quantities, or their bodies failed to recognise it properly.) Blood sugar highs and lows were both dangerous situations for Sultan. Extreme high blood sugar could cause a deadly acute reaction, or, over time, damage his nerves so severely as to cost him his limbs. It could also cause cataracts or other conditions that affected his sight. But low sugar levels were unsafe too. If Sultan's blood sugars dipped from too little food or too much exercise, he would become dizzy and confused. He might even slip into a coma.

Sultan's only hope was to learn to regulate his blood sugar himself, a task that required ferocious self-discipline. First, he had to keep his blood sugar steady by managing his food and exercise. Patiently, with repetition and encouragement, Edric taught Sultan to follow simple 'food rules' – to measure the components of his meals to control how much sugar he ate. Edric also taught him to eat at regular times and monitor his exercise. Delaying a meal or walking an unplanned distance could see his blood sugar dive.

The second challenge was to balance his blood sugar with the correct amount of injected insulin. To do this, Sultan needed to test his blood sugar five times per day. Edric must have wondered how Sultan could do this for an affordable price. Nowadays in New Zealand, diabetics calculate their blood sugar instantly with a machine called a glucometer, which measures glucose in a spot of blood on a disposable testing strip. There was no such machine at Thanarbaid. Even if there had been, in the 1980s, a single glucometer testing strip cost 35 *taka* (NZ$2.10, $US1.40). To test five times a day would have exceeded Sultan's daily wage! One alternative was disposable strips for testing urine, as measuring the glucose levels in urine is a fairly reliable proxy for blood sugar. No machine was required and those strips cost two *taka* each (NZ 12 cents, US 8 cents), or 10 *taka* for five tests per day. But even that price was prohibitive, being a significant portion of a daily wage.

Fortunately, Doctor Ibrahim in Dhaka used an affordable technique that drew on past medical practice. The method used Benedict's solution – a bright blue liquid – to measure the sugar levels in urine. Edric helped Sultan practice the technique until he had it mastered. Five times a day, Sultan would put drops of his own urine into a test tube, add a few drops of Benedict's solution, then heat the blue mixture over a stove. If his blood sugar was within a safe range, the solution stayed blue. A change to green, orange or red meant the blood sugar was too high and Sultan needed to increase his insulin dose.

This method was already inexpensive but Edric reduced costs further, by halving all the input amounts. When I visited in 2016, the method was still in use at a cost of 0.2 *taka* per test, or a total of one *taka* (NZ 2 cents, US 1 cent) for five tests per day. This was one tenth of the cost of using disposable urine testing strips, and one hundredth of the cost of the blood glucose strips for glucometers (five tests costing 10 *taka*

The equipment for testing sugar levels in urine - a container, dropper, test tube and holder, Benedict's solution and a burner or open flame. Photo by Ben McLaughlin.

Patients heating a mixture of urine and Benedict's solution over a flame. A colour change to green, orange or red indicates that they need to increase their insulin dose. Photo from the Kailakuri Facebook page.

(NZ 18 cents, US 13 cents) and 100 *taka* ($NZ1.80, $US1.30) respectively). The equipment for each new patient cost 93 *taka* ($NZ1.70, $US1.20), including a month's supply of Benedict's solution.

Sultan lived at Thanarbaid Clinic while he learned these skills. Each day he tested his urine sugar levels five times and wrote down the results. A change to green, orange or red he recorded with one, two or three tally marks: these mimicked the gradations on the syringe by which he needed to increase his insulin dose. Edric observed closely. Because he ate meals with the patients, he could check that Sultan was measuring his food properly; he could also respond quickly if Sultan miscalculated his insulin and went into shock or coma. After weeks of practice, all Sultan's test tubes came back blue. Edric invited him to become a staff member and Sultan began to teach others.

The number of diabetic patients at the clinic grew slowly, one or two per year. In February 1985, two years after the clinic opened, they had three patients dependent on insulin. By 1989, there were nine. Each new Type 1 patient took a trip to Dhaka, to be formally diagnosed at Doctor Ibrahim's clinic and to register for subsidised insulin. Then the patient would stay at Thanarbaid for two weeks to learn to manage their condition. Thanarbaid also saw Type 2 patients, most of whom took glibenclamide tablets instead of insulin, but they still needed diabetes education. Once a month, one of Edric's team made the journey to Dhaka to collect insulin. With no fridge, they kept it cool in a hole underground.

Over the years that followed, Edric enhanced the diabetes education. Half of his patients were illiterate, so he trained

Sultan Ahmed in about 2013.
Photo by Christine Steiner.

Sultan delivering diabetes education. Photo from the Kailakuri Facebook page.

his staff to teach using diagrams. Simple drawings showed patients what time to have meals, and what quantity of local foods to eat to keep their blood sugar regular. On the clinic site there was an old sundial and Edric encouraged patients to check that to know when to do their blood sugar tests. Sister Margaret Shield from Jalchatra recalled, 'The sundial was an item of interest for everyone walking by. … We used to stop and look at our watches to "see if it was right" when we passed.'

Thanarbaid's nascent diabetes programme was one of the first in the country outside Dhaka. Yet, despite the rarity of this lifeline, the programme faced the same challenges as the rest of the clinic: diabetic patients did not necessarily come to Thanarbaid or stay. Edric decided to ask patients with sufficient resources to pay for their travel to Dhaka (about 120 *taka*), both to reduce the burden on finances, and so that the patients invested in their own treatment. As he put it, 'The patient has to want to get well.' But sometimes the patient's family made their decision for them. Sultan recalled one family who brought a young diabetic woman to the clinic. He begged the family to stay, but despite having the means to pay for treatment, they declined and took their daughter away.

Plenty of success stories balanced out these sad cases. One was a diabetic *kabiraj* who had tried in vain to treat himself. A friend told him about Thanarbaid just as he grew too weak to collect the plants he used for his remedies. He became a patient of the clinic for over 10 years. Another success story was Mohammad Muslim Uddin, known as Muslim Bhai. He was in his fifties when I spoke to him, and had greying hair curled into sideburns and a soft beard. Through chance connections he had managed to find his own way to Doctor Ibrahim's clinic in Dhaka – at that stage, just a tin shed extension to the doctor's home. Muslim Bhai recovered there, but he had to return to the capital every month to collect insulin. These trips cost 60 *taka* for insulin and 140 *taka* for transport, and sometimes he could not afford the journey. His health deteriorated. In 1986, Muslim Bhai learned about Thanarbaid and began collecting his insulin from there instead. When I met him, he had been doing so for over 30 years.

As Edric's clinic was one of the first insulin outposts outside Dhaka, the patients' reliance on it cannot be overstated. In 1985, Edric wrote home that Sultan was terrified he would return to New Zealand, lest this might mean an end to his insulin. However, supplies were never secure. If floods or unrest caused transport delays, lives were at risk. One diabetic told me that he intentionally used too little insulin each month, so he always had a small surplus for emergencies. But even with steady supplies and careful management, diabetics still risk occasional reactions. Muslim Bhai told me, 'Just yesterday I had a reaction, after coming home late from the *bazaar*. I normally eat between one o'clock and half past, but at two I was still at the *bazaar*. I wanted to go home, but the friend I was sitting with said, "Nah, wait for me."'

By the time Muslim Bhai had walked home, his vision was blurred. Looking at his wife he could see two of her! He managed to drink sugar water and recovered. 'Those types of reactions do happen from time to time,' he told me. Such incidents could be dangerous, especially if they occurred frequently. Muslim Bhai explained that, even with help, some diabetics struggled to manage their illness, as do people elsewhere in the world. He had been to 71 funerals of other diabetic patients. 'I kept count,' he said.

Nonetheless, for Muslim Bhai, Sultan and others to successfully manage Type 1 diabetes for 30 years in their remote, low-income area, was a feat nothing short of astounding. Edric's diabetes programme grew to become a key component of his health work and it transformed his region. Patient numbers had grown slowly at first, but by 2019 there were more than 1600 diabetics receiving care. These were people living normal lives, working and raising families, who might otherwise have had their time cut short. As awareness of diabetes spread, stigma reduced and so did the danger of having the condition. Members of the community could now recognise diabetic reactions and other symptoms and refer people to the clinic. In earlier times they may have attacked that person, out of fear.

On my visit in 2016 I noted one heartening sign of transformation. Bangladesh is known for its fondness for sweet beverages. Hosts offer cups of tea at every sitting, so sweet they made my teeth hurt. Yet when I visited the clinic I noticed the teashop just outside the gate provided 'diabetic' (sugar-free) tea.

A paramedic checking an inpatient. Photo by Christine Steiner.

14

Healthcare by the poor

Ten years after Edric left Vietnam, lessons he learned there were still influencing his work, and one such insight was his observation about the power of teaching. Pat Smith had taught the Montagnards well enough to run the hospital when foreigners fled; she later trained them as village health workers who could teach others. At Thanarbaid, Edric would also focus on teaching, but he would rely more heavily on this strategy than Minh Quy ever had. In the early years of the clinic, Edric had no other foreigners in his team, nor did he seek any. He did not try to recruit Bangladeshi doctors or nurses. Although he did encourage staff to attend short courses, he never sent any staff to medical school. The primary way in which Edric grew the clinic's capacity was by teaching people on the job.

This decision was first and foremost practical. Edric knew it worked; to train and employ local people was affordable and it was also sustainable because they were likely to stay long term. They valued having a job that meant that they could make a difference and they had no qualifications that would earn them higher pay elsewhere.

More fundamentally, however, the decision was ideological. Edric told me in 2012 that training local people gave them the dignity of being able to solve their own problems: 'If you want success and you don't want to be paternalistic or maternalistic, then you really want the local people to do it. The person who comes from the outside is like the facilitator or enabler, but it should be the local people that do the work.'

Edric believed that local people could become paramedics who were not only competent, but the *best* workers to be serving their communities. Edric told Radio New Zealand in 2012,

> *In developing countries the people who drop out from the ordinary educational system at a low level are not necessarily going to be low-grade performers. You've got people who are highly intelligent who drop out for economic or other reasons. If you can find these people and train them up, then you can get staff who are appropriately and well trained ... intelligent, hardworking and motivated. You can also get people who understand how the community and the poor people, the patients, think.*

Outsiders lacked this local knowledge and their qualifications could put up barriers. 'Educated, certificated staff do not fit easily into this type of programme,' Edric noted;

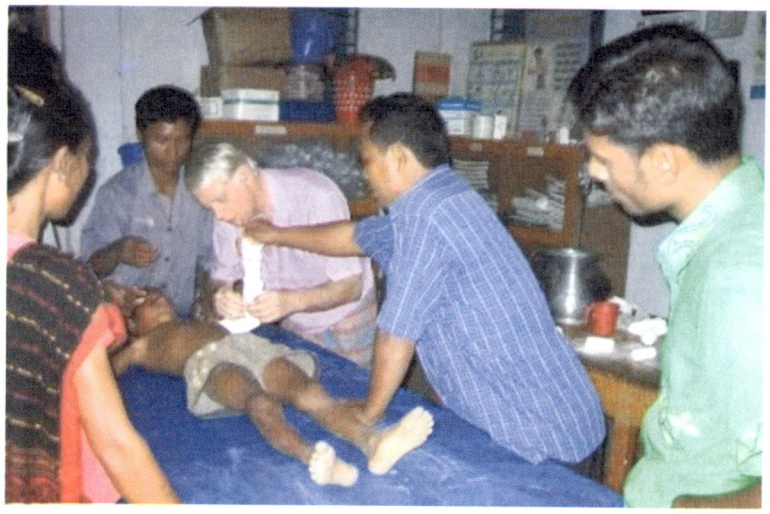

Edric setting a fracture while paramedics watch and assist. The patient had fallen from a coconut tree and broken his arm. Photo by Nicholas Tseffos.

Village health worker Lakhoni Hagidok checks a patient. Photo from the Kailakuri Healthcare Project.

'Their training is inappropriate to it. Their education, their outlook and their opportunities make it very difficult for them to identify with the poor.' Medical schools tended to prepare graduates to treat with the latest expensive technology. The very process of studying medicine often whisked students away into a higher-class world. Thanarbaid locals, meanwhile, had immense potential. When Edric looked at a day labourer eking out his living, he knew that with the right training, such people could prevent illness, mend limbs and save lives.

One such person who realised his potential at Thanarbaid was Bijoy Bormon, a fair-skinned and thoughtful man whom I met in 2016. As a child, Bijoy had longed to become a doctor. Each day after school, he had watched his uncle selling medicines in the market and saw the customers return and thank his uncle for making them better. He completed high school, but soon afterward his family fell into a financial crisis making further study impossible. Bijoy took whatever work he could find to help his family survive.

In 2000 he saw a job opening at the clinic. When called for an interview, his passion for healthcare was so obvious that Edric employed him as a paramedic. Bijoy received training on the job, tailored to assist his own community. He never attended medical school so never became a qualified doctor. Nevertheless, when I asked Bijoy about the lives he had saved, he listed story after story with obvious satisfaction. He advanced from a paramedic to become assistant director of the outpatient section, one of the most senior staff.

Edric witnessed countless such examples of potential being realised. Rejia Begum, the village health worker, became one of the most competent staff despite having studied only

Bijoy Bormon shows Edric an x-ray (obtained elsewhere as there is no x-ray machine at Kailakuri). Photo from the Kailakuri Facebook page.

to about age nine. Another staff member, Chengu Mree, had received no schooling and learned to read and write at the project. Yet when senior staff reviewed all children's weight charts kept by the village health workers, Chengu's were the best. Such examples supported Edric's ideological preference: it was not necessary to bring in outsiders. Local people could be trained to meet the needs of their own communities.

Edric's belief in the potential of local people, however, was part of an even broader philosophy. Edric had now lived in many different countries where there was a void in health-care for the poor, a shortfall beyond any that governments could remedy in a near timeframe. Having wrestled with this problem for years, he had reached a personal conviction: the *only* near-term solution lay in training the people themselves. Judy Walter, a nurse who volunteered at Thanarbaid, explained, 'Edric's philosophy of healthcare was "healthcare *by* the poor, for the poor." That was his mantra. That's what he lived by. ... Edric believed that poverty was so widespread that no government service, nor non-government organisation or private organisation could ever meet the needs of the poor. It was only the poor themselves who could help the poor.'

That lesson had never been so stark as in Vietnam when foreigners had fled the line of fire and left local Montagnards running the hospital. But elsewhere too, Edric had seen that few outsiders would step up to assist the poor. To Edric this point was critical: involving locals was not just helpful but *essential* to meet shortfalls in services. He wrote, 'For the end of the twentieth century the observation about poor people doing healthcare themselves is of equivalent importance to Florence Nightingale's observation that cleanliness lessens infection and Captain Cook's conclusions about [preventing scurvy with] fresh fruit.' It was a new paradigm that ought to transform healthcare practice.

Edric's philosophy made sense to me, to a point. I accepted that poor people had potential that was untapped, but surely outsiders with medical qualifications had more of a role to play? Pat Smith had supplemented her Montagnard team with qualified doctors and nurses. Their skills surely made up for their lack of local knowledge and experience among the poor. Why did Edric not put more emphasis on recruiting foreigners, or better still, Bangladeshi doctors? I was speaking with Bangladeshi medical students when my naiveté was exposed. Regardless of the fact that most of the country's population lived in rural areas, there simply were very few medical grad-

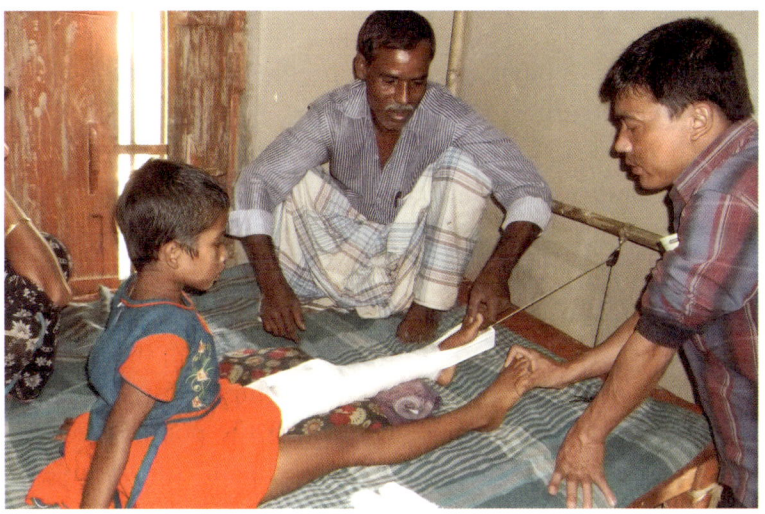

A paramedic tends to a patient with a fractured femur.
Photo from the Kailakuri Healthcare Project.

uates who would go to a place like Thanarbaid. Like medical students anywhere, Bangladeshi students almost universally sought reputable jobs on good pay and in comfortable areas where their children could attain a sound education. One student, Fokruddin Ahmed, known as Tarif, explained, 'Very few of my classmates plan to work in rural areas. Perhaps 4 or 5 in a class of 125.'

It was also rare for students from poor backgrounds to become doctors. To study medicine cost 400,000 *taka* (over $NZ7000 or $US5000) per year in the private system. It was cheaper in the public system at 60,000 *taka* ($NZ1100 or $US760) per year, but only 2200 students were accepted out of 80,000 who applied. Even if Thanarbaid students got a place and secured a loan, they would still need to repay five years of fees. They would then face the same incentives as other graduate doctors, to pursue high pay, progress and comfort. Why would they return to a village?

Given these pressures it is no wonder that Edric never sent any staff to medical school. He could not justify diverting such funds from desperate needs at the clinic, especially when graduates were unlikely to return. He wrote in 2013, 'Doctors produced by the medical colleges have been trained for, and are eager to work in, sophisticated urban situations. ... They have great difficulty with the hardships, frustrations and income levels pertaining to living with the poor. Even with high salaries it is almost unknown for doctors to continue on in remote areas. This is the problem our clinic faces.'

The challenge of attracting professionals to rural areas was not unique to Bangladesh. In 2016, a doctor's practice in New Zealand's small town of Tokoroa made international headlines when it offered an annual salary of $NZ400,000 ($US276,000) to attract a doctor, having searched for two years without filling the position. That strategy would work at Thanarbaid, I thought. Surely there must be a price at which qualified staff would come? Edric must have often refuted such thinking when he explained his model to outsiders. There *were no funds* for the poor of Bangladesh. Graduates *would not come* – not to Tokoroa, not to Thanarbaid – unless they had different motivations from most. A healthcare worker I met in Mymensingh told me that Edric had written off the idea of attracting graduates, 'He always told me – don't bother about the doctors. They won't come here to rural areas. Instead, strengthen the paramedic staff. Then you can strengthen your referral system: paramedics see the patients, then if they find difficulties they can't manage, they refer. This way, the burden on doctors elsewhere also gets reduced.'

Edric had chosen his model because it was sustainable; it delivered paramedics appropriate for their context and complemented the country's healthcare system as a whole. But more fundamentally, it was the *only* approach that Edric believed would work in the near term.

Edric, Onen Mangsang (second from right) and other staff members laugh during a meeting. Photographer unknown.

15

Doctor Bhai
was behind us

To teach other people to deliver healthcare was no easy task, especially not in a foreign language and culture. Edric had studied for 19 years before qualifying as a doctor. Now he aimed to teach similar skills to people who had not necessarily finished primary school. How did he do it?

The answer, as he explained to me in 2012, was teaching 'standard treatments' – the most simple, low-cost response to common health issues. 'These are relatively easy to teach,' he told me; 'The rule must be that everybody, including the professional staff, must follow the standard treatments.' The challenges came, Edric said, when paramedics tried to do things they had not been trained to do; when they were too timid to do what they could; or when they neglected their duties, which was a discipline issue. Ever since he and Sunit Chiran first surveyed the area, Edric had been refining his treatments and compiling them into a book. When any paramedic was unsure what to do, they had to refer to the Standard Treatment Book or ask someone more experienced.

Several paramedics recounted their learning process. A keystone was the weekly lesson which was compulsory for all staff including those in the kitchen and gardens. Edric gathered his team around a blackboard and explained key concepts. He also led practical exercises such as listening to the heart with a stethoscope or giving injections into a lemon. Between those sessions, Edric would teach whenever opportunities arose.

It was often the impromptu lessons that stuck in trainees' minds. One paramedic, Onen Mangsang, told me about an incident that occurred at night. A woman was in labour but the team could not find any female workers to send to her home. Edric told Onen to fetch a kerosene lamp and the two of them set off immediately. Onen remembered holding up the lamp so that Edric could see; and later, the doctor's *lungi* getting drenched as he delivered the baby. 'That will happen,' Edric told him; 'It's no problem, just something you have to deal with.' Later, Onen became a village health worker and put his learning into practice, saving the life of a woman giving birth.

Another paramedic, Suronjon Bormon, recalled the case of an 18-year-old woman who was bent over with bone tuberculosis. She could barely move. Edric gathered all his paramedics and taught them to diagnose her condition. This lesson stayed with them for good reason: the woman was admitted for three months and made a full recovery, astounding everyone.

A paramedic delivers health education while Edric watches.
Photographer unknown.

Weekly training session for all staff. Photo by Christine Steiner in about 2013.

Other lessons were memorable because they were frightening. Suronjon recalled the case of a female patient who was bleeding after delivery. The paramedics were giving her saline but she was still in shock. Edric told them, 'Quickly! Lift her legs and tilt the table upwards, so that blood can run to her vital organs.' The woman survived and the paramedics remembered their lesson.

Edric monitored trainees' progress by checking patients himself, then comparing a paramedic's analysis with his own. Onen told me that Edric routinely supervised in this way. Whenever a new patient arrived, Edric would ask Onen to write out their 'ticket' – a paper slip recording their personal details, signs, symptoms and treatment – then check that Onen's conclusions matched his own. As Edric moved around the clinic, he often checked tickets to see that paramedics had prescribed correct treatment. Senior staff did the same. Paramedics therefore learned through constant supervision, as well as weekly training sessions and lessons around the patients' mats. Bijoy Bormon, now a senior member of staff, told me that he always felt a sense of ease because Doctor Bhai held ultimate responsibility, 'We knew that Doctor Bhai was always behind us. He used to say, "When I'm not around any more, you will have the Standard Treatment Book. Everything is written in there."'

Edric also gave his staff a more holistic education. He knew that social and economic factors were critical to health, and that relationships, housing and employment all affected a patient's recovery. Edric taught staff to consider these factors. Minhaz Ali, a paramedic, explained, 'We have to do "social analysis" to catch the real issue – *why* is this problem hap-

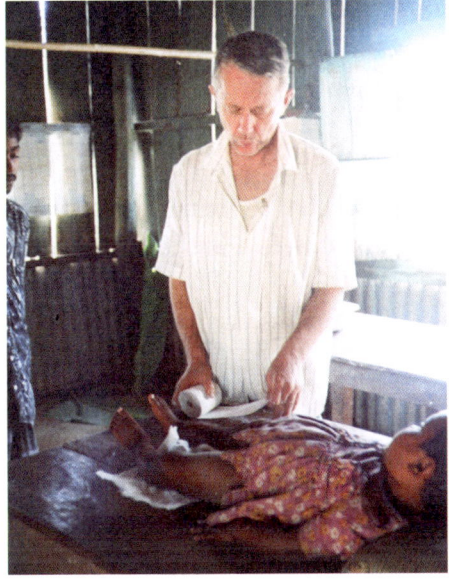

Edric putting leg casts on a girl with rickets, while a paramedic watches. Photo by Judy Walter.

Edric's copy of the Standard Treatment Book used by all staff.

pening? … At face value, our main job is to treat the patient. What they will do after leaving the hospital, we don't care. But Edric also thought about the patient's context.'

Minhaz recalled one couple who were homeless when they arrived at the clinic, having sold all their land to buy various treatments. Minhaz told me, 'When the husband recovered, Doctor Bhai thought, "Where will they go? If they stay homeless, they might fall into the same problem again."' Edric employed the husband, and later the wife, so they could save money for land.

Another paramedic Lipi Khatun told me how the team treated patients who had attempted suicide by drinking pesticide. 'Social analysis' was a crucial step to address the underlying issues. Lipi told me that paramedics first treated the poisoning. They then listened carefully to the patient's concerns and tried to find a solution. For instance, if the problem was an argument with family members, staff would call in the relevant people and encourage them to reconcile before discharging the patient. Lipi recalled, 'Otherwise, Edric thought, the patient may simply go home and try the same thing again.'

Such stories show the strength of Edric's team. Yet, working with paramedics also had limitations. All people made mistakes and this was especially true of workers without formal training. Were errors costing lives, and how did Edric respond?

'If we made a mistake, Edric was not angry. He taught us,' Minhaz told me. In one case a paramedic put two kinds of medicine into one syringe instead of two; Edric corrected him. Another paramedic confused two medicines with similar names and gave them to the wrong patients. That person

A *vangari* driver sleeps after transporting patients. Some patients could not afford transport home or back to the clinic for follow-up and staff had to take that into account. Photo by Nicholas Tseffos.

explained, 'Edric was grateful that I told him. He told me to give the patients saline and rest.'

Paramedic Dipali Bormon remembered Edric using one mistake as a teaching opportunity, 'There was an epileptic patient who was fitting, foaming at the mouth ... One of our paramedics tried to give her some medication by mouth. Edric quickly stopped him and gave the patient an injection instead.' Edric later explained to the staff that it was a choking hazard to give oral medication to patients who were fitting.

Edric had a different attitude towards neglect of duty. Minhaz explained, 'If I had responsibility for a patient but I wasn't there ... Edric did not accept this.' A few people recounted such incidents. One day there had been a celebration nearby and a staff member went to look. Meanwhile, a diarrhoeal baby under that person's care fell into severe dehydration. 'Edric was so angry when he saw that,' the paramedic reflected. 'He told us – patients are the first priority! When he got angry his face got very red.'

Another staff member told me the story of a baby girl. The paramedic on duty had left their post and the baby vomited with no adult nearby. 'Edric was furious – that child could have died! He called the paramedic immediately as well as a senior member of staff. … The next morning Edric called everyone together and ran a training session about how to care for babies. Edric was angry, banging his hand on the table. He said, "You should always stay with a child! If a baby vomits, you have to clean it up. You always have to be there!"'

In one serious case about 2011, a patient did die. When Edric investigated, he discovered that the staff member on night duty had fallen asleep. Paramedics told me that afterwards, Edric was much stricter with the night duty staff. He transferred that paramedic to a different set of duties. While such incidents did occur, local people were under no illusions about the clinic and took a practical attitude. There was no alternative: Thanarbaid was providing services that people could otherwise not access or afford. As Bijoy explained to me, 'Locals know our staff are not well qualified medically, but they see how they serve the people. They believe in the staff and in the foreign doctor.'

The team also provided better care than many public hospitals with qualified staff. In a letter, Edric wrote of a boy with a broken arm who had received inadequate treatment in a government hospital. At Thanarbaid his arm had to be rebro-

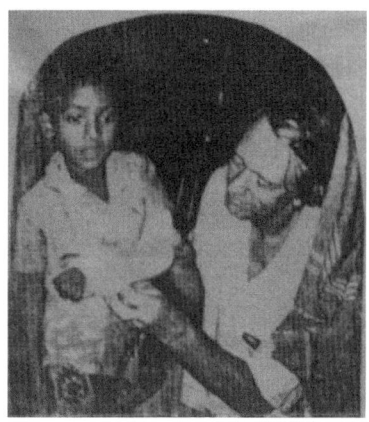

Edric and Kanchon Bormon, aged 8, whose arm had to be rebroken and reset after poor treatment in a government hospital. Photo from a Thanarbaid newsletter.

ken and reset. I heard the story of a man who had suffered an electric shock. Staff at two government hospitals told him he would die and discharged him. Bijoy recalled, 'The man came to our clinic and was completely healed. He decided to go back to the Mirzapur [government] hospital and show them that he didn't die!' Bijoy concluded, 'I tell this example to show that although our clinic does not have qualified medical personnel, it can provide good care and save lives.'

A major test of the staff's capacity came in 1988. In August of that year, the country suffered one of the worst floods of the century. Floods are normal in Bangladesh, so predictable that business people sell peanuts to crowds who gather to see the disruption. The 1988 flood was different. According to the Grameen Trust, roughly two thirds of the country was under water; tens of millions were made homeless and over 2000 people died. In some cities, streets usually crammed with buses and rickshaws became filled with boats. Edric wrote home of the historic event, 'Every year large parts of Bangladesh are inundated … but that floods would come to our highland area was unthinkable.' Paramedic Mohammad Suruzzaman Akanda, known as Suruz, recalled, 'Even my parents had never seen a flood that big before.'

Edric continued his description:

Everywhere, mud-walled buildings collapsed. … People told me that … for 24 hours before the water arrived they could hear it coming. … When it reaches a road it banks up, then falls as a small waterfall as it passes over.

One after another, known villages' reports came – they had gone under water and the people had fled (it reminded me of the advance of the North Vietnamese Army in 1975). When would it be our turn? Thanarbaid, however, remained high and dry from beginning to end. Floodwaters came to the very edge of Jalchatra Mission. Water came into the forest and surrounded two sides of the forest cross-roads near Thanarbaid. … To visit Jalchatra I had to push the cycle through water almost up to the waist!

Edric's response was to mobilise his staff and local volunteers. At that time most people still used open wells – now the floodwater contaminated them and disease began to spread. Suruz recalled, 'As soon as Doctor Bhai knew the flood was happening, he knew the situation would be severe. When people drank water or ate fish they would get cholera. So he called his staff together and gave them some training.' Edric instructed his team to open welfare centres in people's homes. From these bases, his staff and volunteers visited nearby houses and taught people to purify water and treat diarrhoea.

This work continued for days. Travel was difficult and dangerous – 'the roads were as muddy as rice paddies,' one neighbour recalled – but still the refugees came, many of them ill or starving from a lack of clean food. According to Suruz, Edric travelled continually from one welfare centre to another, not arriving back to Thanarbaid until ten or eleven o'clock each night, soaked from the rain and exhausted. He and his team, indeed all local people, must have felt immense fatigue and relief when the waters finally receded after three weeks.

The disaster was an opportunity for Edric's staff to shine. They cooperated with local volunteers and saved countless lives – a significant achievement. Yet Edric's team had already been accustomed to dealing with emergencies. At Thanarbaid they saved lives on a daily basis, on a scale that dwarfed any of their failures.

Edric certainly trusted his team enough to put his life in their hands. In 2012, he told a Radio New Zealand interviewer,

When I am sick, I normally go to be admitted at our centre, because I want to get better. For example, one day ... I got severe diarrhoea. Looking after me on night duty was one of my staff called Pintu who had finished primary school. He looked after me overnight and the next day I asked him, 'How many litres of intravenous saline did you give me?' He said, 'Eleven litres.' So I obviously would have died if he hadn't saved me.

Edric concluded, 'That sort of performance is quite normal. I know we all make our mistakes. I've made many mistakes and our staff members sometimes make mistakes. But on the whole they're pretty good.'

Outpatients lined up at the Thanarbaid gate before being admitted one by one for consultation. Photo by Peter Wilson, 1999.

16

The pressure of the poor does not let up

Towards the end of 1988, a new volunteer joined the Thanarbaid team. Judy Walter was an American nurse who met Edric while she worked as a regional health coordinator for the Church of Bangladesh. In 2016 I corresponded with Judy via email to Kenya, where she then lived. She reflected on her discovery:

> *I was visiting all the church-run clinics and realising some of the major challenges they were facing. It was depressing. I felt overwhelmed. Then I was advised to see the work that Doctor Edric was doing in Thanarbaid. What I found was a vibrant, busy, alive healthcare service. ... This was in contrast to the other facilities where one or two sister nurses alone were valiantly trying to care for the sick with few resources. ... The difference, I gradually*

came to see, was vision, a charismatic leader, motivation, and transmission of basic healthcare knowledge in very simple terms.

Judy became part of the staff for six years. She began as supervisor of the village health initiatives, and later oversaw the midwives and the antenatal programme, living in a hut built for her on the clinic grounds. Apart from Edric himself, she was the first professional to join his otherwise paramedic team.

Since Judy had spent so long with Edric, I was eager to hear her insights into how he sustained himself. Many people told me that he had an insatiable appetite for work. 'There was no end to his work,' Binoy Kubi, the neighbour from Thanarbaid village told me; 'He never rested.' Judy agreed that Edric's workdays were formidable, 'Edric was always available, disregarding his own needs. ... More often than not, he would forget to eat, or wouldn't take time to eat, so Mormiron, our cook, would keep sending for him.'

It took a concerted effort to pull Edric away from patients. Judy continued, 'I remember one little girl of maybe four or five who was with us for almost six months. She became very attached to Edric and would wait for him to come out of the dining room, take his hand and make him walk with her. She was the only one I knew who could slow Edric down.'

Edric's incessant routine had an obvious driver. People told me story after story with a recurring theme: 'If Doctor Bhai hadn't gone to her house, the patient would have died that night.' In a letter home, he summarised the burden: 'The pressure of the poor does not let up.' Rest therefore had an unacceptable price for Edric: someone would suffer or die.

Judy Walter in about 1994.
Photo supplied.

Edric had friends in Mymensingh who were part of Taizé, an international community focused on service and reflective prayer. One of them, Brother Guillaume, told me how Edric made peace with his limitations: 'He had an interesting attitude. Life is God-given. As far as we can help people to live, we can do. We must not obsess on it. We cannot do everything, only what is within our means. He tried hard to save lives, but sometimes he would say, "It's not possible. It's too expensive, too complicated. We have to accept it."'

The reality was that, often, even Edric's best efforts were not enough. Tragedy was a regular visitor at the clinic, often undermining the morale of Edric and his team. Few patients were harder on staff members' emotions than those who suffered burns. In winter, when people lit fires to keep warm, their flowing clothing became a terrible hazard. If the burns covered more than 50 per cent of a patient's body, they were sent home to die, as survival was impossible. If the burns were less severe, Edric's team would do their best, but to watch a patient's struggle for life or recovery was gruelling. The paramedics cut away dead skin, dressed the burns every day or two and kept this up for weeks. They could not relieve the pain.

For Judy, one case that stuck in the mind was that of a six-year-old girl. Helena had suffered third-degree burns. Paramedics dressed her wounds faithfully, but the tragedy of the case was crushing. Judy was so moved that she wrote a reflection for Lent: 'With cries that pierce to the heart, Helena's tiny voice breaks into the silence of the night. Sighs of a young child dealing with the cosmic pain that has been laid on her shoulders. The Passion of Jesus continues in Helena. ... Confronted with such suffering we are powerless, reduced to silence and tears, as was Mary.'

There was only one place to turn in such powerlessness. Judy continued, 'Mother and child together share the burden. Being rooted in Islamic faith, they put all their trust in Allah, the All-Merciful. In the Qur'an we find these consoling words: "Have we not lifted up our heart and relieved you of the burden which weighed down your back? ... Every hardship is followed by ease. Every hardship is followed by ease."' Helena survived this ordeal. Eventually, a day came when she left the clinic, skipping, though she still had disfiguring scars. Years later, Judy wondered what her fate had been.

Such cases took a toll on Edric. He read books about suffering that helped him to reconcile it with a God who was compassionate. 'The suffering of the poor reveals the grief of God,' he later wrote. Yet the tragedy could be too much to bear. When a patient died, Edric would withdraw to his room to rest, read his Bible or pray, no doubt pouring out his anguish to God.

Sometimes Edric's sadness spilled into anger. Judy told me,

I think he struggled a lot with anger over seemingly need-less deaths ... I remember a young child of less than a year arrived at the clinic, not breathing. Edric immedi-ately took the child and did CPR – without any response. He handed the child back to the mother and then banged his fist down on the table and left. I felt his frustration and sense of failure. ... He would even vent his anger at parents or a spouse who waited too long to bring the patient to the clinic. It was one way of coping with the frustration of not being able to help – or he could lash out at staff for some seemingly minor thing.

Staff remembered these flashes of anger. On several occa-sions, Edric threw water at paramedics who did not follow instructions. 'A whole bucket of water,' Nissen Rema, a bystander recalled. 'That was his reaction. He would throw water, then go into his house for a while to cool down. Later he would go to the person and apologise, and say "I'm sorry, I was angry. I shouldn't have done that."'

At least once, Edric threw his dinner on the ground because it was cold, an ironic response given his slow atten-dance at meals. Another time, furious with the behaviour of some patients, he kicked every person out of the clinic and closed the gate until he cooled down. Judy reflected, 'When Edric was angry, he did not turn it inward, but outward ... but it would pass and equilibrium would return. Every-one accepted this as just part of Doctor Bhai and loved and respected him in all his humanness.'

Edric's anger was no doubt a motivating force, power-ing him to find new solutions, but anger was also an unwel-come friend waiting for Edric if he slowed down. Judy told me, 'I think part of his coping mechanism was staying busy, working till exhaustion, then collapsing. When he came to the end of his physical endurance, he then had to face his feelings of anger, frustration, discouragement.'

Judy had another suspicion about what drove Edric: the pressure of the poor did not let up, but neither did Edric's own expectations. Now that he controlled how he worked and lived, the only barriers to living out his revolutionary ideals were within his own mind. Inevitably, Edric fell short of the sacrifice he believed was possible. Sister Margaret Shield, his friend at Jalchatra, described him as 'restless'; indeed, from his bedroom walls, paper cutouts of Nelson Mandela and Mother Teresa called him to greater efforts. Naomi Iwamoto, a Japanese nurse who lived in Dhaka, reflected, 'I once asked Edric what was the greatest of his difficulties. He said, "It is I, myself."'

Edric's lofty expectations were most evident in the extent of his simplicity. He was not unusual for living in a mud hut or eating local fare: many foreigners who arrived in Bangladesh in that period did the same. This was a pushback against earlier missionaries who, with resources and prestige, lived like 'tribal chiefs', as Brother Jacques, of the Taizé brothers, put it. Bishop Mondol hinted at this dynamic, telling me that Church of Bangladesh missionaries tried to be near Bengali lifestyles, getting a 'low' salary of twice the local income instead of 'living on 10 times that.' Some of Edric's contemporaries pushed back further. The Taizé brothers took vows of poverty, in line with their monastic tradition of vowing poverty, chastity and obedience, but as Brother Guillaume told me, 'Edric was more radical than we were in his adaptation.'

Edric on a bicycle. Photo by Christine Steiner.

Edric's bedroom in about 2013. Photo by Christine Steiner.

Two foreigners who came close to Edric's simplicity were American Catholic fathers Doug Venne and Robert McCahill ('Bob Bhai'). These friends of Edric lived in Bengali villages supported by the association Maryknoll. Both embraced the lifestyles of their neighbours; Father Doug even declined medical treatment in his later years to avoid 'wasting' money that could be used for the poor. In 2016 I met Bob Bhai and asked what motivated his lifestyle. 'My role model was Jesus – I thought this way of life was embodied in the gospels,' Bob Bhai told me. He also noted how Gandhi – a Hindu – had criticised missionaries in India with his words, 'A life of service and uttermost simplicity is the best preaching.' Not everyone agreed with Gandhi, however. Bob Bhai recalled, 'Some missionaries thought we were a bunch of monkeys in the *banyan* tree. Those were the words they used.'

Edric also experienced criticism. 'Father Homrich would just say outright, "Edric's crazy,"' recalled Julienne Hayes-Smith, a New Zealander with the Missionary Sisters of the Society of Mary, a group of religious sisters in Dhaka. 'It was hard to get him to accept nice food,' she remembered. 'I used to tease him, "Come on, a little Kiwi luxury." (They would not be considered luxuries in New Zealand.) He didn't allow himself even those.' Judy gave a possible reason: 'Edric came to Bangladesh not to serve the poor, but to identify with the poor, to become one with them.' It was not only that Edric believed Gandhi's words, that simplicity and service were the best preaching. For him, this way of life was the *only* way to live up to his egalitarian ideals, the truest way of emulating Jesus.

Edric and Father Doug sit on the verandah of Edric's house at Thanarbaid Clinic. Photo by Judy Walter.

The Taizé brothers' residence in Mymensingh in 2016. Photo by the author.

Fortunately many things helped Edric cope with the challenges of work, life, and his own expectations. He had the support of friends, especially the Taizé brothers whom he often visited during difficult times. 'We were one of his breathing spaces,' Brother Erik recalled. Edric also drew strength from church services, communion and Bible reading. Judy recalled that he loved to sing sacred songs, rocking his body to his own rhthym. 'Edric must have been tone deaf because … it never sounded like the same melody the rest of the group was singing. I don't think that mattered. He *had* to sing, and sing he did … loudly.'

Prayer was another source of life. Recognising that Muslims, Hindus and Christians shared a common belief in the power of prayer, Edric established daily prayer meetings. Every morning the whole team would gather. Someone would pick red *joba* (hibiscus) flowers to decorate the centre of the room and everyone would pray in silence interspersed with readings from each group's scriptures. These meetings enabled colleagues to show respect for others' beliefs without compromising their own. Edric prayed to Jesus against a backdrop of Christians singing, Muslims praying in Arabic, or Hindus reading their sacred texts. As he listened to Muslim or Hindu readings and prayers, he put a hand on his heart out of respect.

As well as unifying the team, the morning prayers sustained Edric. Whatever emergency may have occurred during the night, the next morning he would have space to pray to Jesus. He would feel his frustrations subside as they sang 'peace' together: '*Shanti, shanti, shanti.*' These prayers bolstered Edric against any tragedy that may come and enabled him to accept his powerlessness. He wrote home, 'Prayer is

Edric and colleagues at a morning prayer meeting. Photo by Tuyen Do.

Staff at a morning prayer meeting. Photo by Christine Steiner.

the power of life when things are grinding to a halt or motivation waning.' Edric later drew on this practice even more heavily, as from 1999 he began taking annual, month-long prayer retreats.

However, there was yet another powerful force that sustained Edric – the work itself. Judy reflected, 'You could feel him come alive as a patient unexpectedly improved.' She recalled one young man who arrived at the clinic near death, having been bedbound for over a year. 'No one expected him to live. Edric started treating him for tuberculosis, and began feeding the patient himself, coaxing him back to life. After a few months he was ready for rehab – he had to learn to walk again. Leaning on Edric, he took his first steps. Edric was beaming. Doctor Bhai's happiness was as great as the patient's, maybe even more so. ... This is what gave Edric life.'

The work was more than joyful and satisfying; it was also indispensable to his relationship with God. Bob Bhai commented, 'It gives *shuk shanti* – joy and peace – to work with the poor. Spirituality is built right into the work. Those who help the poor are helping God.' The nurse Naomi agreed that Edric's work was a spiritual pursuit: 'He needed that context and environment in order to hear God.'

The community of patients and staff was another source of motivation. Brother Jacques from the Taizé community noted, 'It gave him joy to be with the people.' Sister Julienne explained, 'The staff members really do become your brothers and sisters. ... This brings a weakness – sometimes it's difficult to see the boundaries. What's your job, and what's your family?' Brother Jacques continued, 'It was easy to walk away from a job, but not from a family.'

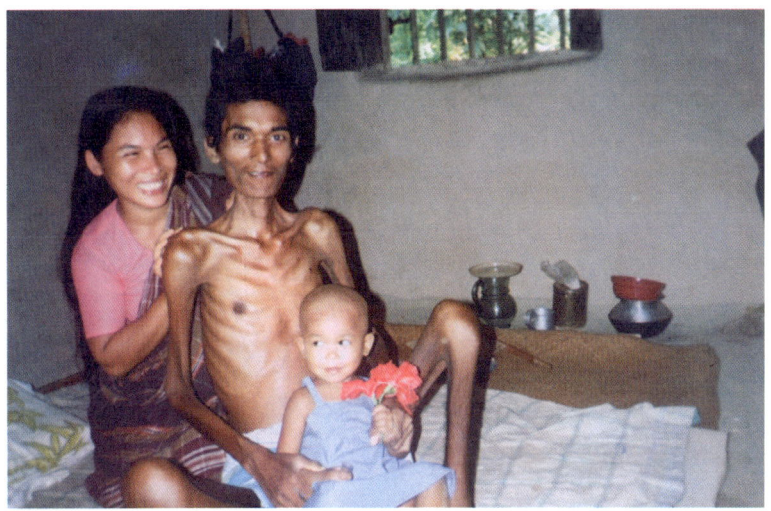

The tuberculosis patient Barnad Maji with his family in about 1992. Photo by Judy Walter. Barnad and his family gave permission for this photo to be published.

Barnad Maji learning to walk again, supported by Edric and a colleague. Photo by Judy Walter.

Edric would not walk away, even when, as the paramedic Onen Mangsang remembered, 'In 1991 there was a time I will never forget. There was an outbreak of cholera throughout our community.' Judy was there:

> As soon as the first patient arrived, Edric realised what was happening and started giving orders as to how to proceed. More and more patients arrived, and within hours, the small supply of intravenous (IV) fluids was finished. … There were many deaths that day. We both worked 24 hours without eating or sleeping.
>
> Sometime in that 24 hours, Edric said he was going to begin making his own IV solutions, boiling the water, adding the salt and reusing the old IV bags! I thought he was out of his mind! But we had no other option. … Because of severe dehydration, most patients' circulatory systems had collapsed, and we couldn't get the home-made IV solutions into the veins, so Edric started to put the fluids into muscle. I was horrified, but with no other option, I followed orders.
>
> Twenty-four hours later I could see that not only were the homemade IV solutions helping save lives, but also patients who were being hydrated via muscle were coming out of shock, and we could use their veins for IV hydration. I had never experienced anything like it before. It went against everything I ever learned in nurse's training. The death rate was high, but the patients who walked away were nothing short of miraculous. That was Edric's pattern – he went into action in emergency situations, and thought outside the box to find solutions.

During this outbreak, the personal risk facing the staff was high. Judy told me, 'I remember being very afraid and praying that I would not die there. ... We hardly ate or drank that first week, for fear that everything at the clinic was contaminated.' Even Edric faced into the possibility of his own death. Judy recalled, 'His request to me was, "If I get cholera, treat me just as one of the patients, nothing special like flying doctors or heroic measures; let me die here like the rest."'

Just as Edric had chosen in Kontum when he declined evacuation, he was choosing again: he would die alongside his patients if necessary. Judy added, 'Psychologists may judge his life as unbalanced, but Edric wrote his own book of life.' He had decided to serve the poor and identify with them; nothing else brought him closer to God and no other lifestyle would satisfy. His mother's observation from his childhood still rang true, 'When Edric made his mind up to do something, that was it: he did it.' He wouldn't accept anything less from himself.

The view from the Kailakuri site out the main entrance, a path that thousands of patients would eventually walk. Photo by Ben McLaughlin in 2017.

17

Kailakuri is born

At the end of 1994, Judy Walter left Thanarbaid to return to the United States and Edric lost the solace of an English speaker in the clinic grounds. The hut built for her sat empty. 'Judy is a deeply religious person and such an inspiration,' Edric wrote, 'It is a great sadness that she has gone.' Three years would pass before another foreigner came to work at Thanarbaid. Over this period, Edric would expand the project, but also, inadvertently, arouse major opposition.

Despite Judy's departure, the project was thriving as the new year got under way. Edric's team had 28 staff. Village health workers served 10 villages and visited more than 500 children. The Thanarbaid and Dhorati sites served an average of 30 outpatients per day, 10,000 in the year, people arriving from everywhere within a 25-kilometre radius. Edric estimated this catchment area to be home to over 75,000 people. He wrote, 'Work never ceases; there are patients upon patients all around us.'

Occasionally patients came from even further afield. In 2016 I met Moses and Mustafa, who, long before meeting Edric, had converted to Christianity and been inspired to become 'ambulance drivers' for the poor. Once they learned about Thanarbaid Clinic, 60 kilometres from their homes, they transported people there by bicycle, often riding with sick passengers for hours through the night. Moses and Mustafa did this voluntarily, they told me, 'because of the relationship we had with Doctor Bhai. He was doing this good work in Bangladesh. So why shouldn't we also do good work?' In turn, the passion of such volunteers spurred on Edric and his team.

At this time Edric saw an opportunity. He sent the paramedic Onen Mangsang on an unusual mission: to lease land in Kailakuri village, four kilometres north of Thanarbaid. Edric's vision was to build a new sub-centre that could focus on tuberculosis and diabetes patients. Both groups required long-term treatment and had to make regular visits to the clinic. A specialised sub-centre would improve their access while also reducing the queues of patients at Thanarbaid.

The location of Kailakuri was ideal for such an outpost. Although the village was little more than a dirt road through barren fields, it was central to many distant places from which patients travelled. Initially though, locals were wary of Onen's proposal, fearing that a new clinic might bring crowds and people with contagious diseases, but he won them over. On Edric's behalf, Onen leased three *paki* of government

The Kailakuri sub-centre in 1998. Photo by Peter Wilson.

land (almost one acre), costing 12,000 *taka*, about $NZ500 ($US300) at that time. Onen remembered, 'There were 14 jackfruit trees on the land. We paid separately for the trees, 100 *taka* for each. They gave us the big mango tree for free.'

For the remainder of 1995 the team prepared the site. The following year, Edric announced,

> *In February [1996] we opened our new clinic for TB and diabetes outpatients at Kailakuri … with three mud buildings and one made out of bamboo. Unfortunately the rain came down and melted about 1000* taka *worth of mud bricks due to the carelessness of the builders. I was really angry but did not have the heart to charge them for it because they were all so poor that it would have meant their families going without food …*

The next few weeks brought nationwide strikes that further complicated the clinic's opening. Yet, the number of patients arriving at the new site soon justified the team's efforts. By the end of 1998, there were 123 diabetics and 83 TB patients receiving treatment at Kailakuri, overseen by 15 part-time workers.

The new setup was a major step forward, and unknown to Edric, a development that would safeguard his vision against troubles to come. Naturally Edric wanted to expand access to treatment even further. He organised his staff to run monthly, one-day clinics in three more remote villages: Dhanbari, Chechua and Nandina. Those clinics were held in existing buildings; no new infrastructure was required. Yet the impact was significant. One diabetes patient told me the change saved him return journeys to Thanarbaid of up to six hours by bicycle or 10 hours on foot.

The opening of the Kailakuri sub-centre gave the team opportunity to refine their programmes. In 1997, Edric's team aligned their TB efforts with the nationwide response led by the Damien Foundation in Dhaka. The chosen initiative was known as the 'Directly observed treatment short-course' (DOTS), which aimed to prevent patients giving up their medication before their six-month course was finished. The role of organisations like Kailakuri was to train community members to observe patients taking their medication each day and to follow up if they did not. This simple intervention reduced defaults. Edric later wrote that DOTS 'displays clearly how motivated local people, trained and supervised in a well-organised programme, get far better results than highly educated, commercially-motivated graduate doctors.'

Kailakuri's TB response thrived after joining DOTS. The nationwide programme aimed for cure rates of 85 per cent. Kailakuri exceeded that every year except 2005, when its cure rate dropped to 84 per cent, but from then on remained above 90 per cent. Edric wrote later, 'Not many countries could compete with this!' The Damien Foundation held annual celebrations for cured TB patients, encouraging them to bring other people in for treatment. Edric wrote, 'I am awed when I am asked to attend ... maybe 100 or more are present, all treated at Kailakuri.'

Edric also took the opportunity to refine the diabetes programme, which had grown from 47 patients in 1996 to 160 in 1999. Edric had bold ambitions: he wanted to set up a democratic structure to enable the diabetes patients to manage the programme themselves. With a lot of work, Edric established four committees, one to govern matters at Kailakuri and one each for the three monthly clinics. These groups took time to become functional, but within a few years the diabetes patient body was meeting annually to elect committee members.

The opening of the Kailakuri site therefore heralded significant developments. Patients with TB or diabetes could access treatment more easily; so too could other patients now that space was freed at Thanarbaid. Across the whole project, patient numbers soared to over 15,000 in 1999. To accomplish the extra work, staff numbers roughly doubled.

This growth brought management challenges. There were hints that the project was becoming unwieldy. Edric wrote in 1996, 'Our programme has got so big that I am no longer able to supervise it.' That was one factor spurring him to set up the diabetes committees. It also prompted him to voice – for

Meetings of diabetes patients.
In the second image, staff members
count votes to determine who will
be representatives on the local diabetes committee. Both photos from the
Kailakuri Healthcare Project.

the first time – a desire to attract other medical professionals.
He wrote in 1998, 'Our deepest longing (before God) is that
Bangladeshi health professionals recognise the importance of
this programme and … determine both to sustain and copy it.'

That was a new direction. Sustaining the clinic had thus
far been up to Edric, Judy and the paramedics – for the very

reason that Edric saw no hope of attracting professionals. He had established his whole model on the premise they would not come. But his days were so busy. Even if just one doctor or nurse came, what a difference it would make! On the off chance, he advertised in his New Zealand communications for a volunteer with medical qualifications.

Another concern in this period was that Thanarbaid villagers were voicing new levels of dissatisfaction. Edric wrote in 1997, 'We have been having serious problems in the village of Thanarbaid. Some of the village people have been very angry. One of my Muslim staff (a 20-year-old diabetic) ran away with a Mandi village girl. Then there was a dispute about a stolen bicycle. … Opposition and anger from the village in which we are working is very un-grounding. One loses one's inner peace and begins to feel very old!' Edric managed each disagreement as it arose, but the discord was unsettling.

Through all this expansion and change, Edric's regular responsibilities never lessened. Somehow, he still found time to show personal care to many patients. One such patient was Antaz Ali, a 17-year-old Muslim diabetes patient who arrived in 1996. To his shame, he could not read or write. When Edric learned of this, he began to teach Antaz himself, providing correction as Antaz read aloud from the doctor's own Bangla study books. In time, the student discovered that meaning was appearing from the pages of Bangla text. Edric was impressed at his hunger to learn and employed Antaz as a member of staff.

Another patient was Suronjon Bormon, an 18-year-old Hindu who survived three bouts of *kala jor* (black fever) at the clinic. Suronjon told me that in 1997 Edric had summoned his parents and told them that their son may not survive. Suronjon overheard, and in the early hours of the night, when Edric was doing ward rounds with a lamp, he found Suronjon awake and crying. Suronjon remembered that Doctor Bhai started crying also, and the two of them prayed together, Hindu and Christian, asking God for healing. Suronjon told me, 'I recovered, as Hindus say, "by the grace of God."' Once well, he begged Edric for work and began training as a paramedic.

Such interactions grounded Edric when questions of governance and village politics weighed on his mind. Yet, patients' hardships also placed on him an emotional burden. Over the years when the project grew rapidly, Edric's most frequent source of worry was the predicament of a young girl. Johura was a homeless 12-year-old with diabetes who became Edric's 'god-daughter'. In about 1994, she had been begging at a railway station when one of the Taizé brothers took her to Thanarbaid. Edric's team tried to find her former home; when they were unsuccessful the doctor informally adopted her. (Two years later, they managed to locate her father but he refused to take her back.) Johura settled permanently at the clinic, sharing a hut with a single mother and her children who had also been homeless. Edric wrote about Johura, 'She called me father – *Umba* or *Bubba* ... Her address was "care of us" and "care of myself".'

Parenting Johura would prove a major challenge. She was a pretty and headstrong teenager and refused to go to school, preferring to put on makeup to attract local boys. She showed a dangerous lack of interest in managing her diabetes. After three years of consternation, Edric wrote, 'I do not

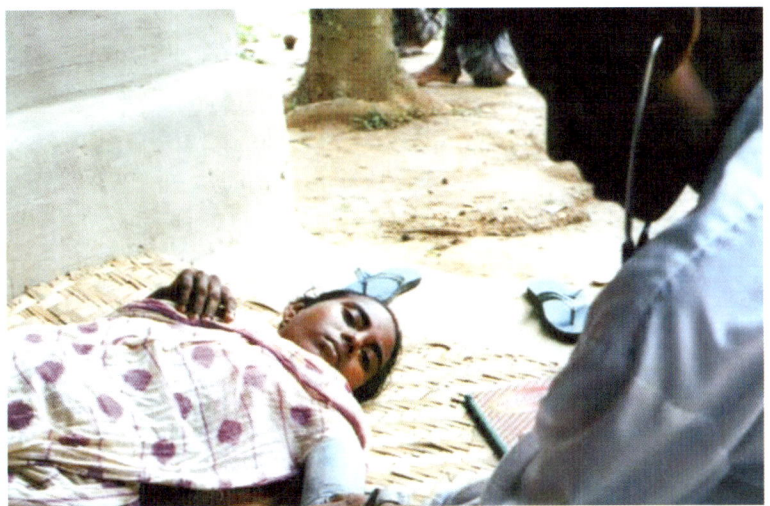

Suronjon Bormon tends a patient. Photo from a Kailakuri newsletter.

know what you will think, but we are considering arranging a marriage for Johura [aged about 15]. I do not like child marriages but her dangers and difficulties are so great that this seems maybe to be the best course …' Marriage did not end her troubles. Johura soon fell pregnant, but her diabetes was uncontrolled; the baby was born prematurely and died.

Edric had much on his mind, therefore, in addition to the project's expansion. Fortunately he had people to turn to for support: his Bangladeshi colleagues; the Taizé brothers in Mymensingh; and his Catholic brothers and sisters in Jalchatra and Dhaka. Nevertheless, Edric must have spent many nights lying awake and asking God for direction, encouragement, and progress for his friends.

A picture of a pohutukawa, an iconic New Zealand tree,
stapled on Edric's bedroom wall. Photo by the author.

18

New Zealand links

In September 1998, as if heaven sent, more support arrived for Edric: a new foreign volunteer landed to join his team. Libby Laing was a bubbly and energetic New Zealander from Taupō who had seen Edric's request for help in a church magazine. Libby had been widowed in her early fifties, and, seeking a new way to apply her nursing skills, she took the plunge. She was 58, one year older than Edric. With support from the New Zealand Church Missionary Society she moved to Bangladesh. She would flourish in this new country and prove a major support to Edric over the next 12 years.

Libby was blessed with a sense of humour and a can-do attitude that more than made up for her inexperience in Bangladesh. She settled in the nearby village of Pirgacha, and there became a daily spectacle: the fair-skinned lady with short, silver hair and glasses who cycled to Thanarbaid and Kailakuri. Learning Bangla was her major challenge. Sister Ruma, one of the Missionary Sisters of the Society of Mary in Dhaka recalled, 'Libby was not fluent in Bangla but she could communicate. She struggled to remember words. I recall one time on the phone, her saying, "I can't see you, I can't see you!"' In a letter to supporters, Libby wrote of her language efforts, 'Some days are better than others but we do have a lot of laughs.'

Libby had a background in mother and child health acquired with the New Zealand organisation Plunket. The village programme therefore became her natural focus. Just as Judy Walter had done the decade before, Libby began to build up the health worker team, cycling with them to distant villages and troubleshooting problems. Genuine warmth and fierce persistence helped Libby overcome her language challenges. Edric later wrote of her, 'Libby is the hands and heart of our mission and the worker who with sweat and tears and damned perseverance carries things through.' Within a few years, Edric handed over to Libby the leadership of the village health programme and she established a staff team who eventually managed it themselves. Edric could not have known then how much he would need Libby's company through the challenging times to come.

At a similar time, hundreds of miles away, a chance encounter set another New Zealander on track to join Edric's support team. In this case it was a reconnection: Peter Wilson, an agriculture expert, had met Edric in 1969 while working for the New Zealand Red Cross team in Vietnam. He had since worked as a consultant in many Asian countries. In 1985, in

Libby cycling to Kailakuri in 1998. Photo by Peter Wilson.

Libby and the village health workers discuss paperwork.
Photo from the Kailakuri Facebook page.

the Hong Kong airport he had by chance bumped into Margaret Neave, the pediatrician who mentored Edric in Vietnam. Speaking to me in his Auckland home, Peter recalled, 'Margaret and I had a hurried catch up. Just as we were parting, she said, "Do you remember Edric Baker? ... He's in Bangladesh now," and we parted.'

In 1998 Peter was invited to do some work in Bangladesh and stayed on a few extra days to visit Edric. He told me his stand-out memories of that trip,

> *Kailakuri was out in the middle of nowhere then, just a few thatched huts amid barren fields as far as the eye could see ... Edric's focus on work was so intense that ... it seemed that it was a bit of a nuisance that somebody came (family aside of course). ... He didn't really talk to me the first day or two. I just observed and wandered around. Only the morning I departed did he tear himself away from work and we had a substantive conversation for a couple of hours. ... I asked him what things were costing; he had no idea then.*

The following year, Peter worked in Bangladesh again and took the opportunity to spend a week at Thanarbaid. 'This time I calculated what it was costing them,' he told me. 'It then cost the project about $NZ0.45 [$US0.24] to serve an outpatient, which included costs of medicine, staff, admin and overheads. It cost $NZ1.27 [$US0.67] per bed night.' Peter shook his head as he put these costs in perspective. 'When Edric visited New Zealand in about 2004, doctors told him that at Middlemore [Hospital in Auckland] it was costing $NZ1200 [$US792] per bed night.' Peter was fascinated by

Peter Wilson analysing the cost of serving patients at Thanarbaid Clinic in 1999. Photo from Peter Wilson.

Edric's project. From that time onwards, he counselled Edric by email or phone through many management difficulties. Peter would become an indispensable part of Edric's support team for decades.

These friendships with Libby and Peter strengthened Edric's relations with New Zealand in an important period. Edric had now spent two decades in Bangladesh, during which he had visited New Zealand only six times – in 1980, 1986, 1989, 1993, 1996 and 1999 – each trip a combination of family time and fundraising. His parents offered to pay for more frequent trips but Edric saw the cost of flights as 'exorbitant' and his work responsibilities too important to leave. Moreover, Edric was not homesick for New Zealand. He told a Bangladeshi child, 'People in New Zealand are like robots.

They have no emotion; they are bland! But Bangladeshis are humans, with life, passion and anger. That's why I want to stay.' Another simple fact kept him from yearning for New Zealand. As he told a colleague, 'My friends are in Bangladesh.' Significant Baker family events – weddings, funerals, and his parents' fiftieth and sixtieth wedding anniversaries – therefore passed without Edric.

The expansion of the project to Kailakuri created new urgency for him to visit New Zealand: he needed to raise funds. Many New Zealanders were already supporting his work. His mother collected donations; his father oversaw his financial affairs; friends collected spectacles and his sister Hilary, a dental nurse, collected dental tools for Edric to take back. From 1996, all these efforts became concerted. Edric's trips became intentional fundraising tours. On a tight schedule, he spoke at dozens of locations around the country and raised tens of thousands of dollars for the project.

Perhaps this new urgency for donations gave Edric greater mental permission to make the journeys. Could he more easily justify travelling to New Zealand now that his trips were helping the people he served? For, although Edric was not homesick, he did not enjoy his separation from his ageing parents, his siblings and their growing families. Betty and John had now retired and shifted to the town of Whakatāne. They mostly kept in good health, but with Edric so far away, their advancing years made the cost of his chosen lifestyle ever more apparent.

In 1999, Edric received news that his father was seriously ill. The scare did not last; he was soon out of hospital. Edric nevertheless returned hurriedly, counting anxious hours in

Betty and John 'J.V.T.' Baker
in about 2000. Photo from
the Baker family collection.

clogged Dhaka traffic, in airport queues and planes that were
the transit to this other world.

How wonderful it was to see family after so many years!
His rare visits brought the Bakers together in lively gather-
ings. Nieces and nephews met in person their uncle who hith-
erto existed only through letters. Others re-encountered the
Edric they knew: someone full of good humour. 'He used to
tell stories about the clinic,' his brother John recalled. 'The
sanitised slice goes into the Kailakuri newsletter; we got the
other stuff. Edric took great delight in telling it. ... he could
spin a great yarn.' Edric treasured such occasions and enjoyed
staying with siblings and friends in their homes.

Edric's extreme simplicity stood out to his hosts. John
remembered, 'He ran pretty skinny on personal effects.' Peter

Wilson agreed, 'When he turned up at the airport, he had no suitcase, just plastic bags, and a shoulder bag, moth-eaten. We gave him a suitcase – when he came on his next trip, that's what he had.' Another friend recalled that, 'Edric dressed like an op-shop. One year Betty gave him an old jersey from her husband. He wore that for 10 years.' Edric's frugality amused some people and unsettled others. Nadine Vickers, a New Zealand volunteer at Kailakuri, reflected, 'His simple lifestyle was something people both admired him for, and felt uncomfortable about, because they felt they would not make the same decisions.'

Family members also recounted his quirks. 'His sense of fairness baffled us,' his niece Rebecca recalled. 'One evening we didn't have enough boiled eggs for everyone. ... Edric wanted to split the two eggs between all six of us plus guests! Everyone had to have the same ... You had to share even a miniscule amount of food.' Rebecca reflected, 'We didn't know what it was like to be poor; we had no comprehension at all.' His family and friends were reminded of Edric's dedication to prayer, as each evening he excused himself to his room to spend time with God and to prepare upcoming talks. Edric also displayed his fastidiousness. His sister Hilary recalled a time when Edric visited her farm: 'We were vaccinating lambs with a scratch under their arm. For Edric, each scratch had to be perfect, just the right depth. It took a long time.'

While his visits were special times of reconnection, Edric also stood out as a foreigner in New Zealand. John told me that the way he talked gave away the length of his absence, 'He spoke in ... Queen's English ... correct but perhaps 30 years old. Because he didn't speak English usually, he spoke in the English he remembered.'

Some of his behaviour was out of place. His brother Les told me, 'One time he had the heaters on ... but also wanted the window open. So he turned the heater on full blast!' On occasion, Edric left hosts waiting for hours because he had got into a conversation elsewhere. In some homes, he even pulled the blankets off the bed, which he found too soft, and slept on the floor.

He also exhibited signs of culture shock. 'There are hardly any people,' he told Radio New Zealand in 2012. 'The homes are so beautiful ...' New Zealanders' wealth was what enabled them to support his clinic. Yet, Edric found any signs of affluence – as he perceived them – hard to stomach. A friend recalled Edric asking, 'Why do you need such a big house?' At times, his consternation spilled into distress, as John recalled, 'I took him to the supermarket once; I never did that again. He couldn't handle the abundance of food.'

Perhaps most shocking to Edric was the comparative cost of New Zealand healthcare. He told Radio New Zealand, 'New Zealand hospitals are just unbelievable ... so sophisticated.' Many people remembered him vocalising comparisons. A family friend recalled, 'Back then it cost 20 dollars to go to the doctor. He'd say what he could do in Bangladesh with that money.' Another friend remembered Edric visiting her in a New Zealand hospital, in which she had a single room. She told me she asked him how his hospital compared. 'He said "Oh," and started measuring with his eyes. "I would have about 22 people in this room."' This habit must have embarrassed some hosts, but Edric was simply seeing New Zealand through Bangladeshi eyes. He wrote to a friend in 1997, 'You asked if I feel pain coming back to Bangladesh from New Zealand. In fact it is the other way. I feel pain in New Zealand. So many things have changed, and not in ways that I would like.'

New Zealand's formal relations with Edric also changed over these years. On 31 December, 1999, the New Zealand Government honoured Edric by making him an officer of the New Zealand Order of Merit for services to humanitarian aid. Ironically, the following year, the New Zealand Medical Council cancelled his practicing certificate as he had spent too long abroad: Edric's commitment to humanitarian work meant he could no longer practise medicine in his own country! But the loss of this privilege did not worry Edric. As his sister Hilda understood, his New Zealand visits were only ever a brief touchdown, 'He came back to see the family, and possibly to get a grounding for what he was doing; to get the contrast. This made him really want to go back to Bangladesh. He would come back to New Zealand, see what was happening, then move on.'

Edric treasured being a Baker brother, uncle and son, but there was no doubt where his heart lay. His New Zealand connections provided him with support and motivation to continue in Bangladesh.

19

The split

The turn of the millennium marked 17 years of Edric's leadership at Thanarbaid and four at Kailakuri. During that time he had rarely, if ever, experienced strong opposition. This was about to change. Edric would soon face open challenge to his leadership, revealing how much power he was willing to yield.

First, however, Edric received a constructive critique. In February 2000, at Edric's invitation, an American doctor Francis McCormack visited for three weeks to evaluate the project. His focus was the quality of medical work and long-term sustainability. Francis found much that impressed him, writing, 'The vision is ambitious, sweeping and revolutionary ... Healthcare has improved, medical knowledge has been imparted to indigenous staff, costs have been kept low, village health promotional work has been established and a staff forged of disparate faiths in service to the poor … each one of these is in itself a tremendous feat.' However, when Francis interviewed staff at Thanarbaid and Kailakuri, he discovered significant tensions. The team felt their salaries were too low. Edric was concerned that higher salaries would make them forget the plight of the poor, but the staff disagreed. The fact that Edric lived on the same low salary as their own did not appease them: the staff members had families to feed, and he did not. Fundamentally, Francis pointed out, Edric's workers were breadwinners, not missionaries. Edric could choose to forgo a higher income, but his staff did not want the same sacrifice made for them.

Further, Francis found that Edric's team wanted to gain professional qualifications and improve facilities at the clinic. In their eyes, the simplicity that Edric maintained felt like an anchor preventing progress. The staff did not wish to remain poor. They wanted certificates that gave them job security in case anything should happen to Edric or the project. They hoped for better buildings and equipment. The staff did not share Edric's concerns that upgrades would attract rich patients and divert their focus from the poor, or that qualifications would facilitate a 'brain drain' as staff sought jobs on higher pay elsewhere. Edric's team wished to improve their lot – as individuals and a community – and resented feeling held back.

The most insightful of Francis' observations was that Edric was reluctant to share power. Francis wrote that the doctor was 'by his own design' excessively overworked; 'wearing too many hats', and creating a 'bottleneck' in decision-making. Staff did not have authority on important deci-

Patients at a drop-in clinic at Thanarbaid in 2017. Photo by Ben McLaughlin.

sions, as Francis noted, 'It is one thing to come to a consensus on where and how to compost, and altogether another thing to jointly decide the payroll.' Nor did staff have experience leading on financial matters and Edric was denying them opportunities to learn. Francis recommended that Edric give more power to the staff, and ultimately relinquish all responsibilities but medical supervision and fundraising. This was a challenge that would resonate for years to come.

For Edric, these observations may have been hard to hear, but they named important realities and therefore demanded attention. In the following months he made significant changes. He raised salaries, handed over management of the village health programme to Libby Laing and her team, and established staff committees to make decisions at Thanarbaid and Dhorati. Yet some elements of governance he would not give up. He was soon to receive a much harsher challenge in precisely the areas in which he would not yield.

Edric had set up the Kailakuri sub-centre as a self-governing project 'owned' by patients. Thanarbaid, meanwhile, remained a project of the Church of Bangladesh. For as long as Edric had been there, that meant he operated that clinic under the authority of Bishop Mondal. When I met this bishop, long retired to his humble Dhaka home, I asked him to describe how he had managed Edric. 'In my time,' the bishop said, 'I tried to say that there would be no committees required by the Church of Bangladesh. Edric could work on his own. ... Yes, the bishop was his boss ... but there was not much bossing going on. I don't understand about medical problems.' A change came in late 2000. Bishop Mondal told me, 'When I retired, another bishop came who liked to have committees all the time.'

This new leader, Bishop Baroi, wanted more influence at Thanarbaid. He directed the Church to set up its own committee to oversee the clinic. They also appointed a Mandi man, Bijon Ghagra, as Project Manager. The role sat alongside Edric's position of Medical Director and held similar authority.

From Edric's perspective, these changes were detrimental. Bijon and the Church could now challenge his decisions at Thanarbaid, which was no small blow to his pride after nearly two decades of sole charge. Edric also feared that they would allow Mandi interests to dominate. That clashed with his goals. After years of investment by the Catholic Mission, Mandi tended to be better off than Muslims and Hindus. Edric had worked hard to ensure that all three groups felt welcome. He worried that greater Mandi influence would unbalance the equilibrium between staff of the three ethnicities, and undermine his focus on the poorest of the poor.

Between 2001 and 2005 that is exactly what occurred. The Church of Bangladesh – intentionally or otherwise – moved the focus towards Mandi. Two visions for the project could not co-exist. Edric resisted the challenges to his authority and direction, and as he did so, his relations with the Church of Bangladesh deteriorated to the point they were no longer workable.

When I asked Edric about this relationship breakdown, he did not identify ethnicity as the source of the conflict *per se*. Instead, the flashpoint he named was that the Church had objected to the project's continued growth. Expansion had been considerable. In 2001, there were 19,000 outpatient visits across Thanarbaid and Kailakuri, up from 15,600 in 1998. Staff member Mohammad Suruzzaman Akanda (Suruz) told me, 'The Church leadership declared that this project was too big. … Doctor Bhai was bringing in lots of patients from further afield … taking on lots of staff … The Church said, "You can't use our money to treat … everyone from this side of the world to the other!"' In fact, it was Edric who sourced the bulk of donations; he even reluctantly gave the Church 10 per cent for overheads. Nevertheless, the Church requested that the project be cut back. Edric told me, 'We didn't think that we should do that, because it was too necessary for the community.'

The Church's objections may have been justified on strategic grounds if they preferred to consolidate and provide higher-level care. However, in stating objections to growth, the Church may in fact have been masking their aversion to another trend entirely: Edric's growing attention to regions where few or no Mandi people lived. Thanarbaid was a Mandi area. In Kailakuri village and further afield, most patients were Bengali Muslims, and staff reflected patient demographics. Therefore, by expanding the project into poorer regions, Edric was drawing resources away from Mandi and offering fewer staff appointments to their community.

Mandi also sought to improve the standards at the clinic. Australian Jenny Clarke, a doctor and one of the Missionary Sisters of the Society of Mary in Dhaka, remembered Edric asking her how to maintain his focus on the poor, 'with the Church of Bangladesh wanting to make things grander and catering for good fee-paying people.' Nissen Rema, a retired staff member, elaborated on these pressures: 'The rich would ask, "Why haven't you made cement buildings? Why are you taking on uneducated people and patients as staff, when you could take on people with better qualifications?"' The implication was that Edric was not doing enough for Mandi, and as he resisted, Thanarbaid locals grew disgruntled. As Brother Guillaume from the Taizé community noted, 'Some people felt they could not, felt they did not, get enough out of Edric.'

In at least one instance, the frustration of Mandi people grew to the point of violence. A local Mandi woman came in as an emergency patient, but Edric did not check her himself; he left this to another paramedic. Staff member Bruno Rema told me what followed,

> *Some other Mandi people became angry, so angry that they wanted to hit Edric … He ran to the office of the priest of the Church of Bangladesh; the padre returned with him to the hospital, met the people, perhaps four or*

five of them, calmed them down, and made them under-
stand that they should not hit Edric. Their complaint was
that for patients of the Muslim community, Edric always
checked them himself. Why not for us, for Mandi?

Edric did not give in to these pressures. On the contrary,
he defended his priorities – just as he had in previous hospitals
to the point he had to move on. As Judy Walter put it, 'During
my time at Thanarbaid, the decisions were always made by
Edric. He was very much in control, and I think this may have
caused friction in these village meetings. Edric was not willing
to compromise his ideals.'

There was, however, a fine line between Edric defending
his ideals and simply his own authority. A Kailakuri villager,
Goren Talbot, described the situation succinctly, 'Edric wanted
to work without conditions.' The result was a slow-burning
tussle for control. The paramedic continued, 'The Church
wanted to take responsibility for the money and do whatever
they wished but Edric did not allow this. The committee was
not happy with Edric, and this attitude spread.'

Unfortunately Edric gave Mandi even more reasons to
grumble: he made a habit of interfering with their customs.
Edric was often involved in informal social work as staff
members asked him for help with their personal problems. In
one instance, a Mandi paramedic had an affair with a first
cousin. The community found out and in keeping with their
traditions, expected Edric – the employer – to dismiss him.
Instead, Edric met with community elders, in an effort to
protect the man and woman from consequences he believed
unjust. When this was unsuccessful, Edric eventually had to
dismiss the man, but found him alternative work elsewhere.

In another case, two paramedics had an affair. Contrary to the community's wishes, Edric allowed both paramedics to keep their jobs, as he was unwilling to let go of his employees. Staff member Pijon Nongmin described Edric's attitude simply, 'What Doctor Bhai will do he will do. He was very strong about his ideology even if this is not perfect or accepted by the community.'

Edric's habit of intervening in support of staff was by no means a habit he reserved for Mandi. Judy recalled a time when Edric intervened on behalf of a Muslim woman staff member whose husband planned to bring home a second wife. He asked influential people to call off the second marriage, and thus made many enemies in that community. Judy reflected, 'I do think at times he became too involved in people's personal problems, infringing on cultural expectations.'

However, it was Mandi with whom his relationship was most strained. The Thanarbaid teacher Mironi Hagidok told me that after Edric failed to dismiss the paramedics who had had an affair, 'Community members were really angry with Doctor Bhai. They wrote to the bishop, saying they didn't want him to be allowed to stay here.' In turn, this teacher and others petitioned the bishop to protect Edric's position at Thanarbaid. But by then the conflict had unsettled the whole community. Mironi continued, 'From that point, Doctor Bhai began thinking that he would not be able to continue his work in this area.'

These years were tense as relationships strained and frayed. In August 2001, Edric celebrated his sixtieth birthday while tension in the community grew. Then in 2002, Libby Laing finished her four-year stint at Thanarbaid and moved

A path leads towards disused buildings on the Thanarbaid Clinic compound.
Photo by Ben McLaughlin in 2017.

back to New Zealand. She would later return for annual visits, but for a time Edric faced a higher workload with less emotional support. Soon after Libby's departure, he wrote, 'Lately we have had a lot of turmoil at Thanarbaid. First we found that we had slipped up on government regulations and so I had to make several trips to Dhaka to get that sorted out. Then we discovered workers had been taking money from the cash box. Then when I had to make some quick changes, our staff went on strike and closed the clinic. It has all been upsetting and disappointing.'

The following year, 2003, brought more difficulties. In July, Edric wrote that the project had grown to four times its original size. There was now a road joining Jalchatra with the rest of Bangladesh, and 'sometimes' electricity at Thanarbaid, yet 'problems and crises continued'.

It was not until November that Edric finally had news to share of progress in his relationship with the Church of Bangladesh: 'We have been through great pangs and labours over the future path of our two clinic programmes,' he wrote. 'Now we see clear paths ahead and are united, but there is much work to be done.' They had negotiated substantial changes to start in January 2004. Edric would shift his focus entirely to Kailakuri. He would resign at Thanarbaid and hand over leadership to the project manager Bijon, although Edric would continue supervising paramedics there until a Bangladeshi replacement could be found. Following church leaders' wishes, Thanarbaid Clinic would transfer to Kailakuri about one third of its services and budget. Kailakuri would become the larger of the two projects and Edric's new home. Edric officially worked a six-day week; he would spend three days

Edric with a patient in about 2001, the time of his sixtieth birthday.
Photo from the former Thanarbaid Clinic website.

at Thanarbaid and three overseeing Kailakuri and providing
medical supervision there.

This plan was a breakthrough of clarity that shifted both
projects forward after years of uncertainty. However, the new
arrangement lasted only 18 months. Sometime before June
2005, Edric and the committee clashed once again. A staff
member told me, 'One day, Edric called in on me at home.
He cried, right in front of me, and told me that there had
been a meeting with lots of people from the village and out
of town and with staff from the Church of Bangladesh. Most
of them had criticised Doctor Bhai, and he described a clash
between the medical and non-medical leadership.' Other staff
members recall Edric saying, 'If they put obstacles in the way
of working with the poor, then I can't work there any more,'

and also, 'I'm providing treatment with money I've collected. Why are they so upset; why do I have to listen to them?'

In June, Edric visited New Zealand. Peter Wilson remembered that he voiced ongoing frustrations. The Church of Bangladesh still focused on Mandi and took 10 per cent of Edric's donations for priorities he did not share. Edric seemed in turmoil about what to do. He then went on a retreat and came back with a decision: he would have to pull out of Thanarbaid entirely. In September, when he returned to Bangladesh, he resigned from all involvement at Thanarbaid.

This parting was amicable and the steps toward it had been gradual. Edric's focus was shifting only a few kilometres. Yet the change was nevertheless momentous. Brother Guillaume reflected, 'Edric was not much of a person to give up. He didn't talk about leaving Thanarbaid in terms of giving up. But it was a terrible struggle for him. To come to Kailakuri was a painful decision I think, a painful period ... For some Christians he became *persona non grata* [unwelcome because of what he had said or done].' Thanarbaid had been Edric's home and community. The clinic had been the greatest investment of his life. Now his involvement there was over. Without so much as a farewell party, Edric left Thanarbaid after 21 years.

20

Edric knows best

In late 2005 Edric was beginning a new era and he would have had mixed feelings. He had ended one chapter of his life at Thanarbaid, but he was now living at Kailakuri and leading an independent clinic, a prospect that brought him relief and also excitement too. To mark the fresh start, his team adopted a new name – the Kailakuri Healthcare Project or Kailakuri for short. Edric could now lead unshackled in the way that he had dreamed.

Edric would not lead singlehanded, however. He chose a Dhaka-based organisation, the Institute of Integrated Rural Development, to help him liaise with government departments. He also continued to draw on his support base in New Zealand. In 2006, Libby Laing, from her home in Taupō, formed a 'Link Group' to pass on donations and arrange Edric's fundraising tours. Accompanying her on this team were Peter Wilson, Edric's parents and sisters and selected friends.

Support from these groups was essential, because Kailakuri had become larger than Thanarbaid had ever been. Now that it served general patients as well as those with TB and diabetes, Kailakuri received over 17,000 outpatient visits in 2006. The same year, the Church of Bangladesh wished to contract its operations even further so Edric brought the whole village health programme – serving 15 villages – under Kailakuri leadership as well. To accommodate all these changes, Edric took on 18 new staff, bringing his team to 68, and expenditure rose by more than half to 5,438,000 *taka* ($NZ118,000; $US81,000). Only with help from the Link Group, and Edric making a fundraising trip to New Zealand in 2007, were donations able to keep pace.

The independent Kailakuri was therefore thriving with a strong team and committed support. The separation from Thanarbaid had been far from simple, but Edric had navigated through. Now, taking stock of the progress, he must have felt that his stubborn pursuit of his goal had been justified, that he had been right not to compromise his vision.

However, there remained imperfections in Edric's management. The doctor Francis McCormack, who had evaluated the clinic five years earlier, had observed that Edric was reluctant to share power. His insights had prompted Edric to hand over more responsibility to Libby and the committees. However, had the separation from Thanarbaid made Edric more inclined to hold on to control?

At least ideologically, Edric was committed to sharing leadership in the new Kailakuri Healthcare Project. He set up

The entrance to the Kailakuri Healthcare Project in 2013.
Photo by Christine Steiner.

Patients wait to register at the outpatient department.
Photo by the author in 2016.

the diabetes committees – although those collapsed at least once and he had to reestablish them. But he was proud of the result. In 2005, he wrote, 'I am awed when I attend the Diabetes Patients' Annual General Meeting. It divides into four area meetings: Kailakuri, Dhanbari, Nandina and Chechua. At each I see 100 or more people, many from distant villages I have never heard of. Most are very poor. ... The meeting is chaired by our staff and led in prayer. With determination these people want and support the programme. It is theirs.'

To govern the wider project, Edric had committees of community advisers and team leaders from his other programmes. At the very least, these provided a place for people to voice their opinions and for Edric to share decisions about governance and finances. In fact, committee members seldom disagreed with Edric. Pijon Nongmin, a senior staff member, told me, 'I can't remember a decision going against Doctor Bhai's wishes, because before the meeting he would prepare the committee members. That was his style.' Edric also took care to appoint people who would defend his focus on the poorest and powerless. One committee member, Abul Kari Munsi, told me, 'Many people around the village who were politically powerful would sometimes try to control this project ... so we didn't include those people in the committee. That's how it worked and is still working.'

Although committees rarely disagreed with Edric, they did hold some degree of power. In one case, a committee nearly went against Edric's wishes. A staff member was found to be beating his wife. Tragically the wife committed suicide by drinking poison and it emerged that while she was dying, her husband had waited two days before bringing her to the

Edric and colleagues at a meeting. Photo by Mirza Shakil, journalist of Dhaka newspaper *The Daily Star.*

A staff meeting. Photo from the Kailakuri Healthcare Project.

clinic. The committee faced a decision – should they fire this staff member for abuse and neglect of his wife? Edric believed they should, but half the committee wished to rehabilitate the staff member. Edric was full of nerves: would the committee vote in favour of keeping an abuser – arguably a murderer – on staff? In the end, they chose to fire the man; Edric got the result he hoped for, but only by a whisker.

Meanwhile, in other aspects of clinic work and beyond, Edric micromanaged. In 2004, before the Link Group was established, Edric proposed to his New Zealand supporters that he himself should take over the fundraising. His father remonstrated by letter, 'It has been established that you are the ideal person to lead medical attendance for the poor in Bangladesh. It has not been established that you are a superman who can do all this medical work and at the same time raise an almost impossible flow of funds in New Zealand ... you *can not* do these two jobs at the same time.' Edric listened to his father and stuck to medical work as he suggested. Yet, he later encroached onto other team members' roles. Nadine Vickers, a New Zealand volunteer, told me she was frustrated at times by him intruding into her tasks. Edric also exasperated Libby Laing by challenging her decisions about the village health programme.

Despite these flaws Edric remained popular. Many people told me that he led from a position of servanthood. One recalled an instance when Edric had fallen over on the road, then, thinking he was unseen, filled in the hole so no one else would have the same injury. At the clinic he fetched medical tools himself, not expecting others to wait on him.

His care for staff and patients was another quality that

Edric speaking with a young patient along the road to Thanarbaid Clinic.
Photo from the New Zealand - Kailakuri Link Group.

they loved in him. One team member Mashud Rahaman Khan
described how Edric had counselled him at times when he felt
overwhelmed with stress. Edric suggested that Mashud write
down all his problems, then take the list to Edric or another
trusted person to ask for their feedback. Mashud told me he
now often used this technique, 'You then take the paper back
and think over it for a day, then you'll find the solution your-
self.' Many staff and patients would seek Edric's support with
personal problems.

Edric was also generous with practical support. In 2016
I spoke to Nor Amin, known as Roton, who had started as
Edric's assistant and become one of the most senior staff.
Roton told me that his family had been extremely poor, and
for his first winter at the project he had nothing to wear but

a thin t-shirt. He reflected, 'One day when I finished work, Doctor Bhai gave me a parcel and said, "An angel gave me this and told me I should give it to you. Open it when you get home." Inside there was a letter and 500 *taka*. Doctor Bhai instructed me to buy a set of winter clothes. I bought one for 350 *taka* and gave the rest of the money back to Doctor Bhai.' Such generosity from Edric made staff members fiercely loyal. In turn, Roton's impeccable honesty saw him become the leader of the project's finance team.

Edric's tendency towards compassion did on occasion cause problems. Some loans he gave out were never repaid. Edric could be soft on discipline, giving staff second and third chances. This frustrated some colleagues who believed it would undermine high work standards, however, Mashud, a Muslim staff member, shared a contrary perspective:

> *I haven't seen any organisation in Bangladesh ... wh*
> *people's mistakes and weaknesses are forgiven. . .t*
> *Kailakuri, if people make a mistake or transgression,*
> *they're not kicked out; they're given advice about what*
> *they should have done. Sometimes they might be sus-*
> *pended for a few weeks so they can think ... Other staff*
> *explain to them that if they act that way, the purpose of*
> *the project is not fulfilled. ... We don't give punishments,*
> *we just explain. We believe that from forgiveness, peo-*
> *ple's wisdom grows.*

People's fondness for Edric stood out in one incident. In 2008, while he was on a visit to Dhaka, rumours spread around Kailakuri that he had been killed! A passerby saw a traffic accident and believed they saw Edric's corpse on the side of the road. The word travelled quickly and reached his hosts in Dhaka. When he returned to his accommodation after a day in the city, they greeted him in astonishment, 'We thought you were dead!' He was confused, 'But I am not!' After returning to Kailakuri, he wrote, 'Multiple people had to hear my voice to make sure it was really I ... many people stared at me in disbelief. ... Everybody was so glad and relieved to see me ... My popularity went up enormously.' But the incident carried a stern lesson. Edric continued, 'In embarrassment and shame I realised, as we all did, that the project has become totally dependent on one person and this should not be.'

By law, the clinic needed at least one qualified doctor to provide medical supervision. Edric was the only one with such a qualification. He was also the project director. When it came to ultimate leadership Edric was not sharing power. Although he had ceded some power to committees, he alone set the vision and direction. Edric knew that a project prioritising the poorest people was something rare and precious and he would not let anyone compromise it again. Edric's attitude would see Kailakuri flourish for over a decade, but ultimately, his approach would also threaten the clinic's long-term survival.

Shilpi Rani (nee Hagidok), a health educator, addressing a meeting of diabetes patients in 2016. Photo from the Kailakuri Healthcare Project.

21

We have not seen a programme like this

Two decades had now passed since Edric searched for insulin for Sultan Ahmed, his first Type 1 diabetes patient. The clinic remained a haven for the poor, especially diabetics who had few other places to turn. Diabetes formed a significant portion of the clinic's workload – it was the reason for two out of every five patient visits – and every week, one or two more patients joined the list to receive ongoing care. In 2004, Kailakuri had nearly 700 diabetics under supervision. By 2006, that had grown to over 1000.

Over this period, diabetes services across the country had much improved but they still fell far short of addressing the need. Doctor Mohammad Ibrahim, the pioneering doctor in Dhaka, had founded a national hospital for diabetes: the Bangladesh Institute of Research and Rehabilitation in Diabetes,

Endocrine and Metabolic Disorders (Birdem). By 2006 it had nearly 60 affiliated centres across the country, the closest one being 25 kilometres from Kailakuri. But poor patients could not access free insulin at these centres unless they could first travel to Dhaka to register for government subsidies. For some patients that task was impossible. In 2001, Edric wrote, 'Apart from the Kailakuri Clinic, so far none of these districts [with a Birdem centre – Sherpur, Mymensingh, Tangail or Jamalpur] has a diabetes service easily accessible to the poor and able to keep diabetes controlled in the majority of patients.'

The result was grim. Across Bangladesh, hundreds of thousands of people were ravaged with diabetic complications. Many were struggling to walk because of foot ulcers and some would even need to have limbs amputated. Others lay incapacitated from wasting or blindness. Both Type 1 and Type 2 diabetics faced these problems. Edric was surprised to see such high prevalence of Type 2 diabetes among an under-nourished population, in contrast to other countries where the condition was associated with obesity. The suffering of all these people spurred on Edric and his team, but at the same time it distressed them that diabetics could access so little assistance elsewhere.

One patient who relied upon the ailing national system was Sujit Rangsa, whom I met in 2016. Sujit was from an extremely poor Mandi family and he developed Type 1 diabetes in 1993. Sponsorship from the organisation World Vision enabled him to register at the Birdem Hospital in Dhaka, and after that, to collect subsidised insulin from one of its regional centres in Jamalpur. However, even with this assistance, Sujit was not able to control his diabetes. The Jamalpur centre had

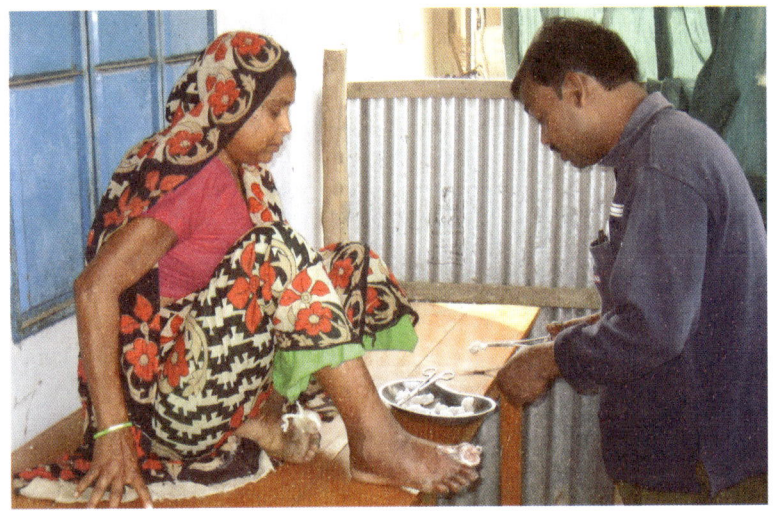

A Kailakuri paramedic dressing the foot ulcer of a patient with unregulated diabetes. Photo from the Kailakuri Facebook page.

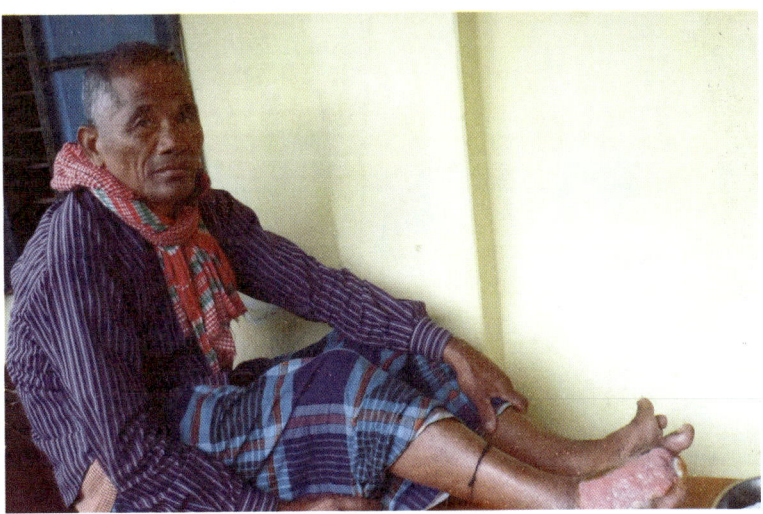

Jiton, another diabetes patient, whose foot was saved from amputation because of treatment at Kailakuri. Photo from the Kailakuri Facebook page.

Sujit Rangsa delivers diabetes education. Photo by Christine Steiner.

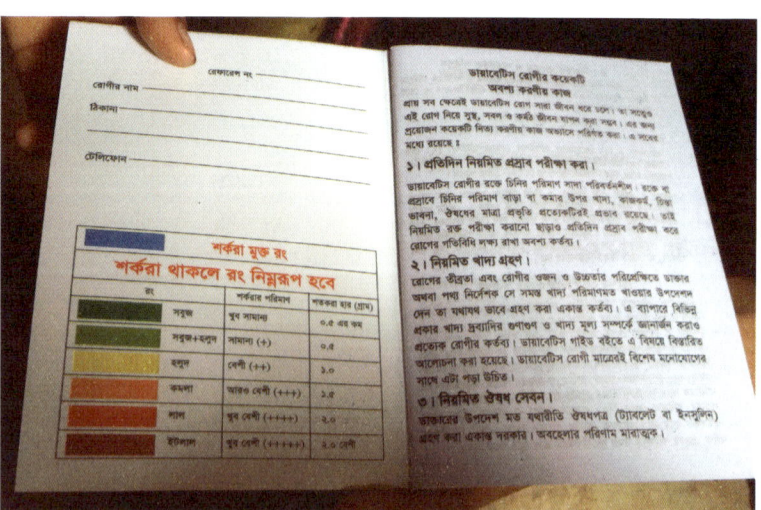

A record book for diabetic patients, supplied by Birdem.
The left page instructs patients how to adjust their insulin dose
depending on the colour of the urine and Benedict's solution after heating.

too few staff for the thousands of patients who needed their assistance. But there was an even more fundamental problem: insulin posted to the centre from Dhaka often arrived up to one month late. Sujit rationed insulin as best he could, but his health was compromised. Only when he heard about Kailakuri in 2000, and started treatment there, did he recover his health. He soon started a job at the clinic teaching others.

Besides the steady insulin supplies at Kailakuri, it was the emphasis on teaching, Sujit told me, that made Edric's programme a success. Diabetes education was as important as insulin or glibenclamide for managing the disease. All diabetics had to learn to monitor their blood sugar, diet and exercise. Those who depended on insulin – all patients with Type 1 and a minority of those with Type 2 – also had to learn to inject insulin and to adjust their dose.

New patients stayed at Kailakuri for at least two weeks to learn these skills. Sujit and other health educators taught them how to check their sugar levels using Benedict's solution, how to plan their meals and to administer insulin. The staff taught using pictures and tally marks instead of words and numbers to advise illiterate patients.

One day as Sujit worked, the young woman Shilpi Hagidok was carried to the clinic. She was blind, wasted and unable to walk. As indicated earlier, she had been unable to find insulin or diabetes education anywhere else. Sujit believed that Shilpi would recover as he had seen other patients return from the brink of death. His female colleagues guided Shilpi around the grounds and gave her meals and insulin. When she gained strength, they taught her to control her diabetes as best she could by sound and touch. Then Shilpi had surgery to

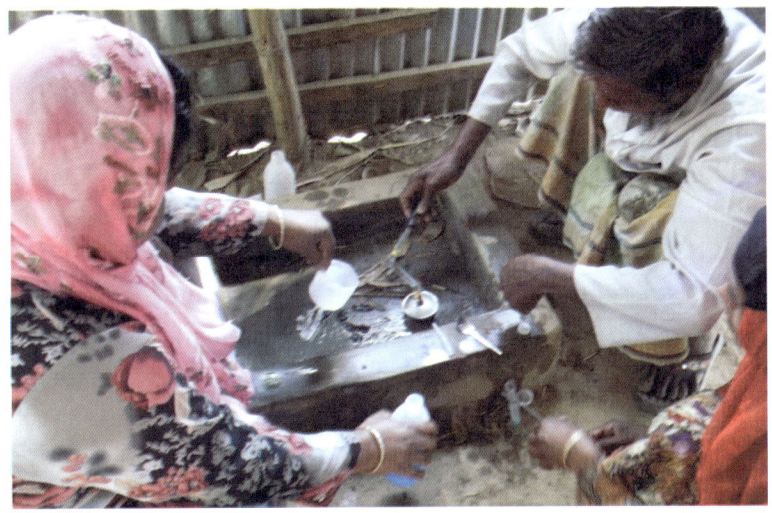

Diabetes patients test their urine sugar. Photo by Christine Steiner.

Shilpi (right) during her recovery. She and another girl are
picking vegetables from the Kailakuri nutrition garden.
Photo from the Kailakuri Healthcare Project.

remove her cataracts. Finally she could see the Benedict's solution and enjoy the satisfaction when her test tubes remained a vivid blue, showing her sugar levels were within a safe range. Once she mastered control of her diabetes, Edric employed her as a health educator too. But for staff members to teach people to manage their diabetes at the clinic was one thing; to help them maintain this discipline at home was another. Sujit, Shilpi and their colleagues coached patients to continue managing their condition amid the demands of marriage, work and social expectations. As far as possible, when someone did not collect their monthly insulin, staff would follow up. If they heard of a patient too afraid to come for treatment, they could go and talk with the family.

Such interventions were only possible because of Edric's paramedic training model, which enabled a higher ratio of staff to patients than was possible elsewhere. In May 2005, Kailakuri had 12 staff supervising 700 diabetics, a ratio of one staff member to roughly 60 patients. In contrast, in 2012 the Birdem-affiliated centre in Tangail had seven staff to 4000 new patients, a ratio of one to 570.[3]

Kailakuri staff could also counsel diabetes patients when they were preparing to marry. This was a critical time as it was common for diabetics to conceal their condition for fear their partner would call off the engagement. Suijt told me of one heartrending case, a Hindu bride who died on her wedding day because the ceremony dictated that she fast then feast on

---

[3] Diabetic Association of Bangladesh, *Statistical Yearbook 2011-2012* (Dhaka: Diabetic Association of Bangladesh, 2012), 502–503, www.ghdonline.org/uploads/BGD_statistical_Report_2012.pdf.

mishti (sweets). She had abandoned her treatment for fear her husband would not accept her. In such situations, the input of caring health workers could make a difference between life and death.

The case of Johura, Edric's goddaughter, also showed the importance of the team's ongoing care. For Johura, diabetes control was a major battle. At one point she suffered tuberculosis and was too unwell to test her blood sugar. Staff at Kailakuri supported her through multiple struggles, improving her health and saving her life repeatedly. But tragically Johura never succeeded in managing her diabetes. During one period of lax discipline in 2012, she died from her disease. Edric was heartbroken. 'He cried a lot,' Sujit remembered. It had been 18 years since Johura had arrived destitute and come to live at the clinic. Edric had so many memories of the cheeky, resilient girl.

There were many deaths and disappointments: these were part of the course of treating diabetes. Nonetheless, Kailakuri was a lifeline for hundreds of people who were enjoying normal lives because they could access insulin, good education and caring support. Such an outcome was remarkable for any diabetic in Bangladesh; for the poor it was extraordinary.

Because of these successes, Edric believed that Kailakuri should serve as a pilot for diabetes care in Bangladesh. In 2001, he invited five diabetes experts to visit from Dhaka, and wrote in his annual report, 'They recognised the unique and important role of the Kailakuri programme and saw that a national, paramedic-based programme on similar lines could be an answer to the country's problem. The parting comment was, "We have not seen a programme like this before in Bangladesh. Very likely there is none in the whole of Asia.'" This was a glowing reference from the country's diabetes experts. Edric added, 'In this context Kailakuri should be seen as a pilot project and given all necessary support.'

In 2013, the programme received another commendation. Researchers from Birdem Hospital compared Kailakuri's diabetes programme with their own by monitoring patients' blood sugars over three months. Birdem had qualified staff, and they used urine testing strips and glucometers, costing about 2 *taka* and 20 *taka* per test. At Kailakuri, the Benedict's solution method cost about 0.2 *taka* per test. Yet, the researchers found that the Birdem and Kailakuri programmes delivered near identical results. Edric's low-cost methods and his emphasis on teaching were effective. They were performing as well as a programme costing as much as 100 times more.

The unsealed road running through the middle of the Kailakuri Healthcare Project. Photo by Christine Steiner.

22

Politics comes to call

Over the years that the Kailakuri Healthcare Project was finding its feet, distant events affected the clinic in ways that were good, bad and unexpected. In 2005, Edric wrote, 'The great outside world is moving in.' Electricity had arrived in the village. The clinic installed electric lights, making night work easier. But electrification also brought new problems. Nearby mosques now amplified their calls to prayer, public messages and teaching. Edric wrote, 'Some of the teachers are very zealous ... Needless to say the speakers are on full volume.' The noise disturbed patients and Edric did not enjoy the 'deafening' announcements blaring across once-peaceful fields. He swallowed his disgruntlement on occasions when they promoted his clinic. But other community members still objected. 'Noise pollution' became the subject of animated village meetings. Volumes decreased only after a politician intervened.

The arrival of cellphones further shattered the area's tranquility. Edric wrote, 'A local shop has a cellphone and is doing a brisk business. Incoming calls are announced by microphone at top pitch, calling recipients from up to a mile away!' This was another major disturbance but it did not last long; the business became redundant as soon as cellphones spread.

In the meantime events around the election in 2006 caused chaos across the nation. The Bangladesh system required an interim 'caretaker' government to take over for the election period. No leader could be found, however, who would satisfy both major parties that elections would be fair. The job fell to the former president. The opposition party was incredulous and led protests that turned violent, resulting in 40 deaths. They then announced they would boycott the election. In an attempt to regain stability, the caretaker government declared a state of emergency, but quickly the military seized control. For a period, democracy in the country stood still. The army held power in Bangladesh until December 2008 when elections were restored.

At first, this political turmoil changed little on the ground at Kailakuri. Village politics and movements of the seasons still had the greatest bearing on happenings at the clinic. In early 2007, Edric wrote, '*Boro Id* is the Muslim festival when the rich are supposed to give gifts to the poor. Today we passed decorated prayer fields and people dressed in their best clothes out walking or riding their bikes. No one would have thought this was one of the world's poorest countries and tangled up in a life-and-death political crisis that has broken down the democratic system.'

Then, due to a chance connection, a man came calling at Kailakuri who provided a link to these faraway events. He had been seeking treatment in other hospitals without success. A Kailakuri villager named Goren Talbot told me what happened: 'The man was impressed that Doctor Bhai spent so long listening for symptoms, and that he sat and ate with other patients.' The patient recovered, and delighted to be well, he shared his story with family members. As it happened, one of his relatives was the Chief of the Army, Major General Moeen U Ahmed, who was running the country. The Major General was intrigued to hear about the rural clinic and its foreign doctor. Goren continued the story: 'He sent army officials to have a look. They reported back to him that Kailakuri provided good treatment, but that the clinic lacked buildings and sufficient milk for patients needing nutrition, and everyone slept on mats on the floor.'

Curious, the Major General decided to see Kailakuri for himself. He visited in April 2008. The event caused weeks of planning and anxiety for Edric's staff, who had to prepare an appropriate reception. Edric wrote, 'The Joint Chief of the Armed Forces visited us … by helicopter … Lots of soldiers came, several thousand village people turned up and we appeared on national television.' Goren pointed over my shoulder as he recounted events: 'The helicopter landed in the field just over there.' Female staff met the visitors with songs and flowers and the Major General was duly impressed. He and his soldiers then spoke with Edric. We can only imagine what the Major General thought as he walked among the clinic buildings, or perhaps sat on a mat covering the dirt floor. Goren continued, 'The Major General saw that the road was muddy, making it difficult for patients to come even on foot. … So, as Acting President, he ordered the road be fixed from Pirgacha to Kailakuri.' He also donated ceiling fans and four cows, though Edric declined his offer of an ambulance as he believed that it would attract rich patients and require costly maintenance.

For Edric and the team, this visit was a phenomenal blessing. The attention raised the clinic's profile. Local government officials chose the occasion to donate a tin building for a new inpatients department. The visit also transformed Kailakuri village. Once the road was fixed to the crossroads near the clinic, patients had easier access and the local economy got a boost. Within a few years a *bazaar* had sprung up and the town had become a thoroughfare for traders. Peter Wilson described the marked difference: 'In 1998, Kailakuri Clinic was in the middle of open country. There were no trees. Apart from maybe three thatched buildings … you could stand and look right around; there was nothing to be seen. Today there are lots of buildings, and at the little crossroads nearby there is a whole little town.' By the time I visited Kailakuri in 2016, that crossroads was a lively marketplace with 200 metres of street-front stores.

But the political intervention brought with it unwelcome developments too. Back in 2003, when a road had been linked to Thanarbaid, Edric wrote, 'Noise and the easy intrusion of outsiders are the cost of this privilege.' The new road to Kailakuri brought similar nuisances. Unpleasant elements from Bangladesh now came to call. Pineapple traders set up a loading zone in the Kailakuri *bazaar*, and to reach it, started driving trucks on a thin, dirt road running straight through the middle of the clinic. This once-quiet track turned to mud under their heavy wheels. Making matters worse, the trucks blared angry horns, interrupting patients' sleep, and drivers took little care to look out for pedestrians, including children, who used to wander the clinic carefree.

Edric was very concerned and sought to get trucks banned from the area. He discussed the problem with the committee members, the local chairman of the police and the Upazila Nirbahi Officer (UNO) – the senior government official of Madhupur sub-district. But there was no quick solution. Unlike the Major General, who could deliver a road in a flash, the clinic team petitioned local authorities for years without response. Edric told me, 'My opinion is that ... the UNO has

Edric walking along the road that runs through the Kailakuri Healthcare Project. Photo by Christine Steiner.

been won over by rich people who bring the trucks in.'

In 2012 they got a partial 'solution' that made matters worse. Edric described in a letter, 'The authorities dug the road up for sealing, but the budget ran out and so it was just left.' When the rains came, he wrote, 'Now to walk from one side to the other is walking through water and mud halfway up to the knee. Our Japanese doctor [a volunteer who arrived in 2010] fell over in the mud and twisted her ankle.'

The mud-river became a feature they were forced to live with every rainy season. Edric continued,

> *Our enterprising staff dug the road up a bit more to make a high path on one side so that pedestrians, cyclists and motorbikes can get past without going through the mud – provided they don't veer off the high path. Last night I did just that. My bike and I tumbled down into a filthy, muddy pool. I was covered with mud from the top of my head to the soles of my feet. ... A young Muslim man rescued the bike and helped me back to the clinic. Sekandor was there waiting for me, another young Muslim who often comes to see me! He pumped water into a bucket from the well and washed my bike as I cleaned myself up by torchlight. This is what ordinary Muslim people are like.*

Of all the frustrations Edric faced, it was the road that repeatedly piqued his anger. A Kailakuri resident told me that one day, when there was a particularly noisy truck, 'Doctor Bhai was furious. So he went to the truck, leaned in the window and hit the driver [by punching him in the shoulder]. The driver was stunned that a foreigner had just hit him! The other people standing around were supporting Doctor Bhai. The driver just drove away.' On the bus journey in 2012 Edric had even confessed to me, 'I sometimes go out and shout at the truck drivers ... I'm afraid I lose my cool at times and throw the toys out of the cot.'

The matter was no mere inconvenience, however, and in 2013, an accident highlighted what was at stake. Edric wrote on 18 March to the leader of the sub-district:

Dear UNO Saheb,
It is my sad duty to inform you that we have just had an accident on the road outside our health centre entrance. A tempo *[three-wheeled enclosed scooter] was taking a pregnant woman with bleeding for a caesarian section at Madhupur. [It overturned.] We managed to get the pregnant woman to Madhupur City Hospital in another* tempo. *Unfortunately she suffered severe bleeding on the way. ... The baby died. Our worker has sustained a fracture of the forearm. ... Please may I remind you that we have been disturbed and endangered by trucks, which have also destroyed the road, for several years. It was the badly destroyed road that caused the* tempo *to overturn. ... Do we have to wait for a death before the authorities will act?*
We need:
1. Truck loading moved at least two kilometres from our entrance south of Kailakuri.
2. Forbidding of truck loading nearer than that.
3. Repair of the roads.
...
Please help us.

Paramedic Nekbor Ali after the *tempo* accident. Photo by Christine Steiner.

Only in late 2013 was the loading zone shifted away from the clinic, after intervention from Chairman Yakob, the former leader of the sub-district. The change reduced the noise but did not stop the heavy trucks coming past. Unfortunately Edric never saw the road repaired. Only in 2016, when I visited, was the work in progress at last.

23

Vulnerabilities

The years of political crisis were chaotic for the nation. For Edric, however, the following years were even more turbulent. He had to handle financial problems on a new scale and deal with many personal losses as well.

The New Year of 2009 dealt Edric a mighty blow. On 13 February Edric's father John 'J.V.T.' Baker died in Whakatāne. John was 96 and his body had gradually shut down. Five months earlier, Edric had been with his parents in New Zealand and must have wondered whether those hours with his father would be his last. At that time John had been frail, yet full of life. News of his death felt sudden. Edric did not return to New Zealand for the funeral, though no doubt he felt the distance acutely as the event passed without him. He opted instead to visit later in 2009 when he spent hours by his father's grave.

For Edric, John had been a symbol of intellect, hard work and good humour and a loving and attentive father. He had also been a staunch supporter of Edric's work. For years he handled donations and other financial affairs in New Zealand. The regular letters between Edric and his father are a mixture of bank transfer details, family business and sage advice. John's death was a deep loss for Edric and it would have been hard for him to have been apart from his mother at such a time. Betty was still in good health, aged 93.

John's death came amid an already difficult period for Edric. Funds were always tight at the clinic, but from 2008 onwards, there was an unprecedented funding shortfall. As Edric shouldered this concern, so too did Libby Laing, who led the New Zealand Link Group. Sadly, amid this stress their friendship deteriorated.

Kailakuri was funded by donations. Only five per cent of their income came from patient fees. To manage in such circumstances, Edric's team had to exercise faith – holding their own responsibility and agency alongside the belief that God would provide the finances they needed. Edric wrote to a donor in 1997, 'Sometimes it seems to me like a wonder or a miracle that people from far away send help to us so that we never run out of money! Our work increases. Our programme enlarges ... there are so many people to help ... but the money does not run out! In the name of Jesus and of the poor I thank you.'

The year 2008, however, brought a perfect storm of factors to threaten the clinic's funding. The global financial crisis dried up charitable giving, meanwhile natural disasters and political turmoil in Bangladesh pushed up costs. At the same time, patient numbers continued to increase (that year the team saw 29,600 outpatient visits and supervised 1402 diabetes patients). At Easter, the funding situation became critical. Edric and the leadership team had no choice but to ask staff who were better off – as Roton, the finance officer, described, 'those who could afford food without their wages' – to take leave until the crisis was solved. Those staff instead opted to work without pay. Edric appealed for donations and managed to end their severe hardship. He then went to New Zealand from July to September to seek more funds. The Link Group discussed the bleak reality that reserves could run dry.

There were points of encouragement during this challenging time. In May, Edric's sister Hilary and her husband Nelson visited the clinic, buoying Edric's spirits. Not long after came interest from a Japanese doctor, Mariko Inui, who discovered that Kailakuri reminded her of her childhood in Japan. Mariko would later give years of service to the project.

Another breakthrough was support from Gareth and Joanne Morgan, New Zealand philanthropists. In September 2008 they agreed to fund Edric long term as one of a number of 'Kiwi heroes abroad'. In 2012, Gareth described Edric as 'New Zealand's own Mother Teresa', and wrote in the New Zealand *Listener*, 'Baker is my hero. If I were a religious person I would describe this man as a modern-day saint.' The Morgan Foundation became the clinic's largest donor.

Then in October 2008, New Zealand's cricket team, the Black Caps, toured Bangladesh. The Link Group invited them to visit Kailakuri. Although the team's schedule did not allow a visit, the captain invited Edric to present the players' caps before the second test match. This capping ceremony in

Dhaka was a prestigious occasion. Sister Julienne Hayes-Smith told me, 'I remember thinking, Edric, I hope you've got some decent clothes! … But the event helped me see another side of Edric: he could mix in that circle [of New Zealand celebrities] as well.' This connection attracted more media exposure and donations from the team.

Yet, as 2008 drew to a close, the funding situation remained tense. Edric predicted a deficit of $NZ20,000 ($US13,300) for 2008 and a further $82,000 the following year. In early 2009, while Edric grieved his father, the situation did not improve. In April, Libby wrote to him, 'Good to hear the Japanese doctor [Mariko Inui] is keen on Kailakuri. Maybe she can help with funding too, otherwise she may not have a project to come to.' Father Doug Venne, the Maryknoll priest, counselled them, 'The thing to do is to live within the funds that we have, no matter how deep the cuts have to be made. Kailakuri operated on a lot less funds five years back and can continue. Do what we can. God will do the rest.'

Against this backdrop of stress and concern, Edric and Libby came into conflict. Minor tensions had prickled throughout their ten-year friendship. Libby had intimate knowledge of the project: she had led the village health programme for four years, then, from her home in New Zealand, managed the Link Group in between annual visits to Bangladesh. Yet, Edric seldom took her opinions on board. Sister Jenny Clarke, of the Missionary Sisters of the Society of Mary in Dhaka, told me, 'Libby had the same complaint as any woman who ever worked with Edric: Once he had made up his mind about something, that was that. In fact, Libby was strong willed and had also made up her mind about things. But Edric always won.'

Libby and Edric. Photo from the Baker family collection.

Libby was someone who pushed back, often with humour. Edric wrote, 'She once threw a banana at me in the course of a friendly debate. She was always buying bananas for me and we were always having friendly debates.' But some frustrations wore her down. Sister Jenny told me, 'When she got fed up with her men [Edric, and Father Homrich, with whom she stayed], she would come down to us [in Dhaka].' In late 2008, with funding still critical, Edric and Libby argued about whether or not to raise staff salaries. Food prices had risen and staff members were struggling. Kanon Bala Bormon, a village health worker, remembered, 'In the end Libby won, the salaries were raised. Doctor Bhai then had a difficult job to find more money.'

This conflict, or perhaps another at a similar time, created fertile ground for a miscommunication between Edric and Libby. During the tense early months of 2009 – while funding worries continued and Edric grieved his father's death – the pair discussed Libby's next visit to Bangladesh and the message Libby heard was that Edric did not want her to return. According to Peter Wilson, 'Edric told me he was concerned that Libby was proposing to come at the hottest time of the year as she had not been in good health and did not handle the heat well. He was in fact suggesting that she come later when the weather was cooler.' But somehow there was a misunderstanding. Libby wrote to Father Doug in April 2009, 'Seems like I have been made redundant from Kailakuri this year but I will probably come to Bangladesh anyway.' She based herself in Dhaka, not Kailakuri, for that visit, though she continued to help with the Link Group finances.

Because their friendship was under strain, Edric did not have Libby's emotional support when he suffered another shock. On 28 December 2009 Father Doug, the Maryknoll missioner and Edric's longtime friend, died from leukaemia aged 81. Doug had spent 34 years in Bangladesh, mostly living in a small hut among local people. He had elected not to receive medical treatment so as not to 'waste' money that could be used for the poor. Doug had been an inspiration to Edric; he had also been a long-term supporter of Kailakuri, attracting donations from the United States and helping to write Edric's newsletters. His death was a deep loss for Edric and one he faced without support from Libby.

Only a few months later, Edric suffered his third blow in 14 months. On 7 April 2010, Libby herself died, aged 69. She

Edric with Libby Laing and Father Doug Venne. Photographer unknown.

had visited Kailakuri less than two weeks before. Edric wrote of their last time together, 'She came to our area for about a week before Easter. The day she returned to Dhaka I gave her a large, delicate wildflower I had picked at the side of the road. I apologised because it got crushed in my pocket. Tears came into her eyes.' That would be their final interaction. As Edric described it, 'A few days later she had her massive stroke, "in the arms" of the sisters, and did not regain consciousness. Muslims, Christians, Hindus, everybody wept at our Kailakuri prayer meeting.' Edric traveled to Dhaka, a ten-hour round trip, to see her body in the morgue. Sister Julienne recalled, 'He was so distraught. It had been a strong relationship because of their common devotion to the poor. ... There was deep, deep respect and feeling for each other, for what each one was trying to do.' Where Edric had had a bubbly friend and partner in supporting Kailakuri, now he had emptiness and sorrow.

In two years, Edric lost three key supporters. He no longer had his father's regular letters of encouragement, or Doug and Libby's camaraderie as foreigners who shared his life among the poor. The cloud of money worries still hovered in Edric's mind, but grief now dwarfed those concerns. In its shadow, everything felt muted. His heart ached.

24

What will the clinic do without you?

Encouragement at this time came from afar, by letters. Muriel Stracy, a New Zealand supporter, recalled that Edric had circulated a request through mission support networks for someone to write pastoral letters to him. Muriel told me she had hesitated because, 'What ordinary housewife would feel qualified to write [such letters to a missionary]? A job for a parson surely?' However, when she heard of the deaths of Libby and Doug, she began sending simple letters of encouragement. 'Your letter is like a lifesaver,' Edric replied to Muriel and her husband Dan in June 2010. I don't know whether you have bad days. Today is one of mine ... Please forgive me if I share with you.'

Bangladeshi media had discovered the clinic and it felt like a dazzling spotlight was on Edric when all he wanted was to hide away. His letter continued,

> *We all know the story of the clown who droops in lonely melancholy after the crowds have gone home ... We have been discovered by the Bangladesh media. First we had a television newsflash then a column in the leading Bengali Daily. Now a half-hour television commentary has gone twice across the country. We are so worried about finances that we need the publicity in the hope of in-country donations, but it all seems to focus on me rather than the project which is not the way it should be.*

Edric was in no mood for such promotion. Yet, this attention was in fact one of Kailakuri's most significant breaks yet. The media 'discovery' was the result of wise networking. The Link Group and supporters within Bangladesh had rallied their contacts in order to publicise Kailakuri and attract donations. Their efforts worked: financial support from Bangladeshis trickled in, helping to replenish funds. But this progress did not lift Edric's gloom. Neither did the arrival of two significant new staff at Kailakuri: Pijon Nongmin and Mariko Inui. Pijon filled a gap as Project Manager. His warm humour and level-headedness would carry the clinic through many challenges. At a similar time, the Japanese doctor Mariko Inui settled in to work with the inpatients department; she stayed for the best part of three years.

Despite these steps forward, responsibility and depression weighed on Edric: 'It is a lot of work,' he wrote in the September 2010 newsletter,

> *Quite likely you have had the experience of having to feed, clothe and educate a large family; funds are short*

Edric and Doctor Mariko Inui in 2013. Photo by Christine Steiner.

Pijon Nongmin.
Photo from the Kailakuri
Healthcare Project.

and you just don't know what to do. That is what Kailak-uri had become like. Doug died. Libby died. The international economic situation is bad. You worry and you can't sleep. You start to become irritable and depressed. People say 'Just trust God', which is very correct, but the psyche is still at work. Finally I knew I just had to get away and retreat.

Annual retreats were a key part of Edric's self-care. In about 1999, he began the practice of travelling to a different part of Bangladesh to spend one month in solitude and prayer. Although it took strong discipline to turn away from queues of patients, Edric always returned with new motivation and direction. One New Zealand doctor told me that short spells of overseas medical work exhausted him; he could not understand how Edric sustained himself. Retreats and daily times of quiet prayer were essential nourishment for Edric.

His retreat in August 2010 would stand out from all others. Edric set off for Diglakuna, a tiny Bangladeshi village near the Indian border where he could find peace and solitude among jungle-covered hills. One day after a long walk, Edric stopped at a friend's house and left as the sky was darkening, declining his host's offer of a guide. However, late that night, Edric had not returned to the retreat centre.

Back at Kailakuri, around midnight, senior staff Pijon Nongmin and Sujit Rangsa received a phone call informing them that Edric was missing. The pair set off at once for the six-hour motorcycle journey to Diglakuna. Pijon told me, 'We worried that maybe he had got lost in the jungle, attacked by an elephant or another wild animal, or that an Indian terrorist group had kidnapped him.' The morning brought no relief, as local police had heard nothing of Edric's whereabouts. Pijon and Sujit now spent a full day fearing the worst. 'We thought we might be bringing back his body.'

That night, news came, at last: Edric was in India! In the dark jungle, he had taken a wrong turn and stumbled over the unmarked border. He was now at a police station being questioned by bemused officials. However, border crossings were an international legal incident. Even if Edric had simply made a wrong turn, he could not just step back over the border. There was a formal procedure. Pijon explained, 'If the two countries have a matter to resolve, they hold a "flag meeting" where they meet at a neutral point at the border. The side that called the meeting has to give a gift of *mishti* and biscuits, then there are other protocols.'

Pijon accompanied the Bangladeshi border police as the process got under way. The Indian police arrived and there was discussion. Finally more vehicles came, and out of one, stepped Edric. He had spent roughly 40 hours 'abroad'. He later wrote that once he stepped onto Bangladeshi soil, he felt like singing the national anthem. He even hugged the police commander – the first Bangladeshi he encountered. Pijon told me how the story ended, 'The Border Security Force asked … me to give Edric a physical checkup to make sure there were no allegations of mishandling. … I just asked Edric if he was alright and he said he was. … As soon as he got permission he gave me a hug, and asked how everyone was, since he knew a lot of people would have worried about him.'

Edric wrote later, 'I have nothing but praise for the way I was treated by the Border Security Force and the Indian police. I feel honoured to think that my misadventure has allowed me to be an ambassador of goodwill between Bangladesh and India. ... Thanks to God, all is now well. A very sincere thanks to all who laboured behind the scenes to enable my speedy return.'

The incident ended jovially and made a lively story for his September newsletter. Yet it also highlighted – again – the clinic's fragility. What would happen if Edric fell ill or died? Only a few weeks later, he caught a serious bout of malaria and spent a short time hospitalised. The series of events underscored the danger the project was in. It was a throwback to the 2008 incident when Edric had been mistaken for dead.

This vulnerability was made even clearer in 2011 when Edric required prostate surgery. Frustrating and alarming his staff, he was reluctant to accept any intervention that a poor person could not afford. He therefore turned down expensive treatment in Dhaka and opted to undergo risky surgery at the Mymensingh public hospital. A New Zealand medical student, Louis Kirton, was volunteering at Kailakuri at the time. He visited Edric after the operation and described the scenes:

As I approached the hospital ... I encountered the noisy hubbub of hundreds of people queuing in long lines for the emergency paramedic service. In the hospital itself corridors were spewing with patients and their families, crammed into every possible space. ... Post-operatively Doctor Baker had been sent to the intensive care unit (ICU). ... I couldn't help but notice people queuing for the bathrooms at the end of the ward. As a test of my nerve he suggested I take a look. No words can describe the assault on one's senses. ... Even more disturbing to Doctor Baker was the treatment patients received in the

ICU. … After Doctor Baker noticed that the patient in the next bed had become unresponsive, he called for the nurse. There was only one nurse in the 15-bed ICU. After an hour the nurse reluctantly arrived and … pulled up the sheet covering the poor fellow's dead face.

Although Edric avoided any life-threatening complications, his surgery at this public hospital was not successful. Brother Guillaume reflected, 'The doctors at the Mymensingh hospital weren't so good. He had two operations, but … it didn't work out. Eventually he had to go to a good hospital. Doctor Bhai had perhaps too much radicalism in that case!' In August 2011, Edric celebrated his seventieth birthday, with his body still recovering.

Soon after came another breakthrough for Kailakuri. In September, the clinic made the front page of *The Daily Star*, an English-language newspaper read nationwide. Then in December it featured on *Ityadi*, one of Bangladesh's most popular programmes, viewed by over 40 million people. There, on screens across the country, was a shot of Edric riding a bicycle. 'That captured the imagination of the Bangladeshi nation,' Peter Wilson told me. 'In the Bangladeshi psyche, the only reason to study medicine is to make money … and to buy a flash car … so a doctor in a rural area is a failure. Here was a doctor on a bicycle! That's what caught the headlines.'

Again, the media spotlight glossed over real challenges at the clinic. Funds remained perilously tight and in late 2011, a bank error caused a cash flow crisis. The clinic had to limit patient numbers while Edric and the Link Group asked donors for help. Roton, the finance officer, told me what happened next: 'Suddenly we had an offer from Gareth and Joanne

Morgan.' The New Zealand philanthropists who had supported Edric since 2008 now more than tripled their annual contribution. 'I remember we all cried and hugged each other,' Roton continued. 'That donation solved the crisis.'

But by now the list of vulnerabilities was adding up. Kailakuri relied on Edric having good health, avoiding mishaps and appealing to donors for funds. Consequently, it was unsustainable. People had told him this for years, but it was a reality he had never properly faced. As early as 1993, his father had raised the question in a letter, 'What will the clinic do if you can't carry on?' In 2012, nearly 20 years later, Gareth and Joanne Morgan visited Kailakuri and reiterated the same message: if Edric did not attend to succession, the clinic would be in trouble.

The stakes were high if the team failed to secure sound leadership. Edric had seen an example of this close to home. Towards the end of 2010, Thanarbaid Clinic, which Edric had nurtured for two decades until 2005, shut its gates. The Church of Bangladesh had been unable to sustain or grow the health centre and the once-flourishing project had run into the ground. Watching its sad end had made Edric confront his limitations. The teacher, Mironi Hagidok, told me she had begged Edric to save the ailing clinic, saying, 'Thanarbaid is like your first son, surely you can't turn your back on it!' As she remembered, Edric sat for a long time with his head down. Finally he replied, 'I can't take on this responsibility.' Kailakuri and existing sub-centres needed his full attention.

The events of 2009 to 2011 were therefore timely wake-up calls. Edric's health problems and misadventures had emphasised his mortality, as had the deaths of his father,

Doug Venne and Libby Laing. His father's words rang in his ears: What would the clinic do when he could not carry on? Supporters echoed the same question. Finally, Edric accepted that he must prioritise finding a successor.

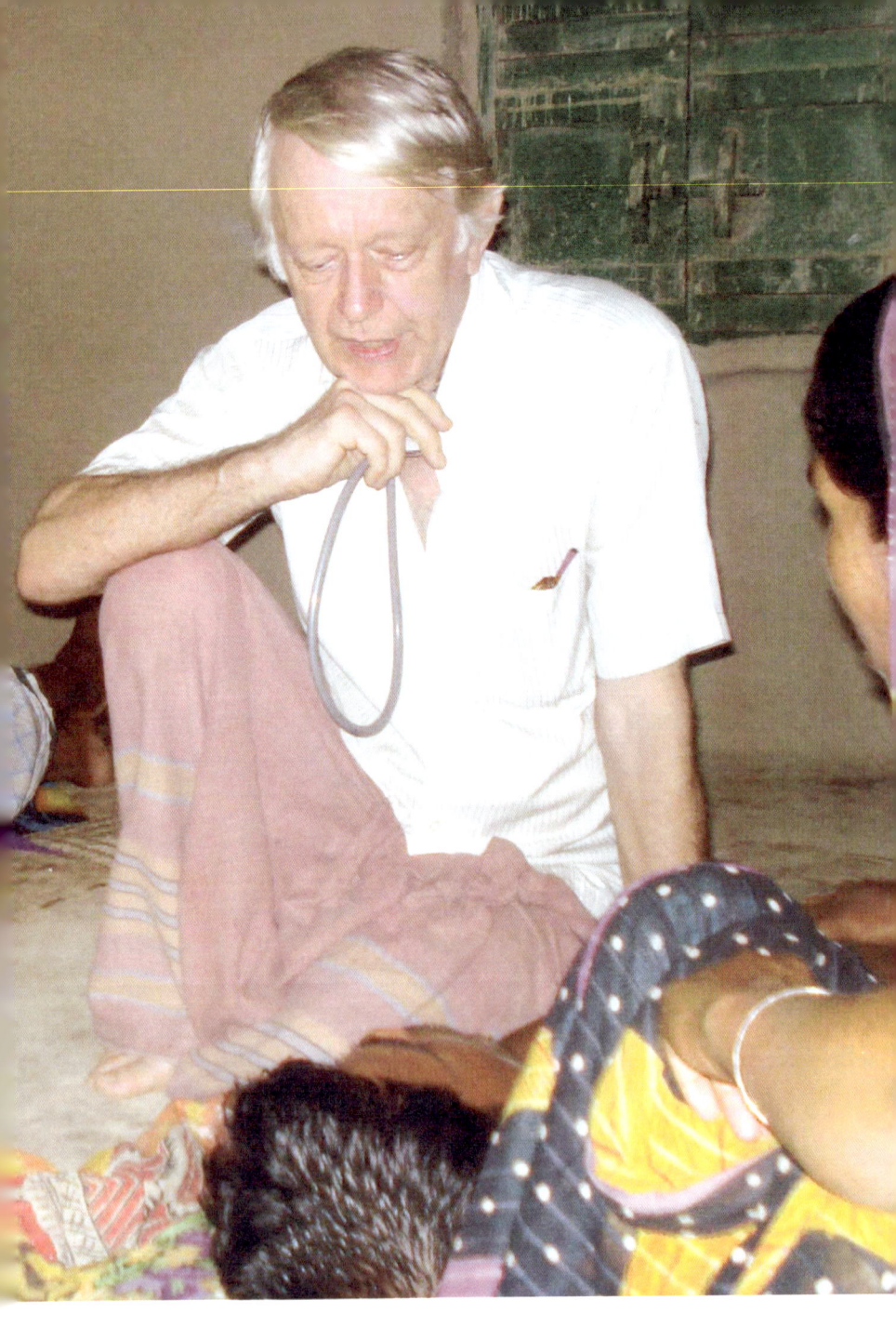

Edric sitting with a patient. Photo by Mirza Shakil, journalist of *The Daily Star*.

25

Only heroes need apply

In November 2012 an article by Gareth Morgan hit the pages
of *GP Pulse*, the publication of the Royal New Zealand College
of General Practitioners. 'Only heroes need apply,' read the
headline, under which the author called for workers to serve
at Kailakuri. Requests for Edric's successor – a Bangladeshi or
foreign doctor – now appeared in nearly every publication or
media interaction about the clinic. But, as Hilda, Edric's sister,
put it, 'It takes a special sort of person.'

The difficulty of this search cannot be overstated. 'Edric's
extreme ideals ... made him suffer,' Brother Guillaume told
me. 'Local people admired him but no local doctor ever felt
they could live in the same way.' Edric knew that even with
high salaries, it was almost unknown for doctors to work in
remote areas. He nevertheless would continue searching for
an exception.

Edric lamented the difficulty of finding doctors with the necessary self-motivation or religious inspiration to assist the poor. Elizabeth Mackie, a former staff member of the New Zealand aid agency Christian World Service, told me, 'He used to grieve that he couldn't find a Bangladeshi willing to have that degree of sacrifice for their own people.' His heartache was for the poor but also for himself. 'Edric so longed to find someone to take over from him,' Sister Margaret Shield told me. Even through the years that he had clung to his project, protecting it, part of him must have ached to be free of his responsibilities. Now this was his priority, could he find safe hands to whom he could entrust the project and rest? Sister Margaret continued, 'I remember Edric saying that I was "lucky" because God was sending young Bangladeshi women to become religious sisters who would take over or adapt our work when we were no longer able.'

Still, Edric had high expectations of a successor and he would wait rather than lower his standards. His idealism and optimism resonated with others. Peter Wilson wrote, 'We just have to trust God on this one.' Monirul Khan, a staff member at the Damien Foundation, voiced determination: 'There are only a few people who would sacrifice themselves for the poor like Doctor Baker. We have to find out whom.' But as 2012 drew to a close, they had found no one.

While the search continued, Kailakuri attracted new supporters. After the media attention, many Bangladeshis visited the clinic and were inspired to donate. Ataur Rahman, New Zealand's honorary Consul General for Bangladesh, created some of this interest. 'Every time I talked to people in Bangladesh, I tried to get them to take ownership,' he told me. 'My message was: do you want foreigners to be donating to your country forever? ... We have plenty of wealthy Bangladeshis. They have a problem getting their head around a charitable clinic like Kailakuri, because we don't have a welfare state. The people who donate tend to do so in their own area. ... That is the challenge in channelling resources from wealthy to impoverished areas.' The story of Kailakuri was an inspiration to many Bangladeshis, but the need for a successor remained.

Short of the ideal option – someone filling Edric's shoes – he and supporters brainstormed other possibilities. Would new medical graduates come and volunteer? Would they stay a few years in exchange for study costs? What about doctors offering their own specialties for a few days at a time? With Ataur's help, Edric explored the idea of merging with other hospitals that did charity work. The pair met with several who were interested, Ataur told me,

> *But they wanted to take the whole project under their control and run it their way. Edric didn't think that would work. He said profit-making organisations, even with a charitable arm, would always face conflicts of interest. Another organisation suggested Edric add a form of income generation because relying on donations would never be sustainable. ... Edric listened to everything. But the feeling I got ... was that Edric wanted another Edric Baker to come in and run his model. ... Edric was headstrong and wanted to do it his way, so we tried to stick with his model.*

One idea that Edric would entertain, at least as an interim measure, was that of interns. Students who spent time at

Kailakuri would be awakened to the value of the work. After a few months supervising paramedics, they might commit long term. Edric explored the possibility with several Bangladeshi medical schools. The most promising was Gonoshasthaya Kendra, 'The People's Health Centre', founded by Doctor Zafrullah Chowdhury, a champion of healthcare for the rural poor. Edric later wrote, 'Their medical college is excellent, but suffers from the same problem [as Kailakuri], how to get the graduates to go to the poor. I was invited to help with motivation.'

Finally, in 2013, hope for a long-term replacement came. It was an American couple, Jason and Merindy Morgenson – both of them doctors. Jason was a relative of Doug Venne, the Maryknoll father and Edric's late friend. On Father Doug's invitation, Jason visited Thanarbaid in 1999 during his first year of medical study. He spent a week at the clinic and was fascinated. The following year he visited again and helped Edric by using the nearest computer – in Pirgacha – to type up the English version of the Standard Treatment Book. In 2006 Jason brought his wife Merindy to see the clinic. She was amazed at the low-cost treatment, later telling me, 'Treating burns and managing diabetes are things we spend millions on.' The couple told Edric that they wished to return to Kailakuri for the long term.

For the clinic team, it was hard to dare to hope. Had their prayers been answered? Would this couple replace Doctor Bhai? In March 2013, the project newsletter announced the Morgensons' intention to 'become long-term medical missionaries at Kailakuri', arriving in 2014. It felt like a miracle after

Doctors Jason and Merindy
Morgenson in 2006.
Photo from the Kailakuri
Healthcare Project.

over a decade of prayer. But the couple's path to Kailakuri
would not be smooth as health and family needs delayed their
arrival.

At the time of this announcement, Edric's team was filled
with optimism. In February, Nadine Vickers had arrived to
replace another New Zealand volunteer, Christine Steiner. As
Nadine began work, the team compiled an Annual Report
with impressive figures. In 2012, with 93 staff and 17,100,000
taka ($NZ260,000; $US215,000), Kailakuri had provided
health education to 23,000 people. They had managed 42,000
outpatient visits and treated 1300 inpatients, 1400 diabetics,
and 77 TB patients (with a 96 per cent cure rate). The village
health team had served 992 children under four and 370 pregnant mothers. So many people were being helped!

By the middle of 2013, calls were coming for Edric to replicate his model. His team had expanded locally and they were now opening a sub-centre on the old Thanarbaid site. Yet supporters in New Zealand and Dhaka pushed for more. Gareth Morgan believed the model could be replicated across Bangladesh. He explored possible collaborators, but all required that Edric change aspects of his model and he did not think that would work. 'Edric's purity cut off a lot of partners,' Gareth reflected. 'But his response would have been – how long is a compromised model going to last?'

Wealthy Bangladeshis also invited Edric to open more clinics. Shofikul Islam, a civil servant, told me, 'I asked him to send people to my area.' But establishing a health centre was not that simple. Edric asked Shofikul to find a suitable leader – 'someone willing to sacrifice themselves' – and he could not.

While these conversations went on, Edric's focus never shifted from his existing project. 'Edric was never very interested in implementing a replication programme,' Peter Wilson told me. 'He saw his role as getting the system working right, and considered that replication would be for somebody else after he had gone.' Elizabeth Mackie of Christian World Service agreed, 'He felt he didn't have the capacity to replicate and still keep his finger on everything happening where he was. … He did scale up a bit, in fact quite a lot. It was always funding that prevented him from scaling up more. … I think he just rooted himself in that place and did everything he could to improve the lives of those people – I think that was enough for him.' But other people's excitement clearly encouraged Edric. He wrote in the Christmas 2013 newsletter, 'Gareth Morgan … has said Kailakuri is the model which should be rolled out across the country ... A famous Bangladeshi businessman ... agrees that the model should be extended all over the place for the poor. But he says, "Find me 100 suitable doctors!"'

This was a bold thought to entertain when Edric did not have a fixed arrival date for his own successors, Jason and Merindy Morgenson. Edric's team had searched high and low in order to recruit them. What prospect did they have of finding 100 suitable doctors? I met an intern at Kailakuri who said, 'It's impossible. Where are you going to find – for 64 districts [of Bangladesh] – 64 Doctor Bhais? You won't find that.' John Gould, another former staff member of Christian World Service, expressed similar scepticism: 'We were of the opinion that, exceptional as Kailakuri was, the model was not easy to replicate because of its dependency on one remarkable individual.'

Supporters might be enthusiastic, but no doctors were lining up to sacrifice themselves to lead new clinics. Meanwhile Kailakuri itself was extremely vulnerable because the Morgensons' arrival was still some time away. The team was not even certain that one clinic could be sustained. The idea of finding more remarkable individuals seemed laughable.

Edric in November 2014.
Photo by Stephan Uttom for the Union of Catholic Asian News.

26

Special treatment

In July 2012, when Edric made his last visit to New Zealand, aged 71, the once tireless doctor was slowing down. A few years earlier, Edric had started commenting on a lack of energy, Peter Wilson remembered. He had kept an eye on his friend's health since a concerning event in 2008 when he, Edric and a friend had been walking up Symonds Street in Auckland and he had turned to see Edric far behind, out of breath. They had shrugged off the incident after a Kiwi doctor gave Edric a clean bill of health. But later, when Edric's health deteriorated, he and Peter would look back on the day on Symonds Street and wonder if that was the beginning of his decline.

Age had not dampened Edric's fervent commitment to a simple lifestyle. He still rode a bicycle, wore a *lungi* and washed in a bucket of water from the tube well. He took a wage comparable to his colleagues, roughly $NZ150 ($US120)

A bicycle outside Edric's mud-walled house. Photo by Ben McLaughlin.

One of Edric's colleagues giving him a haircut. Photo by Christine Steiner.

Edric and colleagues working at a table outside.
Photo from the Kailakuri Healthcare Project.

Edric with New Zealand volunteer Nadine Vickers. The project began
using a computer onsite in 2011. Photo by Christine Steiner.

per month. At some point he had upgraded his bed from a pile of straw to a mattress which doubled as an iron to press his shirt flat beneath. The clinic now had intermittent electricity, enabling lighting and even fans in communal spaces. In 2010 Edric had begun using a mobile phone and from 2011 he accepted the presence of a computer at Kailakuri – this was used by the New Zealand volunteer, Christine Steiner, who assisted with donor communications and administration. Otherwise, Edric's living conditions looked much as they had for three decades.

Edric's supporters accepted his modest lifestyle to a point. Thanarbaid volunteer Judy Walter recalled an incident in which his simplicity went too far and staff pushed back. Edric had lost his bike seat and insisted on riding without it. 'Staff kept reminding him that it wasn't safe … but he ignored them. Finally, staff decided to replace the seat without telling Edric. He was furious and wanted to know who authorised the expenditure. No one spoke up. The seat remained on the cycle.' On the whole though, over the years his supporters admired his commitment to living in solidarity with those around him.

It was when Edric extended his principles to his own health that he made people uncomfortable. His 2011 prostate surgery was one saga that demonstrated his ideals in action. 'He got third-class treatment,' one of the Holy Cross Fathers recalled, 'I went for an operation at the same time, at a big hospital in Dhaka – I who took a vow of poverty! This is why I say he was more religious than we are.' Indeed, Jesus had sacrificed his wellbeing for others, so it was natural that his followers would consider doing the same. But Edric's choice left supporters aghast. His New Zealand friends were accustomed to free healthcare for all; they had no concept of comparing treatments on the basis of cost, or the possibility that, due to scarce resources, their choice to accept healthcare might cause someone else to miss out. Edric had gained a different perspective in his work. He routinely chose lower-cost options in order to save money for others. His own prostate surgery was just one example. The choice had unfortunately resulted in complications, longer recovery time and greater cost than intended, but he had tried to do what he felt was right.

In 2013, a similar dilemma arose again. Edric needed surgery, this time for early-stage cataracts in both eyes. Again he pushed to receive the treatment option that was accessible to the poor. Sharifuzzaman Parag, coordinator of the Doctor K. Zaman Bangladesh National Society for the Blind Hospital in Mymensingh explained, 'There are two types of cataract surgery. A simple operation costs between 2500 and 4000 *taka* ($NZ46 – 73; $US32 – 50) for each eye, and a high quality one costs more than 10 times as much. The hospital recommends the simple surgery only for people who do jobs such as managing cattle; it allows the patient to recover sight well enough to walk around. For fine work, like reading and writing, high quality surgery is needed.'

Edric wanted the simple surgery. According to Parag, 'Doctor Bhai thought, if a poor person can do a simple cataract surgery lying on the floor, why not me?' His supporters – both Bangladeshis and foreigners – were horrified. Doctors' eyesight allows them to diagnose, to research and write: it is the basis of their ability to help the poor! Was Edric going to throw away the quality of his sight in a needless show of solidarity? Parag shook his head as he remembered: 'Doctor Bhai argued quite a lot. We told him, don't worry about the money! We know you can lie down on the floor! We eventually made him understand that he must do the good quality surgery, because society needed him.' This time, the choice was taken from Edric. Parag's hospital provided his surgery for free.

The dilemma arose a third time in October 2013. While on a visit to Dhaka to speak to a class at the medical school Gonoshasthaya Kendra, Edric experienced chest pain and such tiredness he could not walk. The colleagues who were with him kept the incident secret, although they told Pijon Nongmin, the project manager, asking him to keep the matter private. Pijon explained why, 'Doctor Bhai didn't want the other staff to hear about it. He didn't want them to lose their motivation or to worry about the future.' But Edric himself was worried. From that time on, he began to research the cause of his tiredness and chest pain. Back at Kailakuri, these symptoms recurred and Edric sometimes had difficulty breathing. He continued working and cycling, though his trips became shorter and shorter. The senior staff urged him to see a doctor, but he kept putting it off. Near the end of 2013, as Edric and senior staff held this worrying secret, there came an unexpected announcement. Merindy Morgenson was pregnant with triplets! She and Jason could no longer come to Bangladesh in 2014 as intended. This complicated the succession plan. The couple still intended to come. But – triplets! Would they be able to honour their commitment? In fact, the Morgensons would not arrive until June 2019, five years later than originally planned. They brought with them their triplets and a subsequent child.

Ityadi presenter Hanif Sanket congratulates Edric on his honorary citizenship in front of a live audience of thousands and a television audience of millions. Photo from Hanif Sanket.

While the Morgensons' arrival date remained up in the air, another uncertainty was laid to rest. Edric wished to become a Bangladesh citizen. He told a friend, 'I am not going back to New Zealand. I will die in Bangladesh.' The process of gaining citizenship was not straightforward. Edric sought help from Shofikul Islam, an official in the Ministry of Home Affairs, who explained to me, 'Under the law there is a provision – if you want Bangladesh citizenship, you have to surrender your own citizenship. No one wants to do that. Edric was not willing to surrender his citizenship. So I decided, I will have to change the rules.' In August 2014, the government awarded Edric honorary citizenship under a new provision to recognise significant contributions to Bangladesh without the recipient needing to revoke their previous citizenship. He was one of the first foreigners to receive this honour, and he remains one of a very small number of honorary Bangladeshi citizens. Soon after, Edric was invited onto the TV show *Ityadi* and the story was broadcast to tens of millions of people.

For Edric it was a great relief to have citizenship. Yet with the Morgensons' arrival still some time away and Edric's health deteriorating, the team remained uneasy. One day, while visiting the Taizé brothers, Edric collapsed. As Pijon recounted it, the brothers insisted that Edric go to a doctor 'or they would kick him out of the compound!' Edric visited a cardiologist in Mymensingh who advised him to come back for a conference with other specialists.

In September 2014, Edric was diagnosed with a rare disease known as 'idiopathic pulmonary artery hypertension'. It was a terminal illness. The prognosis was death within five years of when the first symptoms showed. We can only imagine Edric's thoughts as he studied and underlined in his textbook, 'Cause of death is usually … right ventricular failure' [a form of heart failure]. Edric's symptoms had first appeared one year before, with his chest pain in Dhaka. At most, he had four more years, or had his symptoms begun earlier, in 2008, with his breathlessness on Symonds Street? That was six years ago. The clock was now ticking as it never had. He was on borrowed time!

In October, while Edric was still in the haze of this discovery, internee doctors from the medical school Gonoshasthaya Kendra began working at the clinic. They came in pairs for two-month placements as part of their school's requirement to do four months' rural service. This scheme was a godsend for Kailakuri. The interns took some of Edric's load and provided much help to his colleagues. However, students were no replacement for a fulltime medical director. The issue of succession remained urgent.

But Edric's illness would not wait. Within months of his diagnosis, he was having episodes of shortness of breath and he was no longer able to cycle or walk for long distances. Volunteer Nadine Vickers remembered that on one bike ride he apologised, as he could only manage to ride as far as Hagurakuri bridge – a 25-minute round trip. Despite his condition Edric did not want to stop work. Pijon told me, 'He would try to work anyway, but he would get exhausted, and take two or three days off ... As he was able to do less, the staff took on more responsibility, which Doctor Bhai had approved in principle, but he didn't want to let go of the jobs.' This reluctance was no longer about lack of trust. As his sister Hilda noted, Kailakuri was, 'Edric's baby, and letting go was not easy'.

Despite his worsening condition, Edric did not want to accept treatment. What good was solidarity or his belief in equality, if, in a matter of life or death, he leant back on his privilege? Pulmonary hypertension did not fit the criteria of conditions that Kailakuri could address. The illness was rare. One medication he needed, bosentan, cost $NZ10.50 ($US7.40) per day and only slowed inevitable decline. Edric could not justify such a medication for his patients, so he refused to take the treatment himself.

Supporters would not accept this. As with his cataract surgery, they would not allow Edric to sacrifice his health for the sake of a show of solidarity. Moreover, they thought his position illogical. His treatment would not come at the expense of Kailakuri patients because, for Edric, additional funds would be found! Their subtext, again, was that Edric deserved special treatment. He was a New Zealander, a doctor and the clinic's leader. Money could be found to prolong his life.

Also, although this was not Edric's intention, his position challenged supporters personally by raising an uncomfortable question: *Healthcare was a right, was it not?* The Holy Cross Brother who took a vow of poverty still opted for first-class treatment. Pat Smith had flown from Kontum to the United States for surgery she needed. Yet Edric's friend Father Doug had refused treatment to avoid 'wasting' money that could be used for the poor. If Edric made a similar choice, what did that mean for his supporters and the healthcare they felt they deserved?

In the end it was pragmatism that determined Edric's treatment. Peter Wilson recalled, 'It took some effort to persuade Edric that he had a duty to lead until a successor arrived, so he *had* to accept drugs.' Meanwhile, his networks of supporters offered him free medical care and medication (even bosentan, courtesy of a Bangladeshi friend and a medicine company). Eventually Edric agreed to be treated at a Dhaka hospital on the condition that he would never be admitted as an inpatient there or receive any expensive interventions, and that Kailakuri would bear no costs.

Although Edric agreed to this course of action, the special treatment always jarred with his values. On his first visit to the specialist he arrived into a waiting room full of people, but he was marched straight in. It was hard not to find such favouritism distressing. In past years, Edric had tried in vain to persuade such hospitals even to see his patients. Yet the treatment they were offering was world class and amid his dismay he found gratitude. Edric wrote to George Christian, his fellow captive in the jungle camp in Vietnam, with whom he had reconnected: 'I doubt whether New Zealand could give me better care than I am getting here. ... I am well looked after and this is where I will retire.' He also wrote to supporters Muriel and Dan Stracy, 'I have a wonderful Muslim doctor. He is one of the top cardiologists in Bangladesh and he does everything free for me. He is so gentle and caring!'

Paramedic Sultan Mahmud transports Edric on a bicycle.
Photo by Mirza Shakil, journalist of *The Daily Star.*

27

I will die in Bangladesh; Kailakuri will be my retirement home

Although the special treatment unsettled Edric, it did prolong his ability to assist the poor. In January 2015, with a revised drug regime he could manage light duties for up to seven hours, provided he rested for one or two hours during the day. Jason Morgenson visited for three weeks and Edric briefed him on management and administration of the project. Edric still held the key leadership role.

But the illness was taking its toll. In February, Edric's sister Hilda and niece Heather visited Kailakuri. They found Edric frail and unable to walk far. His colleagues were transporting him about on the back of a bicycle. 'He was still mentally on the go, and never stopped,' Hilda recalled. 'He was very worried about succession.' To see close family must have encouraged Edric but also confronted him with the magnitude of the situation. Hilda continued, 'We both knew we would never see each other again when Heather and I left. On looking back I saw Edric waving with his eyes shut. I felt he was struggling to cope, as I was.' In New Zealand, their mother Betty, aged 99 and too frail to travel, faced the likelihood that she would outlive her son and be unable to see him again.

At Easter, the Catholic brothers from Jalchatra offered Mass at Kailakuri. 'Edric was in very bad health,' Father Alex Rabanel recalled. 'His co-workers brought him in almost on a stretcher. He could hardly stay for the whole service, nevertheless he was going to join in.' Fortunately, the student interns were settled: Doctor Mariko Inui would arrive the next month and Sister Jenny Clarke, a qualified doctor, was also providing support. She would be a mainstay of the team in later months.

The further decline in Edric's health brought forward an historic day. On 20 April 2015, Edric officially handed over his leadership to a team of three senior staff: Sujit Rangsa as Acting Medical Coordinator, Pijon Nongmin as Assistant Director of Management and Nor Amin (Roton) as Assistant Director of Programmes. Though the occasion was understated on account of Edric's health, what was happening was momentous. Edric was handing over his life's work. His efforts had earned him the New Zealand Order of Merit, his honorary Bangladeshi citizenship and the appreciation of millions. A few months earlier, the TV show *Ityadi* had again featured the project, noting that Kailakuri had served 27,000 people and provided 47,000 outpatient visits and other services in 2014. The clinic did so for 22,861,000 *taka* ($NZ381,000; $US297,000), a sum that would cover one or two professional salaries at a New Zealand hospital. John Gould, a former staff

Edric with Nor Amin (Roton) and Pijon Nongmin, right.
Photo by Christine Steiner.

'Sister Doctor' Jenny Clarke (as Edric called her), Doctor Mariko Inui, and Mironi Hagidok, a member of the Community Committee. Photo from the Kailakuri Healthcare Project.

member of Christian World Service later reflected, 'You'd be hard pushed to find any other project where more illness and death was prevented per dollar spent.'

Edric was not in a mindset to celebrate these achievements. On the contrary, the milestone brought him a sense of loss. Pijon reflected, 'He was thinking – what's my position now? He asked us if maybe he could stay on as a "medical consultant". So that's what he was called on the paperwork.' From then on, Edric refused to take his monthly salary of 8,807 *taka* ($NZ152; $US112), as he no longer considered himself to be working. Volunteer Nadine Vickers found that decision astonishing. She told me, 'He was so generous to others, and so tough on himself.' Edric still held himself to the ideal of complete self-giving for the poor. In this area of his life, he felt compelled to achieve formidably high standards, arguably perfection.

A letter Edric wrote on 20 April to Reverend Michael Hewat, a New Zealand supporter, suggests that he felt an ongoing restlessness and dissatisfaction about the limits of what he had achieved. He described the tough conditions suffered by people living on Bangladesh's northern border, and wrote, 'Sometimes I wonder whether we should pick up our Kailakuri project and move away to where we can be with those who are the very poorest!' Could he never let himself rest, I wondered. Did he not feel he had achieved enough?

When Doctor Mariko arrived in May, she found the paramedics treating Edric with tender care. 'The staff are the most loving, caring, concerned group of people I have ever met,' she wrote. 'They will, and do, do everything for Edric. They wash him, dress him, and take him about on the back of a bicycle.' Close staff members such as Antaz Ali, Pintu Hagidok, Sujit Rangsa and Bijoy Bormon were always at hand. 'If Edric needed anything, he would ask one of us,' Bijoy told me. 'When he became very sick, he wanted to stay close to these people.' When Edric grew too ill to attend morning prayers, staff came to his hut to pray. Doctor Mariko noted, 'Prayer was like a tranquiliser for him.' With Mariko there to assist interns and support Sujit in his new role as Acting Medical Coordinator, Edric could rest more easily.

But the team still lacked ongoing medical supervision and an English-speaking volunteer to seek funding. As illness weakened Edric's body, worries weighed on his mind. In May, Edric wrote to supporters Muriel and Dan Stracy, 'My health has not been good. … We are all concerned about what happens to our project in the time before Jason and Merindy get settled in. … I am wondering if you know of anybody who would be eager to come over and help us?'

Edric even contacted Judy Walter, his colleague from early Thanarbaid days who had left the project over 20 years before. He wrote, 'Dear Judy, maybe you have completed in Kenya. … Is there any chance that you might be able to come back and help us for a while? … Please forgive me for asking. Please remember to pray for us.' She graciously declined his invitation.

The May newsletter would be the last that Edric wrote. In it, he mentioned a successful clinic elsewhere in Bangladesh that went into demise following the death of its leader, a French nursing sister. Edric wrote in bold, underlined text, 'We do not intend to allow this to happen to Kailakuri!' He now spent all his time lying in his hut, and fears about the future of the clinic sat in the room with him. Although weak, he was not in pain. But the pressure of his concerns, coupled with his tiredness, shortened his temper and made the usually gentle doctor prone to snap.

In June, Edric was cheered by another visit from family, this time from his other sister Hilary and her husband and daughter. Hilary recalled, 'Edric was still in such good spirits that we didn't appreciate how sick he was.' Her daughter Rebecca agreed: 'He still had enthusiasm and zest for life, and the energy I had seen in him in New Zealand. For instance, I was worried about the huge spiders. He said, "Don't worry about them, there's a one-metre lizard!" That was actually true: we saw the tail.'

Soon after their visit, Edric wrote to Jason with news that a volunteer had come forward who would take over English communications: 'Then I will be a full-time free patient in the Kailakuri nursing home.' But giving up these tasks was painful. Pijon reflected, 'English communications was Edric's last remaining job. With the volunteer's arrival, he was being made redundant. He was thinking – I'm no longer working here, how do the others see me?' The role was also Edric's only tie to some English-speaking friends and he found excuses to delay the handover. Eventually, however, his body gave him no choice but to relinquish these tasks.

In early August, Edric wrote to one supporter, 'I am now practically completely retired. I am reading a book that points out how important it is to keep up contemplative prayer in Christian mission. This will now be my new role.' In another letter he wrote, 'It is such a challenge adjusting to not being able to do anything.' He described a book he was reading by a

Edric's bedroom turned into a memorial after his death.
Photo by Ben McLaughlin.

Catholic archbishop imprisoned in Vietnam who had to make a similar adjustment. 'One day [the archbishop] felt Jesus was saying to him, "Your commitment is to me not to the works you do for me. You must learn to distinguish been God and his work." ... What an essential lesson for me!'

It was the voices of these wise authors and his gentle carers that kept Edric company while he accepted his condition. Later in August, it was time for Doctor Mariko to return to Japan. Edric shook her hand in a fond farewell. Two interns now held the most senior medical authority at the project. There was nothing Edric could do besides pray, but he did not relinquish his cares. In perhaps his final letter, on 27 August to supporters in Europe, he wrote: 'Sometimes I think it is perhaps better not to know the news ... but still I try to keep up each day. There are many things to pray about to our heavenly Father. And how the world needs the love of Jesus!'

Tuesday 1 September was a rainy day. About noon, Edric's condition became critical. The paramedic Bijoy Bormon told me that someone called him over to Doctor Bhai's house. Edric could speak only faintly and had difficulty breathing. Bijoy and the others sent for a priest. Father Donel started coming from Pirgacha but was slowed by the rain on the rough roads. Meanwhile, as Bijoy, Pintu and others waited with him, Edric phoned Peter Wilson in Auckland. 'He could hardly talk,' Peter remembered. 'He asked that I ring back and talk to the management staff. This I did. Although we said it was premature, we talked about how the health centre would function post-Edric.'

Less than one hour later, in the company of his closest carers and friends, Edric died. From the silence of that room, in which the shocked group knelt around his mattress, the news travelled with small-town speed. Doctor Bhai is dead! Father Donel, hurrying with the sacraments received the news en route. 'Along the way I got the message,' he told me, 'I was so shocked – I was too late. I reached him five minutes after his death.' Edric's attendants stayed at his bedside. Among them was Bijoy, who since childhood had dreamed of becoming a doctor, and who had now used his medical skills to care for his teacher as he died.

Edric had requested a simple, Christian funeral service and burial in a dirt grave behind his house, all with little fuss or expense. The complication was the crowds. People started gathering immediately. By nightfall they filled the clinic grounds, and they stayed up sharing stories ahead of the funeral the next day. One person there was Muktadir Aziz, the senior government official of Madhupur. In 2016 he met me at his new workplace – the Prime Minister's office – and recalled that unforgettable day. 'Pijon called me and told me,' he remembered:

> *I said, 'I am coming …' I phoned my boss, the Deputy Commissioner, and the Officer in Charge of the Police and told them to come. I told them, 'A man who served the people without anything, just his life … we should respect him.' I ordered my staff to make a bouquet of flowers. I also ordered the Officer in Charge of Police to pay a straight salute to Baker [a tribute usually reserved for freedom fighters from the Liberation War]. He told me Doctor Bhai is not entitled to this salute. I told him, 'I order this. If there are any problems I will explain to my superior.' I never had to explain, because everyone loved him.*

Edric could no longer argue against such accolades. Neither could he insist upon simplicity or solidarity with the poor. At long last, friends could honour him as they wished. When Shofikul Islam, the civil servant, saw that Edric's clothing was tattered and mended, he gave him an expensive shirt to be buried in. Mandi friends put on Edric a *kothup* headdress. This was the highest honour that could be given in their community, akin to a crown.

The funeral was the next morning. A world away in New Zealand, Edric's mother Betty and his siblings, relatives and friends sat in the mute disbelief of distanced grief while other Kiwis passed the afternoon oblivious to the significance of the

Men carry Edric to his final resting place. Photo from the Kailakuri Healthcare Project.

A woman touches the face of Doctor Bhai one last time.
Photo by Mirza Shakil, journalist of *The Daily Star*.

The crowd gathered for the funeral. Photo from the Kailakuri Healthcare Project.

Thousands of patients, colleagues, locals and well-wishers.
Photo by Mirza Shakil, journalist of *The Daily Star*.

day. At Kailakuri Church, Father Donel led Edric's funeral service in front of the largest crowd the village had ever seen. Hundreds waited outside, then all walked back together to the clinic. Among the guests was Doctor Zafrullah Chowdhury from Gonoshasthaya Kendra medical school, as well as other esteemed doctors and journalists to report the story to the nation. Also in the crowd was Suronjon Bormon, the paramedic who had been saved three times from black fever. Nearby was staff member Dipali Bormon's son, who as a baby had been treated for pneumonia by Edric. Among the guests were countless other children who owed their lives to the health workers who had guided their safe entry into the world. Shilpi Hagidok was in the crowd, as were Sujit Rangsa, Antaz Ali and dozens of other diabetics who had learned to manage their illness, then pass on the knowledge to others.

Few in the crowd had not received some form of benefit from Edric's work, and few had not been moved by the man himself. One paramedic echoed philanthropist Gareth Morgan's view that 'Doctor Bhai was a saint'. Chairman Yakob reflected, 'He came from so far away, and although he was a Christian, he served all these different groups ... If Doctor Bhai could do that, why couldn't I?' Muktadir Aziz, the civil servant whom I met in the Prime Minister's office, offered simple, but high praise of Edric: 'I felt like he liked me.'

Back in the cool shade of the clinic grounds, perhaps the most stone-faced were Edric's staff. He had brought them all so far together. He had seen their potential and spurred them to realise it, giving them reason for pride. 'Doctor Bhai was a gold medal man,' a diabetes patient told me. Nor Amin (Roton), one of the leaders to whom Edric entrusted the project, took the image further: 'Do you know that story in which gold touches iron and turns it to gold? Doctor Bhai was gold ... and he turned other people to gold. People who came here, Doctor Bhai turned them into paramedics.' Edric's team now blended in among the countless patients they had brought back to health, and the way the crowd pressed made it hard to see who was Muslim, Hindu or Christian.

Finally, the last farewells had been said. The guests moved to the garden behind Edric's house. Their friend had been crowned by Mandi, saluted by officials and honoured as both a leader of the people and one of them. There, at last, in a grave surrounded by flowers, his friends laid their fellow Bangladeshi, their Doctor Bhai, to rest.

Edric's grave behind his house, decorated for the first anniversary of his death. Photo from the Kailakuri Healthcare Project.

Some of the 80+ staff at Kailakuri Healthcare Project, including Sujit Rangsa, centre, and Nor Amin (Roton), right. Photo by Ben McLaughlin.

Epilogue

In December 2019, a bus from Dhaka pulled up at Kailakuri and 60 well-dressed passengers stepped into the dust. They had heard about the clinic three weeks earlier on *Ityadi* – the programme that had first beamed the 'doctor on a bicycle' to its audience eight years before. Four years after Baker's death, a new feature updated viewers that the clinic continued to serve the poor. Just 118 *taka* ($NZ2; $US1) paid for an average visit for an outpatient. To treat someone with diabetes for one year cost 3720 *taka* ($NZ64; $US44). In 2018, the clinic had served 28,000 people for an average cost of 760 *taka* ($NZ13; $US9) per person. Now, *Ityadi* showed, American doctors Jason and Merindy Morgenson had arrived to assist. The short clip must have tapped into the nation's mood, because in the six weeks that followed the screening, over

2000 people – officials, journalists and ordinary Bangladeshis – visited the clinic.

Receiving this stream of guests were Pijon Nongmin, Nor Amin (Roton), and Sujit Rangsa, the senior staff that Doctor Baker had selected to lead the project. For four years they had shouldered immense responsibility and remained united. Funding had become even more scarce, while costs inflated and the needs of the poor grew. The project ate into reserves, which forced the new leaders to make tough calls. But their resolve was rewarded. By the end of 2018 they had reduced spending with only a slight decrease in patient numbers.

At the same time, in order to protect Edric's vision long term, the team had registered the project as an independent organisation: 'Doctor Baker's Organisation for Wellbeing'. Pijon submitted the necessary documents, but 18 months later the goverment had still not given official sign-off. In the end, the *Ityadi* presenter appealed on the clinic's behalf. The government provided the signature the next day.

For the senior staff, the greatest challenge since Edric's death was maintaining medical supervision. With the Morgensons' arrival still some time away, the team had continued the search. For two years, Sister Jenny Clarke and Sister Julienne Hayes-Smith, a doctor and nurse, supported the interns, as did several short-term volunteers. Then a breakthrough came in September 2017: with funding provided by Jason and Merindy, the project employed a graduate doctor, Rakibur Islam, to oversee until the couple's arrival. Doctor Rakib was a former intern who had been transformed by the experience, just as Edric predicted. Here was one 'remarkable individual' willing to forego a higher income and serve the poor. Soon after,

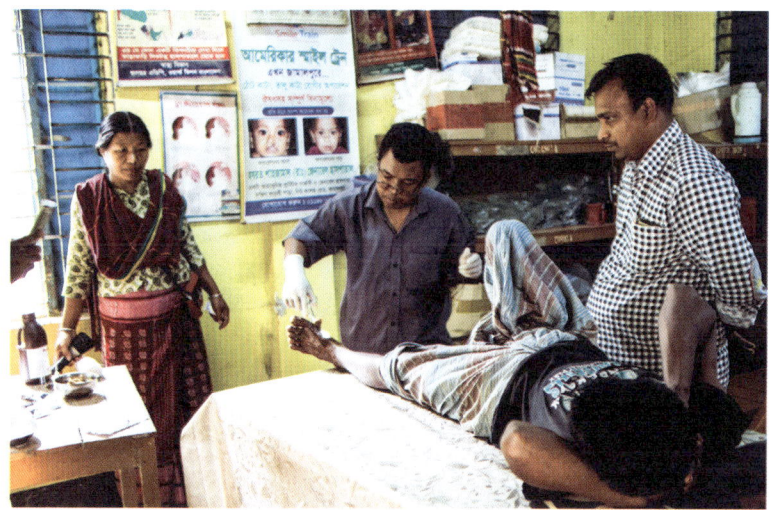

Sujit Rangsa, the Acting Medical Coordinator, treating a patient's foot.
Photo by Ben McLaughlin.

Dr Rakib (left), the first Bangladeshi doctor employed at the project.
He and colleagues are celebrating a donation of medical supplies.
Photo from the Kailakuri Healthcare Project.

The Morgenson family at Kailakuri. Photo by Mirza Shakil, published in *The Daily Star* on 3 December 2019.

another Bangladeshi doctor joined as a short-term member of the team. Edric's vision of Bangladeshi doctors sustaining Kailakuri had been realised.

On 1 June 2019, Jason, Merindy and their family arrived at Kailakuri. Their youngest child was aged three and the triplets almost five. These fair-skinned children joined the bustle of patients and staff. Jason and Merindy added their skills to the team. Jason wrote, '[Doctor Baker] trained [the paramedics] very well. The care that the staff give the patients at Kailakuri rivals that of well-trained nurses and doctors in the United States. … We pray that God will help us pick up where Edric left off in praying with the staff, teaching them, and supporting them in every way that we possibly can.'

Besides these new arrivals, the clinic was much as it had been in Edric's time. Gonoshasthaya Kendra medical school continued to send interns. Sister Margaret Shield shared with me an email that the school's founder, Doctor Zafrullah Chowdhury, wrote to her in 2015. He stated his wish that all medical students would visit Kailakuri to learn about their work and 'to pay respect to the Albert Schweitzer of Bangladesh'.

The simple idea – that every person should have healthcare – therefore continued to captivate people, just as it had driven Edric and his team. In December 2019, it was that vision that filled buses with Bangladeshis keen to witness Kailakuri's work. Each visitor knew places in Bangladesh that needed such a project. The emergency of poverty continued and diabetes was only growing more prevalent. The potential of Edric's model was as rich as it had ever been; lessons from Kailakuri were ripe to be spread.

It was that same simple but captivating idea that pulled me into Edric's story. During the five-year project of writing his biography, I feel that I have 'lived with' Edric – an odd feeling given that we met only twice. The experience has given me a good dose of perspective. I shaped some of these chapters while in a New Zealand hospital before my son's birth, feeling sobered to receive care not accessible for women at Kailakuri.

It would be impossible to spend time with Edric and not catch some of his passion. As Maryknoll father Doug Venne wrote, Edric was 'burning with fire to help the poor' and that fire leapt from his hundreds of letters. Edric's example has stoked my belief in equality and called me to greater generosity. I now share his excitement that 20 dollars can buy a year's antenatal care. Giving to Kailakuri brings a smile to my face.

These five years with Edric have also called me to more radical commitment. I envy the ability he had to be single-minded and reject compromise: for all that those attributes made his life difficult, they made it easier too, by eliminating alternative paths. Yet, while my life seems scattered and my energy divided, Edric's example shows what can be gained from focus and sacrifice for worthwhile goals. His life also points me to the nourishing discipline of prayer so I can last the distance.

I will admit that living with Edric has been dispiriting at times. As John Bonifant, Edric's colleague at Wellington Hospital said, 'Saints can be difficult to live with'. Reflecting on a life spent minute by minute saving lives, I have doubted my own value and the efficacy of my training. Should I instead pursue medical work? But then I have remembered the people who made up Edric's big team – from his family, teachers and mentors who formed him through to his paramedics, cooks and funders, even the people who carried water from the tube wells. Edric's successes cannot be separated from the contributions of these people. I was also heartened to reflect that while Edric was still a boy, authors Charles Joy and Melvin Arnold were writing a book about Albert Schweitzer, and that book turned out to be consequential. So biographers have a role to play too.

Over these five years I have discovered that I can write a biography after all. Edric was right: with enough support, it is possible to do things without formal qualifications and to train on the go. I have therefore learned that I have a part to play in Edric's dream of healthcare for everyone. Although there are significant barriers to that dream being realised, as Edric knew when he recruited his paramedics, the vision compels you to learn all you can and get involved. There are different roles to play, and, as Edric learned from Pat Smith and the Montagnards, with the right encouragement people can 'find the job that fits them'. Qualifications or none, Edric believed that I have something to offer towards this dream. You do too, reader, whether a few dollars, your direction of study, or a year – or five – of your life.

Acknowledgements

My heartfelt thanks to the big team who made this book possible. First to the New Zealand – Kailakuri Link Group and the Baker family for your trust and encouragement to research Edric's story. Thanks to St John's Theological College, Christian World Service and other donors for their financial support.

Huge thanks to the 150+ people who shared memories and photos of Edric and patiently answered my follow-up questions. Thanks to John Havican for hosting me in Vietnam and enabling me to trace Edric's footsteps in Qui Nhon and Kontum; to Hilary Smith for sharing her wonderful books on Minh Quy; and to Kerry Heubeck, James Tuohy, Dennis Montgomery and the family of Peter Eccles-Smith for the photos that brought these places to life.

To the team who hosted me in Bangladesh and translated interviews, I am so grateful. Nadine Bormon (nee Vickers), Roton Bormon, Pijon Nongmin, Suijt Rangsa, Nor Amin (Roton) and colleagues, this book could not have happened without you – nor would there be any project to write about without your ongoing work. My thanks to *The Daily Star* journalist Mirza Shakil, Ben McLaughlin and many others for your photos of this special place.

I am grateful to Deborah Shepard for her deft work editing the manuscript; to Stephanie Day for proof-reading; and to all who gave feedback on drafts: Graham Langton, Peter Wilson, Nadine Bormon, Hilda England, Hilary Lynch, John-Luke Day, Faith Alexander, Sister Julienne, Brother Erik and others. Thanks to Jason Morgenson, Nick Laing, Rowena Woodhams and Sujit Rangsa for sharing their medical expertise; to Emma Bevernage for beautiful graphic design; and to everyone who encouraged me through this long project – my family, the morning prayer group at 309 Mansfield, Frances Cherry's writing group, friends at St Timothy's and St Tom's churches and others – you know who you are.

A special thank you to my mother, Faith Alexander, who accompanied me on most of the travel for interviews in Bangladesh and New Zealand. She scanned thousands of documents, provided an excellent sounding board and found the project as fascinating as I did. At times, my progress was solely due to her and my father, Keith Alexander, hosting me for writing retreats away from the busyness of life. When our son arrived, it was only because of their enthusiastic grandparenting that I could continue any writing! (Meanwhile Wilfred had a ball.)

Special thanks to Peter Wilson – whose own life deserves a biography – for his steadfast support of this project and of me. His wise contributions have made the story stronger and along with the inspiring conversations we have shared, showed why he was such a valued friend to Edric.

Final thanks to my dear husband John-Luke. When I asked for his advice one 2012 day – should I book flights and a bus trip immediately? – he said 'Go for it,' and he has encouraged me ever since. My time and energy poured into this project has always been a joint contribution. When we hold the completed book and see Edric's story reach more people, the satisfaction will, like all things in our lives, be shared.

Index

About the author

Kate Day is a researcher and advocate living in Wellington, New Zealand. She works on a variety of social and environmental campaigns and supports the church to speak up on such issues. Having a longstanding fascination with Asia, she has spent time living in China and Cambodia. She is married to John-Luke and they have two children. *Call Me Brother* is her first book.